C.S. PACAT   JOHANNA THE MAD   JOANA LAFUENTE

FENCE ™

RISE

Published by

BOOM! BOX™

FENCE: RISE, August 2022. Published by BOOM! Box, a division of Boom Entertainment, Inc. Fence is ™ & © 2022 C.S. Pacat. All rights reserved. BOOM!™ Box™ and the BOOM! Box logo are trademarks of Boom Entertainment, Inc., registered in various countries and categories. All characters, events, and institutions depicted herein are fictional. Any similarity between any of the names, characters, persons, events, and/or institutions in this publication to actual names, characters, and persons, whether living or dead, events, and/or institutions is unintended and purely coincidental. BOOM! Studios does not read or accept unsolicited submissions of ideas, stories, or artwork.

BOOM! Studios, 5670 Wilshire Boulevard, Suite 400, Los Angeles, CA 90036-5679. Printed in Canada. First Printing.

ISBN: 978-1-68415-843-0, eISBN: 978-1-64668-612-4
BOOM! Exclusive ISBN: 978-1-68415-864-5

MIRABILE VINCULUM

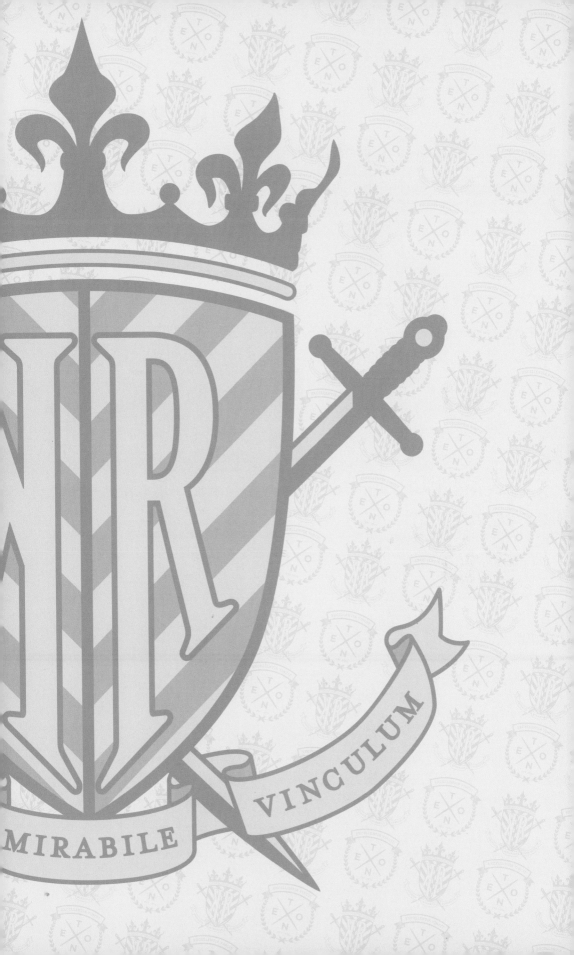

EXCELLENTIA V

T

E

N

EST. 1874

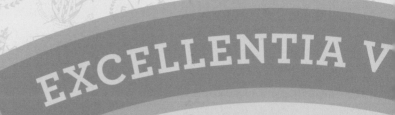

WRITTEN BY
C.S. PACAT

ILLUSTRATED BY
JOHANNA THE MAD

COLORS BY
JOANA LAFUENTE

LETTERS BY
JIM CAMPBELL

TECHNICAL CONSULTANT
PIETER LEEUWENBURGH

SCHOOL LOGO DESIGNS
FAWN LAU

MAIN COVER AND BOOM! EXCLUSIVE COVER BY
JOHANNA THE MAD

DESIGNER
VERONICA GUTIERREZ

ASSISTANT EDITOR
KENZIE RZONCA

EDITORS
**SOPHIE PHILIPS-ROBERTS
AND DAFNA PLEBAN**

CREATED BY
C.S. PACAT & JOHANNA THE MAD

CHAPTER
SEVENTEEN

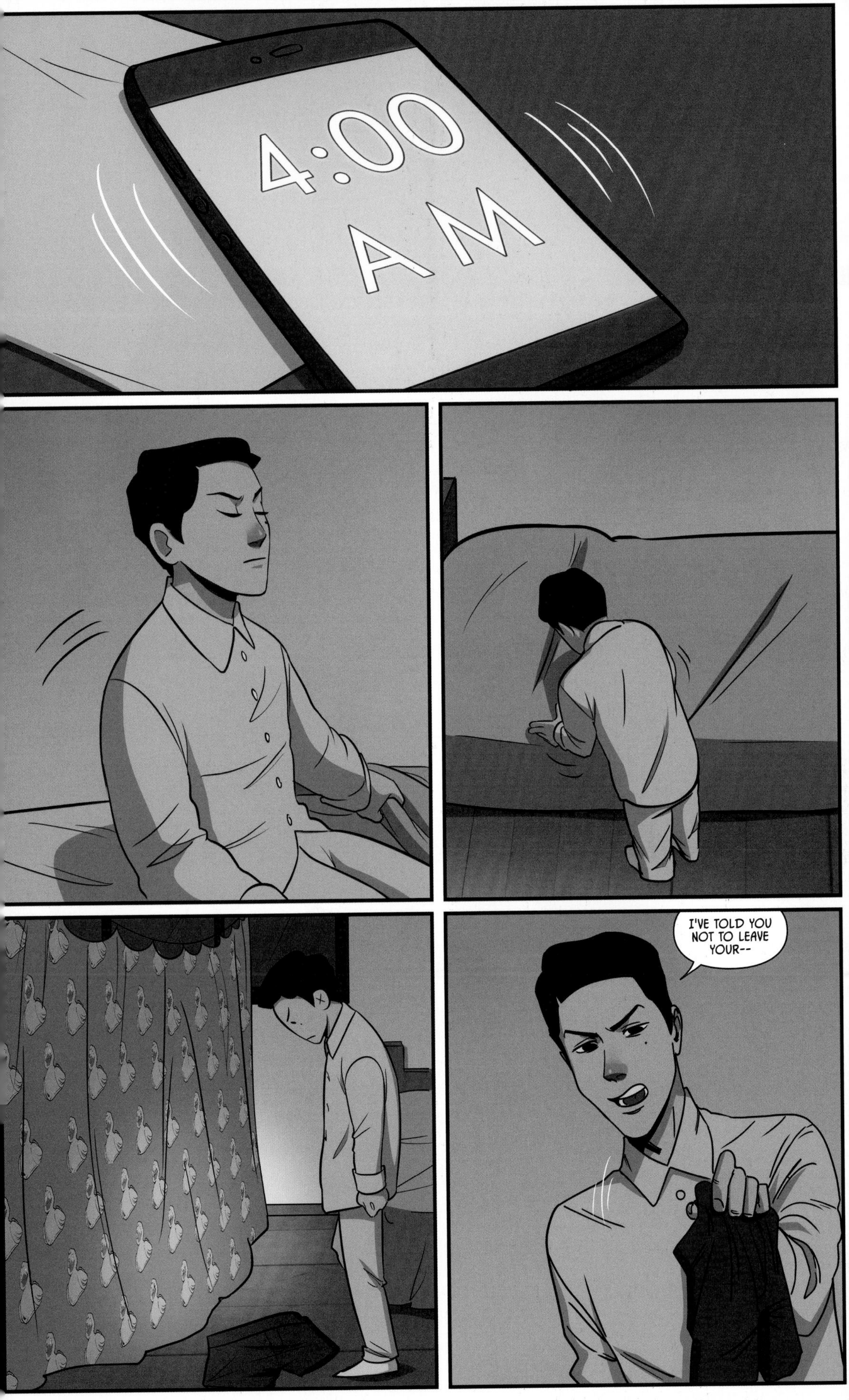
4:00 AM
I'VE TOLD YOU NOT TO LEAVE YOUR--

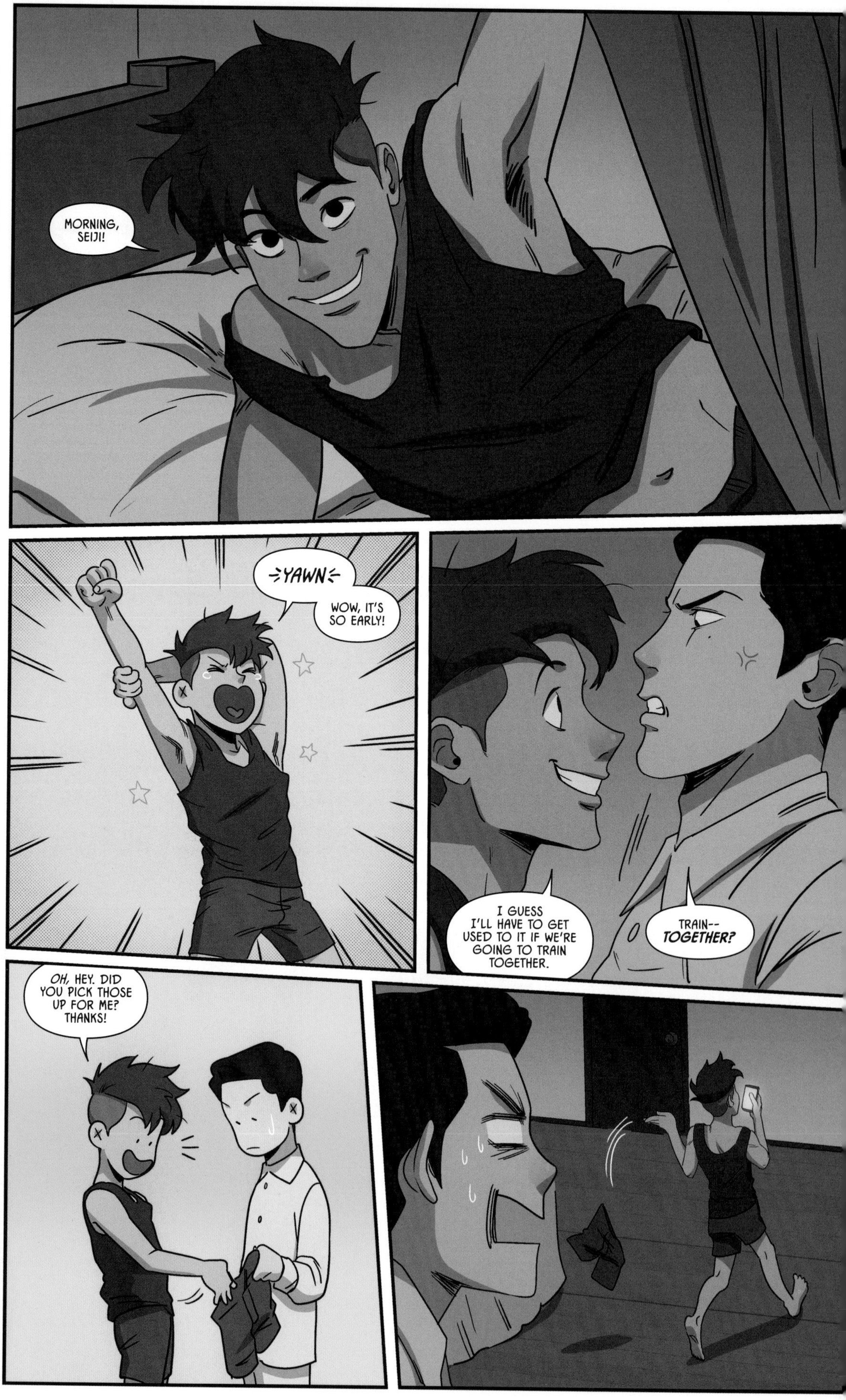

MORNING, SEIJI!
≠YAWN≠
WOW, IT'S SO EARLY!
I GUESS I'LL HAVE TO GET USED TO IT IF WE'RE GOING TO TRAIN TOGETHER.
TRAIN-- *TOGETHER?*
OH, HEY. DID YOU PICK THOSE UP FOR ME? THANKS!

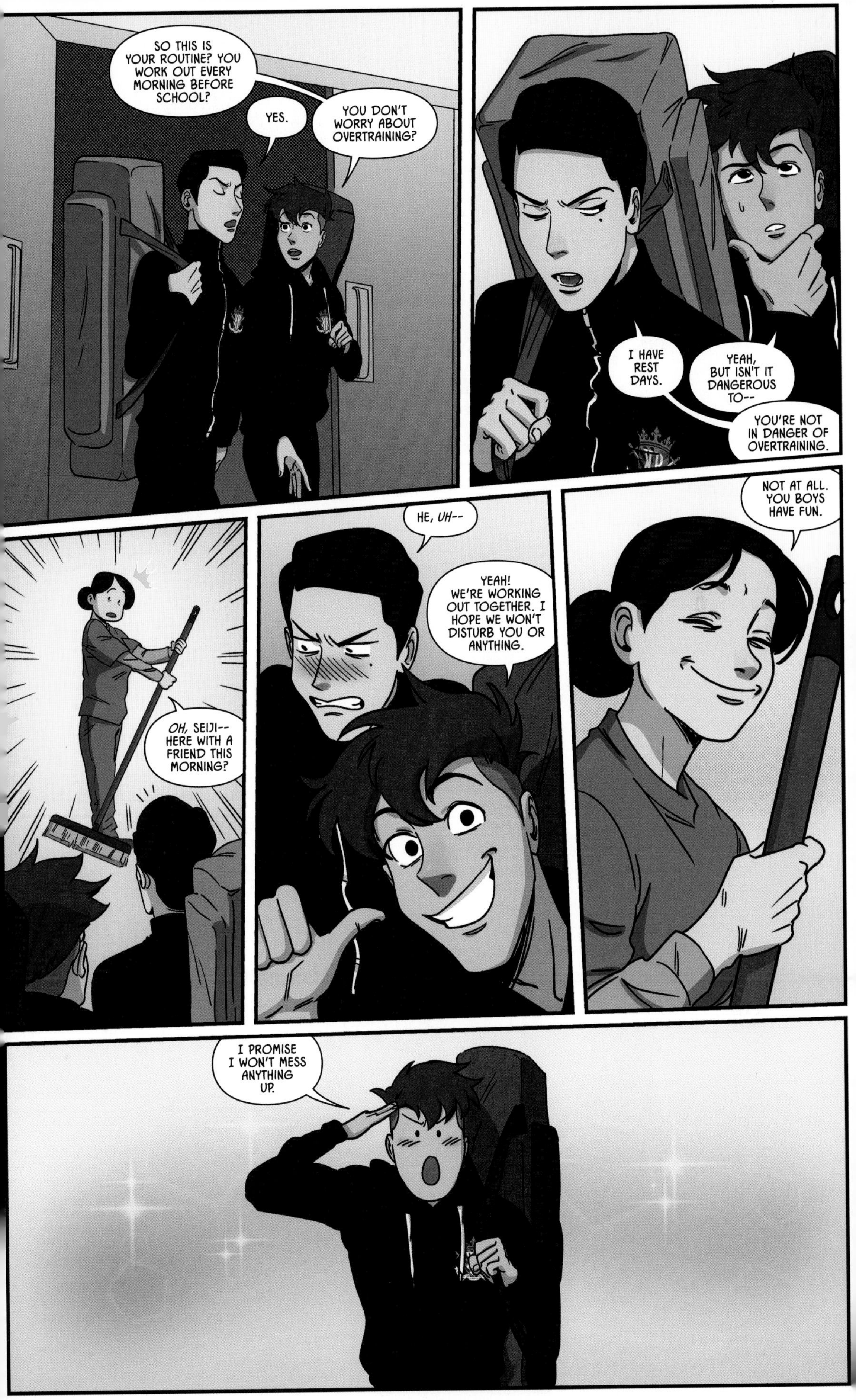
SO THIS IS YOUR ROUTINE? YOU WORK OUT EVERY MORNING BEFORE SCHOOL?
YES.
YOU DON'T WORRY ABOUT OVERTRAINING?
I HAVE REST DAYS.
YEAH, BUT ISN'T IT DANGEROUS TO--
YOU'RE NOT IN DANGER OF OVERTRAINING.
OH, SEIJI--HERE WITH A FRIEND THIS MORNING?
HE, UH--
YEAH! WE'RE WORKING OUT TOGETHER. I HOPE WE WON'T DISTURB YOU OR ANYTHING.
NOT AT ALL. YOU BOYS HAVE FUN.
I PROMISE I WON'T MESS ANYTHING UP.

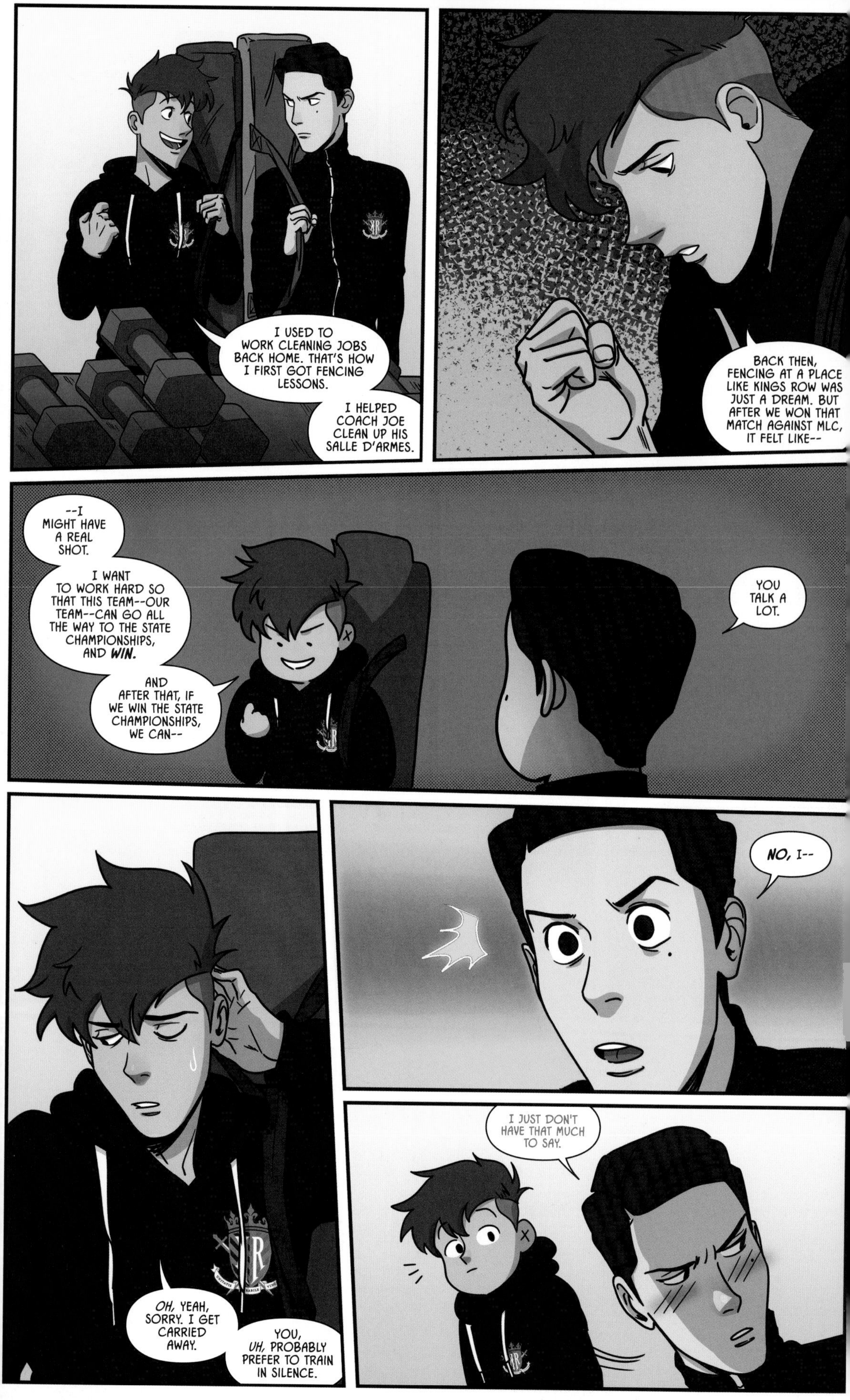
I USED TO WORK CLEANING JOBS BACK HOME. THAT'S HOW I FIRST GOT FENCING LESSONS.
I HELPED COACH JOE CLEAN UP HIS SALLE D'ARMES.
BACK THEN, FENCING AT A PLACE LIKE KINGS ROW WAS JUST A DREAM. BUT AFTER WE WON THAT MATCH AGAINST MLC, IT FELT LIKE--
--I MIGHT HAVE A REAL SHOT.
I WANT TO WORK HARD SO THAT THIS TEAM--OUR TEAM--CAN GO ALL THE WAY TO THE STATE CHAMPIONSHIPS, AND *WIN.*
AND AFTER THAT, IF WE WIN THE STATE CHAMPIONSHIPS, WE CAN--
YOU TALK A LOT.
OH, YEAH, SORRY. I GET CARRIED AWAY.
YOU, *UH,* PROBABLY PREFER TO TRAIN IN SILENCE.
NO, I--
I JUST DON'T HAVE THAT MUCH TO SAY.

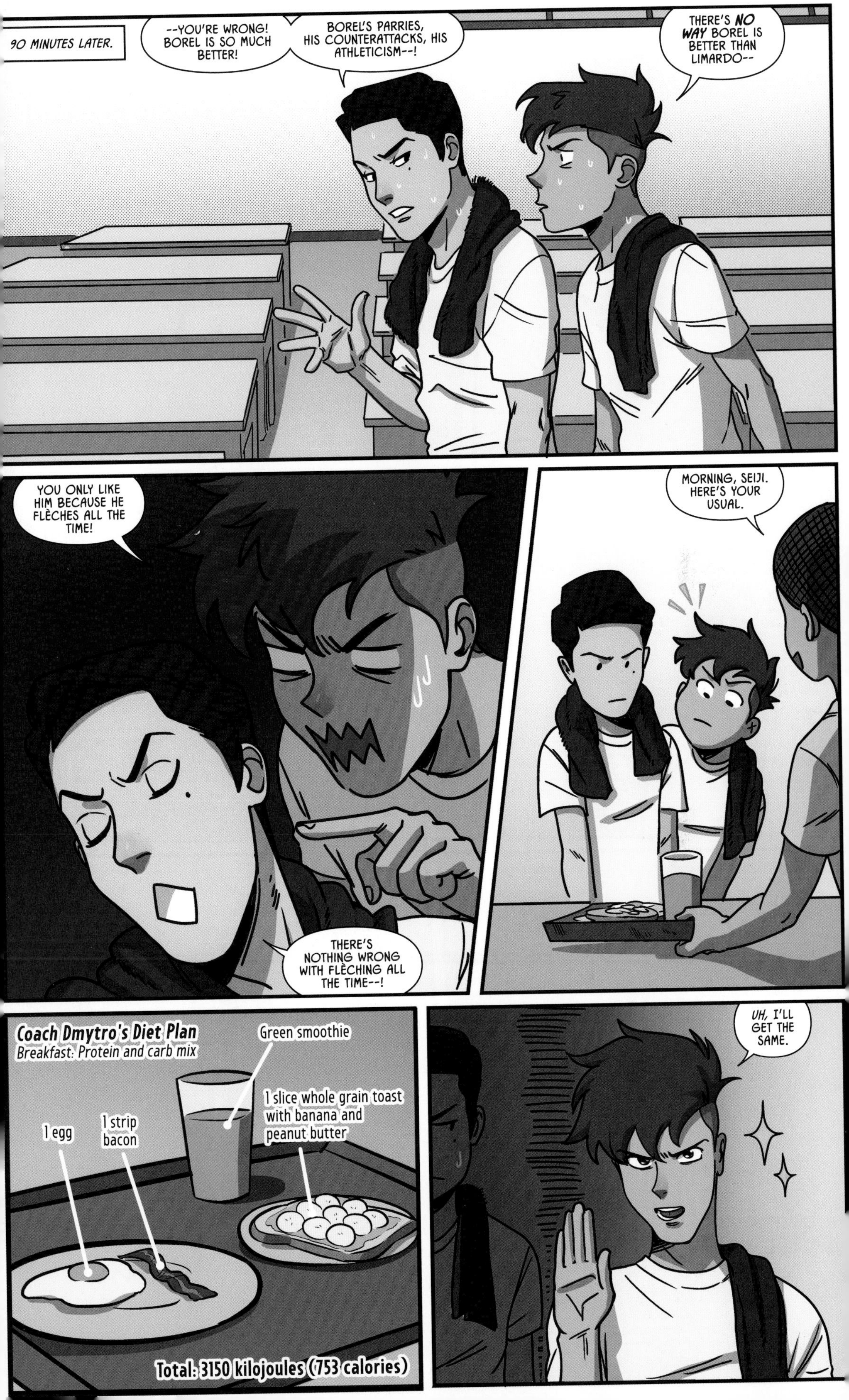

90 MINUTES LATER.
--YOU'RE WRONG! BOREL IS SO MUCH BETTER!
BOREL'S PARRIES, HIS COUNTERATTACKS, HIS ATHLETICISM--!
THERE'S NO WAY BOREL IS BETTER THAN LIMARDO--
YOU ONLY LIKE HIM BECAUSE HE FLÈCHES ALL THE TIME!
THERE'S NOTHING WRONG WITH FLÈCHING ALL THE TIME--!
MORNING, SEIJI. HERE'S YOUR USUAL.
Coach Dmytro's Diet Plan
Breakfast: Protein and carb mix
Green smoothie
1 slice whole grain toast with banana and peanut butter
1 egg
1 strip bacon
Total: 3150 kilojoules (753 calories)
UH, I'LL GET THE SAME.

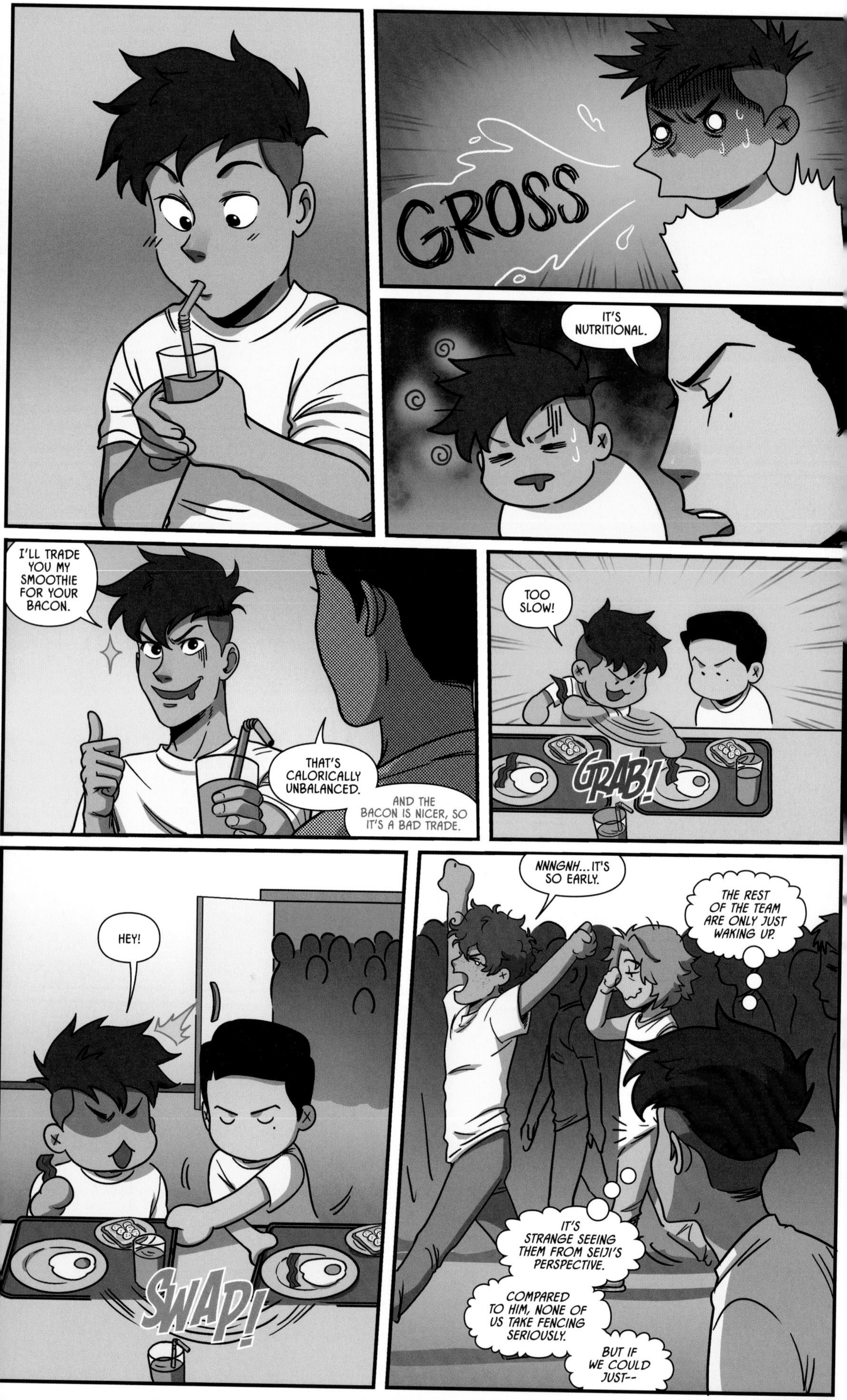
GROSS
IT'S NUTRITIONAL.
I'LL TRADE YOU MY SMOOTHIE FOR YOUR BACON.
THAT'S CALORICALLY UNBALANCED.
AND THE BACON IS NICER, SO IT'S A BAD TRADE.
TOO SLOW!
GRAB!
HEY!
SWAP!
NNNGNH...IT'S SO EARLY.
THE REST OF THE TEAM ARE ONLY JUST WAKING UP.
IT'S STRANGE SEEING THEM FROM SEIJI'S PERSPECTIVE.
COMPARED TO HIM, NONE OF US TAKE FENCING SERIOUSLY.
BUT IF WE COULD JUST--

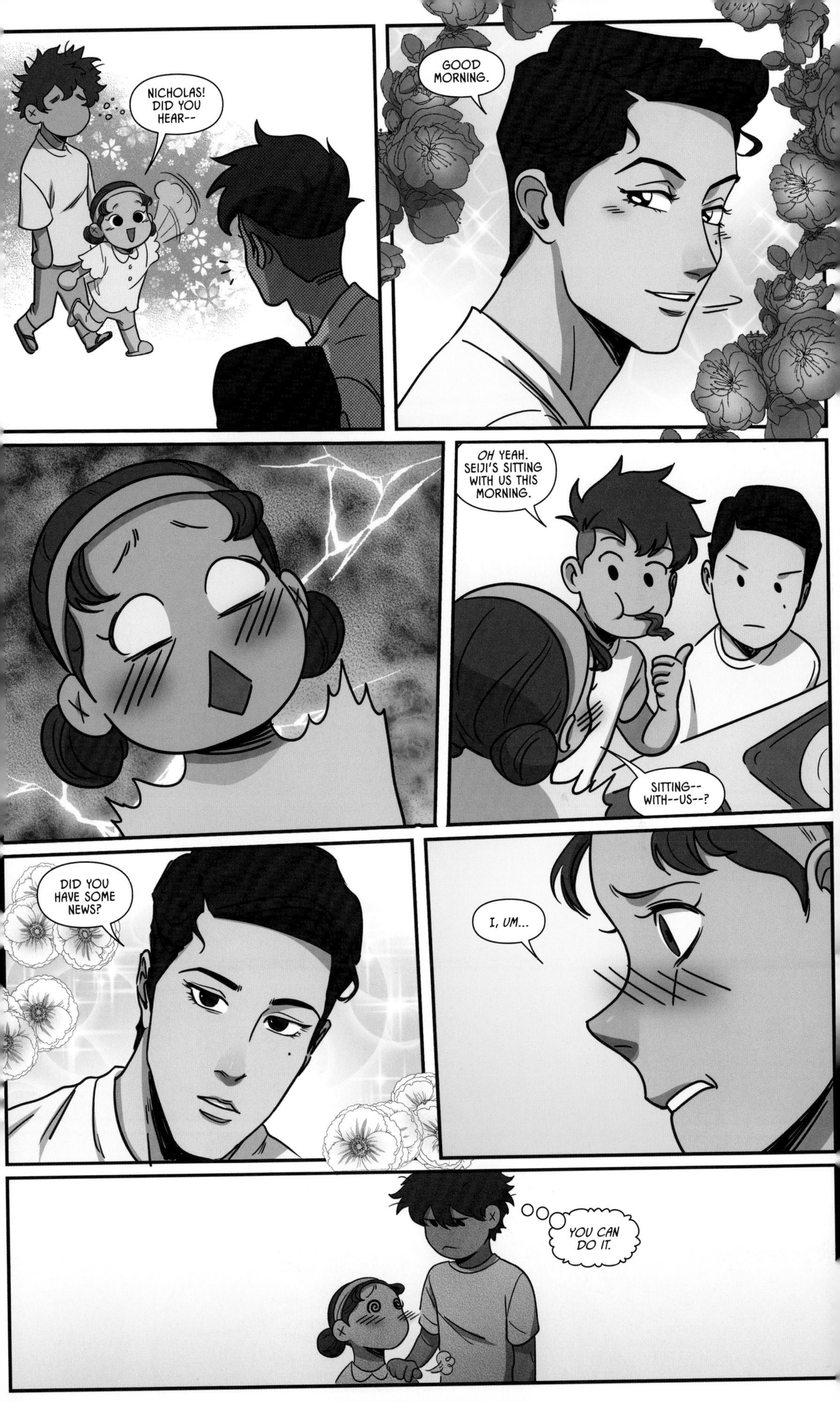
NICHOLAS! DID YOU HEAR--
GOOD MORNING.
OH YEAH. SEIJI'S SITTING WITH US THIS MORNING.
SITTING-- WITH--US--?
DID YOU HAVE SOME NEWS?
I, UM...
YOU CAN DO IT.

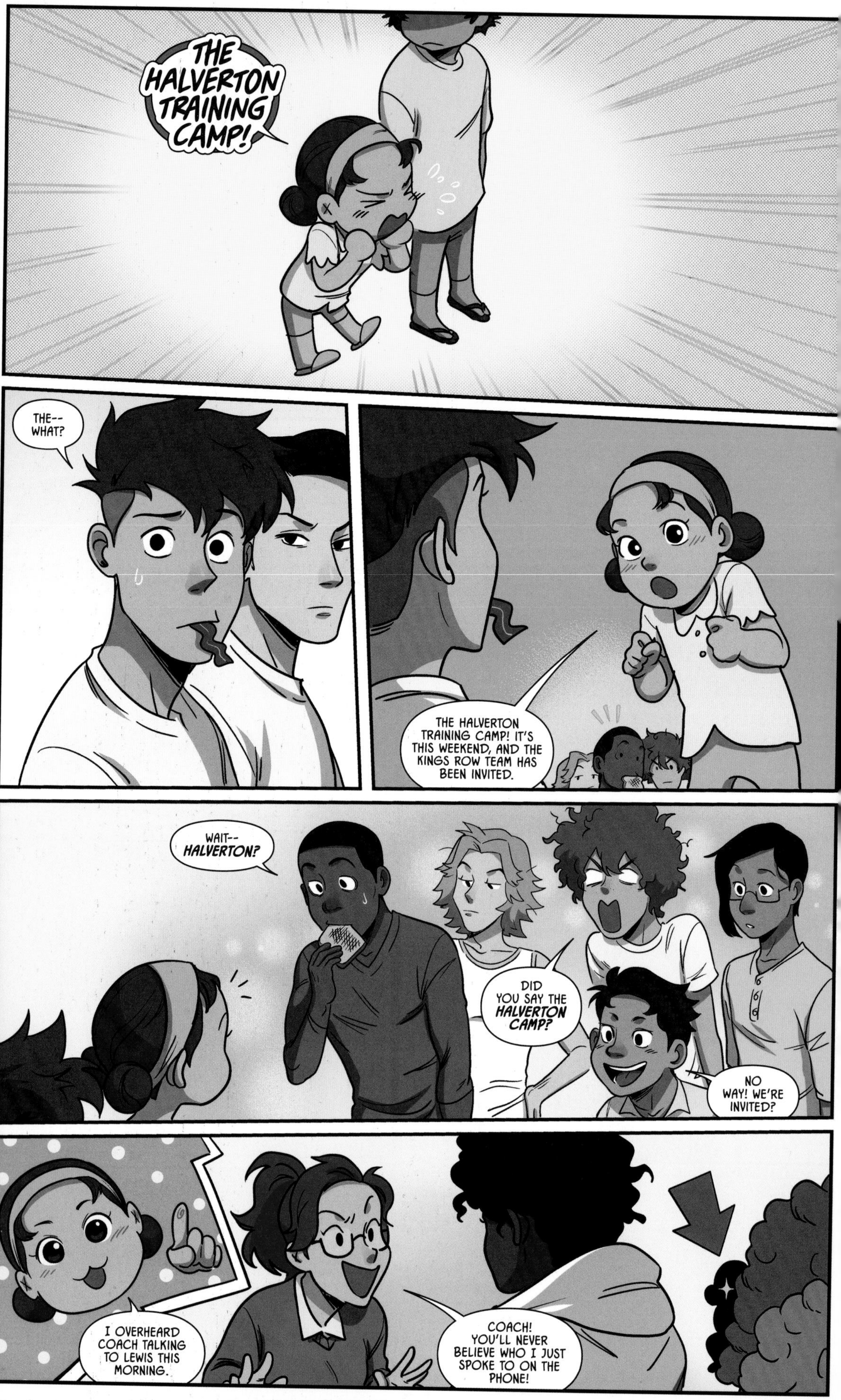
THE HALVERTON TRAINING CAMP!
THE-- WHAT?
THE HALVERTON TRAINING CAMP! IT'S THIS WEEKEND, AND THE KINGS ROW TEAM HAS BEEN INVITED.
WAIT-- HALVERTON?
DID YOU SAY THE HALVERTON CAMP?
NO WAY! WE'RE INVITED?
I OVERHEARD COACH TALKING TO LEWIS THIS MORNING.
COACH! YOU'LL NEVER BELIEVE WHO I JUST SPOKE TO ON THE PHONE!

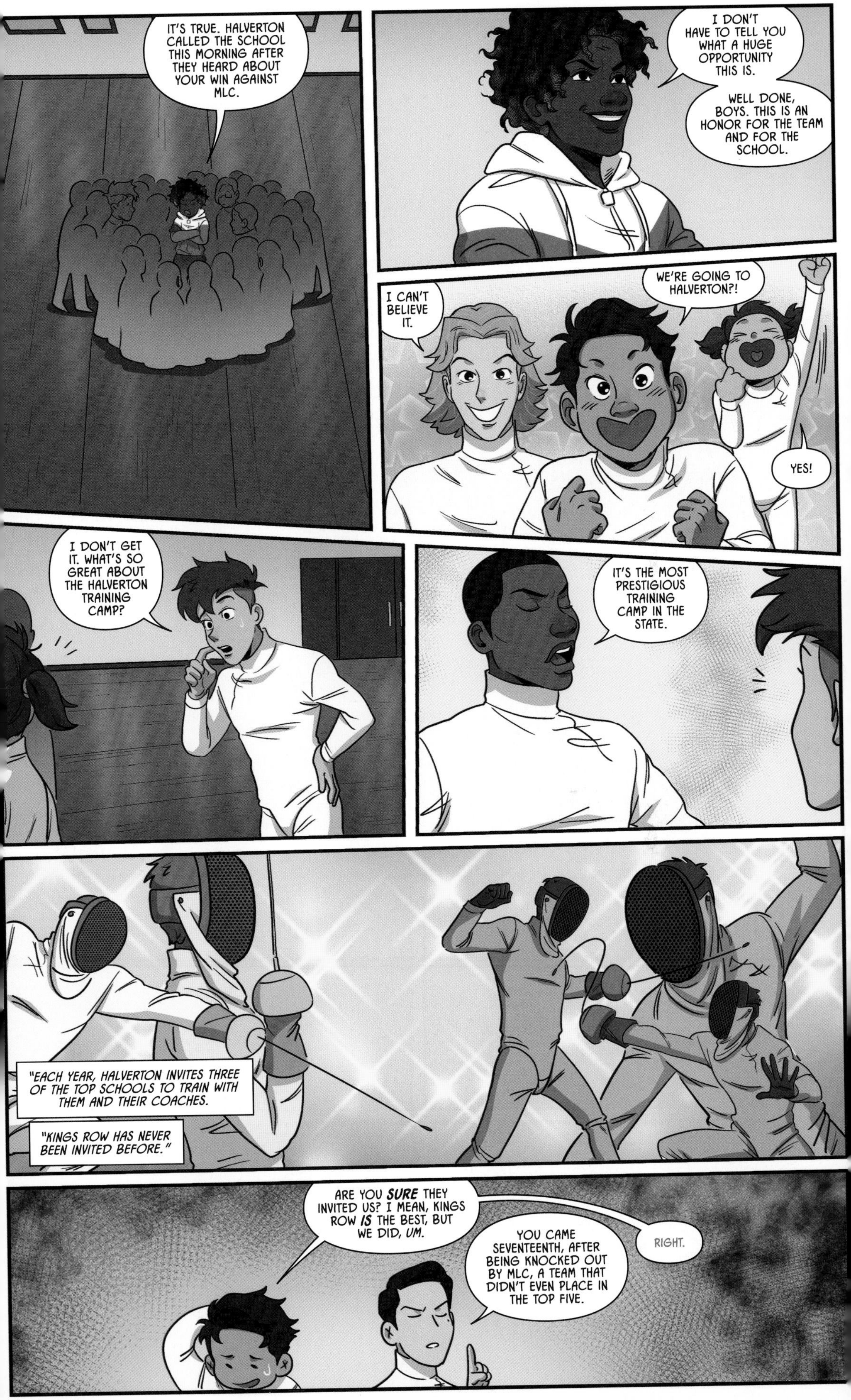
IT'S TRUE. HALVERTON CALLED THE SCHOOL THIS MORNING AFTER THEY HEARD ABOUT YOUR WIN AGAINST MLC.
I DON'T HAVE TO TELL YOU WHAT A HUGE OPPORTUNITY THIS IS.
WELL DONE, BOYS. THIS IS AN HONOR FOR THE TEAM AND FOR THE SCHOOL.
I CAN'T BELIEVE IT.
WE'RE GOING TO HALVERTON?!
YES!
I DON'T GET IT. WHAT'S SO GREAT ABOUT THE HALVERTON TRAINING CAMP?
IT'S THE MOST PRESTIGIOUS TRAINING CAMP IN THE STATE.
"EACH YEAR, HALVERTON INVITES THREE OF THE TOP SCHOOLS TO TRAIN WITH THEM AND THEIR COACHES.
"KINGS ROW HAS NEVER BEEN INVITED BEFORE."
ARE YOU SURE THEY INVITED US? I MEAN, KINGS ROW IS THE BEST, BUT WE DID, UM.
RIGHT.
YOU CAME SEVENTEENTH, AFTER BEING KNOCKED OUT BY MLC, A TEAM THAT DIDN'T EVEN PLACE IN THE TOP FIVE.

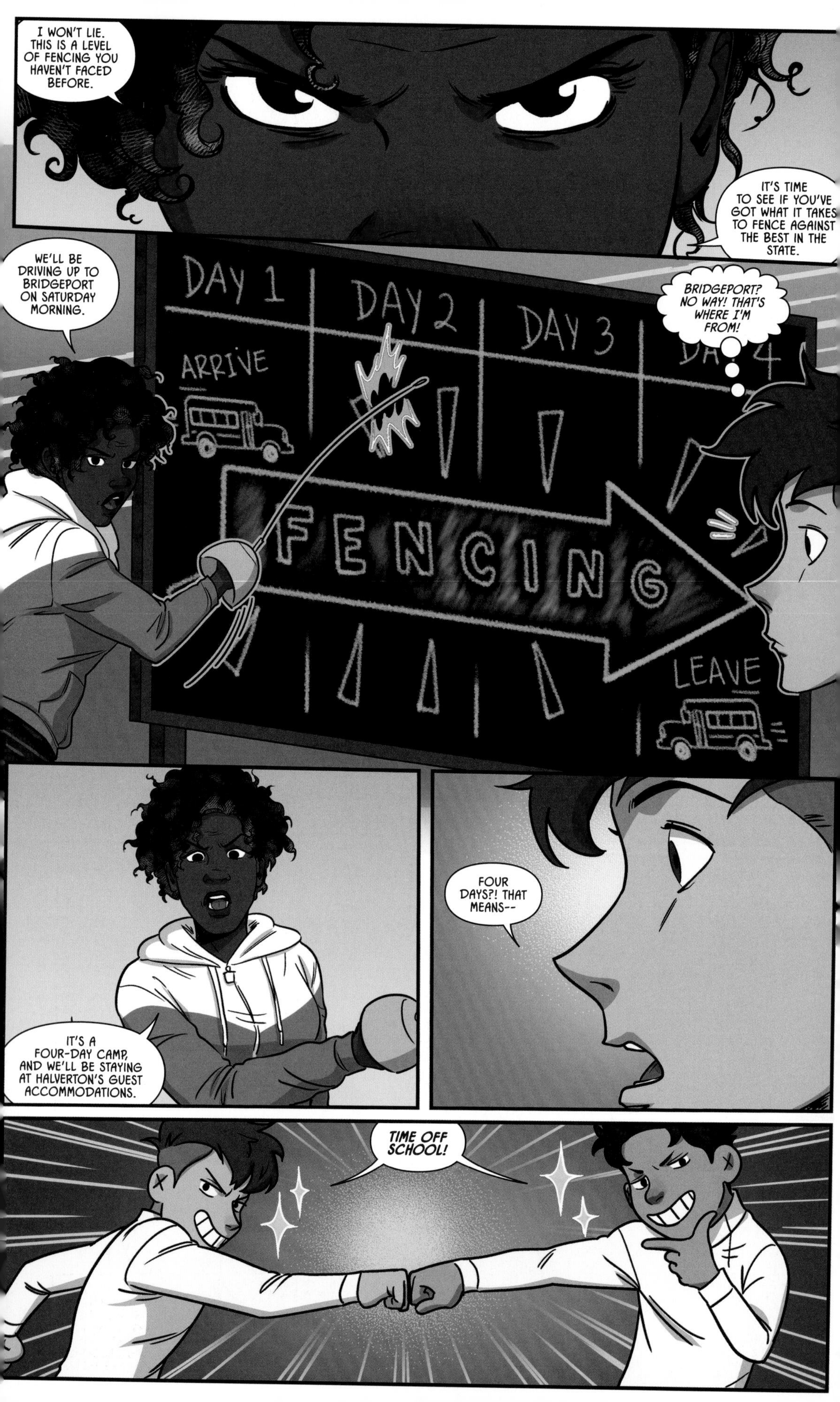
I WON'T LIE. THIS IS A LEVEL OF FENCING YOU HAVEN'T FACED BEFORE.
IT'S TIME TO SEE IF YOU'VE GOT WHAT IT TAKES TO FENCE AGAINST THE BEST IN THE STATE.
WE'LL BE DRIVING UP TO BRIDGEPORT ON SATURDAY MORNING.
DAY 1
DAY 2
DAY 3
ARRIVE
FENCING
LEAVE
BRIDGEPORT? NO WAY! THAT'S WHERE I'M FROM!
IT'S A FOUR-DAY CAMP, AND WE'LL BE STAYING AT HALVERTON'S GUEST ACCOMMODATIONS.
FOUR DAYS?! THAT MEANS--
TIME OFF SCHOOL!

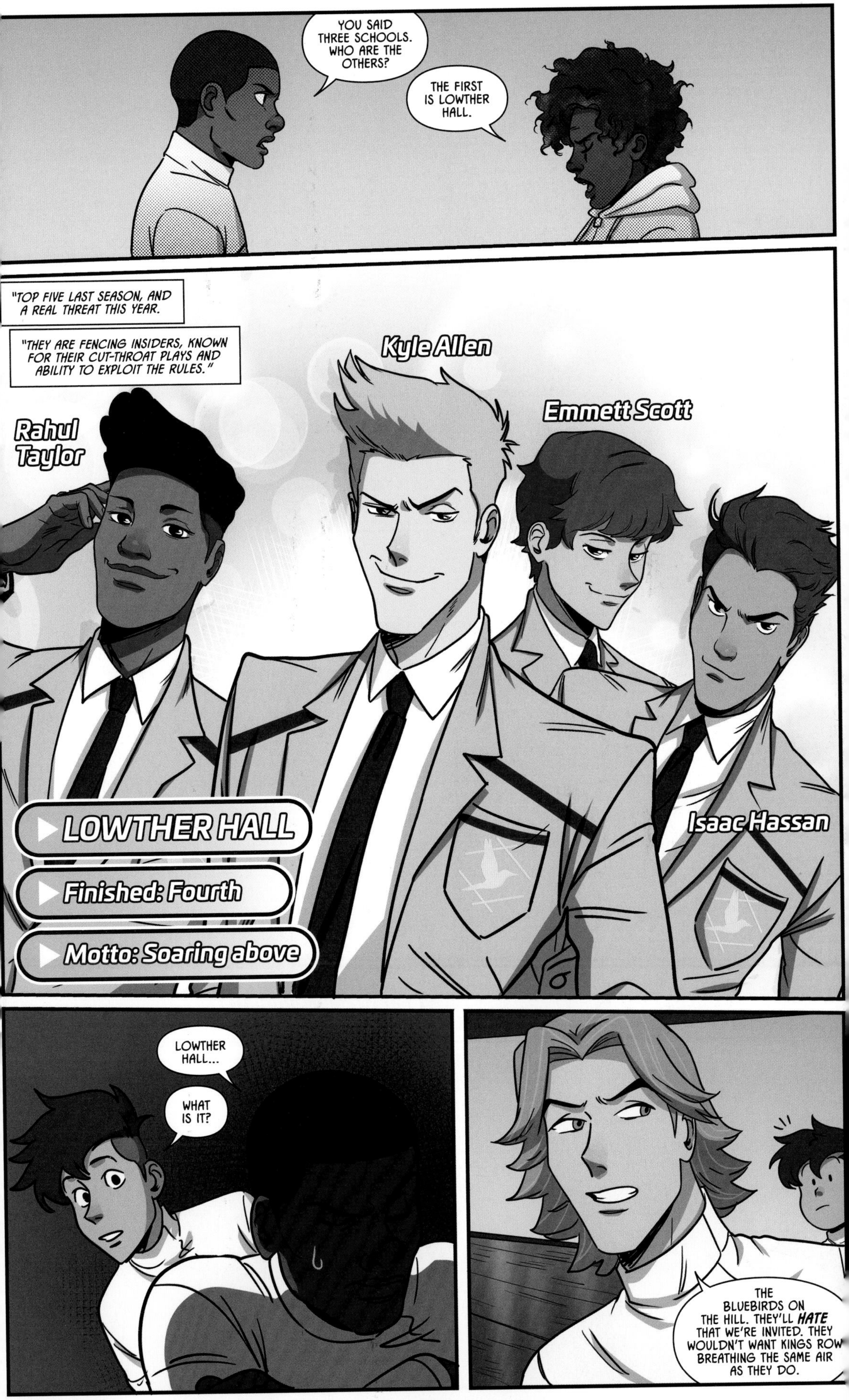
YOU SAID THREE SCHOOLS. WHO ARE THE OTHERS?
THE FIRST IS LOWTHER HALL.
"TOP FIVE LAST SEASON, AND A REAL THREAT THIS YEAR.
"THEY ARE FENCING INSIDERS, KNOWN FOR THEIR CUT-THROAT PLAYS AND ABILITY TO EXPLOIT THE RULES."
Kyle Allen
Emmett Scott
Rahul Taylor
Isaac Hassan
LOWTHER HALL
Finished: Fourth
Motto: Soaring above
LOWTHER HALL...
WHAT IS IT?
THE BLUEBIRDS ON THE HILL. THEY'LL ***HATE*** THAT WE'RE INVITED. THEY WOULDN'T WANT KINGS ROW BREATHING THE SAME AIR AS THEY DO.

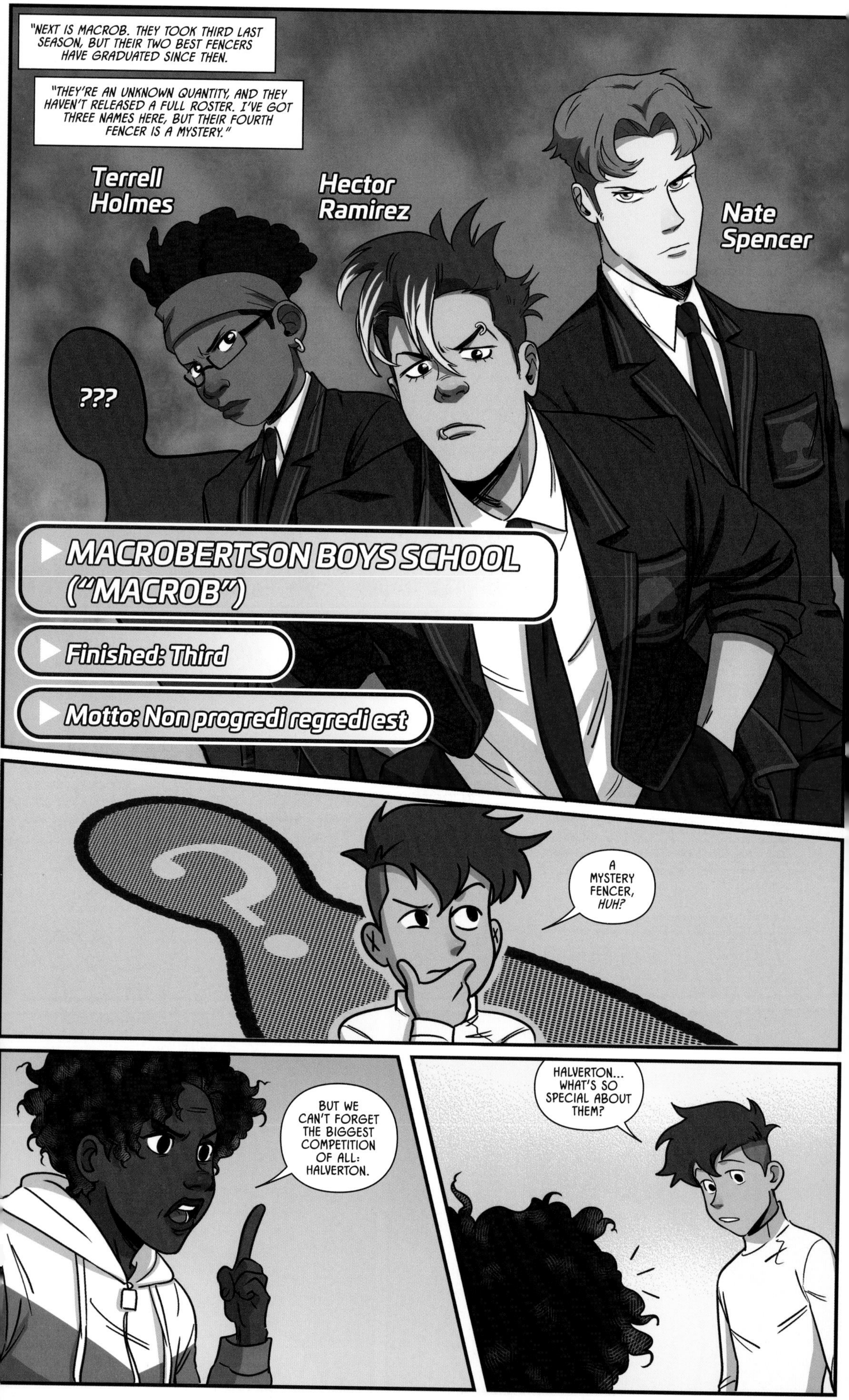
"NEXT IS MACROB. THEY TOOK THIRD LAST SEASON, BUT THEIR TWO BEST FENCERS HAVE GRADUATED SINCE THEN.
"THEY'RE AN UNKNOWN QUANTITY, AND THEY HAVEN'T RELEASED A FULL ROSTER. I'VE GOT THREE NAMES HERE, BUT THEIR FOURTH FENCER IS A MYSTERY."
Terrell Holmes
Hector Ramirez
Nate Spencer
???
MACROBERTSON BOYS SCHOOL ("MACROB")
Finished: Third
Motto: Non progredi regredi est
A MYSTERY FENCER, HUH?
BUT WE CAN'T FORGET THE BIGGEST COMPETITION OF ALL: HALVERTON.
HALVERTON... WHAT'S SO SPECIAL ABOUT THEM?

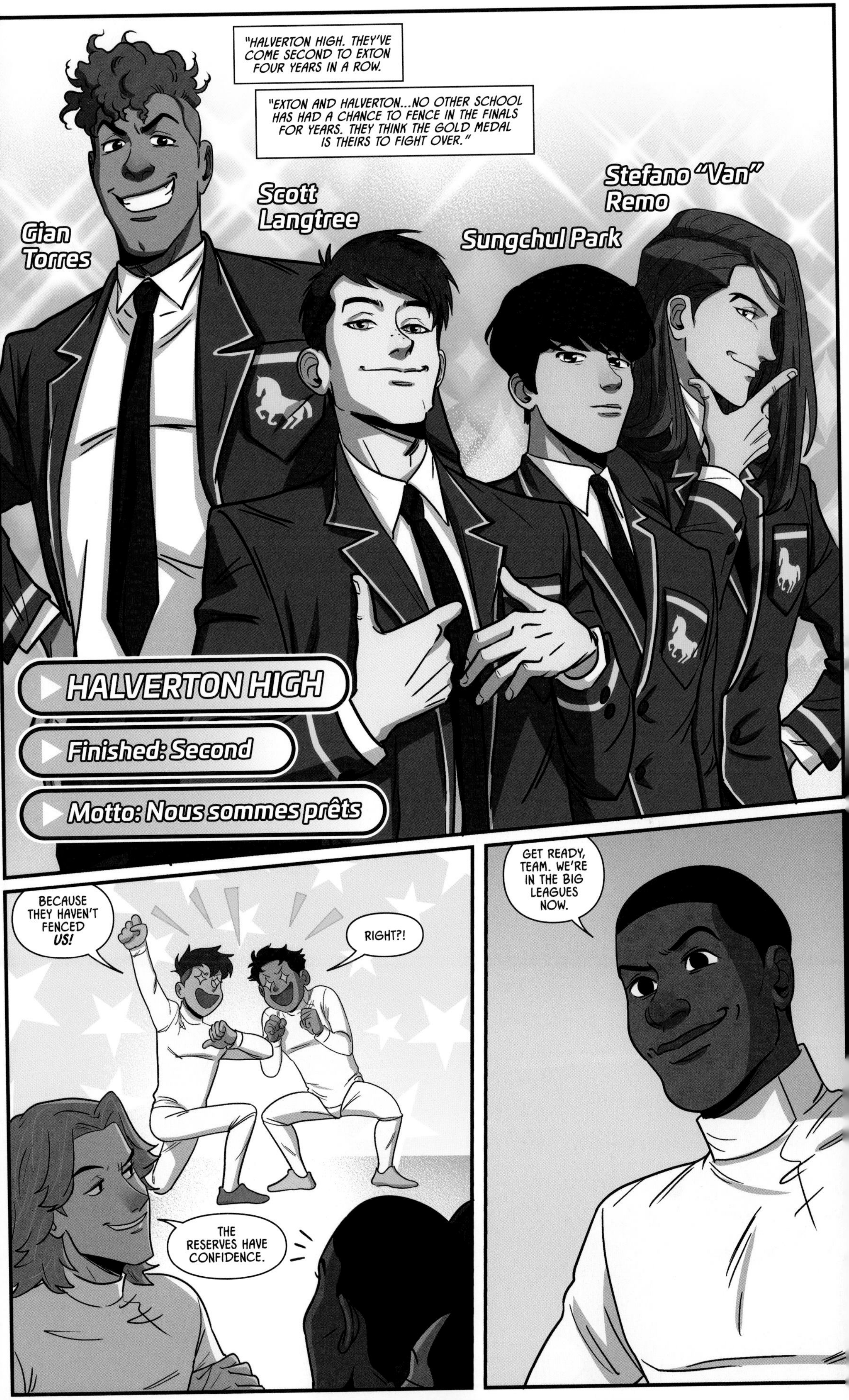
"HALVERTON HIGH. THEY'VE COME SECOND TO EXTON FOUR YEARS IN A ROW.
"EXTON AND HALVERTON...NO OTHER SCHOOL HAS HAD A CHANCE TO FENCE IN THE FINALS FOR YEARS. THEY THINK THE GOLD MEDAL IS THEIRS TO FIGHT OVER."
Gian Torres
Scott Langtree
Sungchul Park
Stefano "Van" Remo
HALVERTON HIGH
Finished: Second
Motto: Nous sommes prêts
BECAUSE THEY HAVEN'T FENCED US!
RIGHT?!
THE RESERVES HAVE CONFIDENCE.
GET READY, TEAM. WE'RE IN THE BIG LEAGUES NOW.

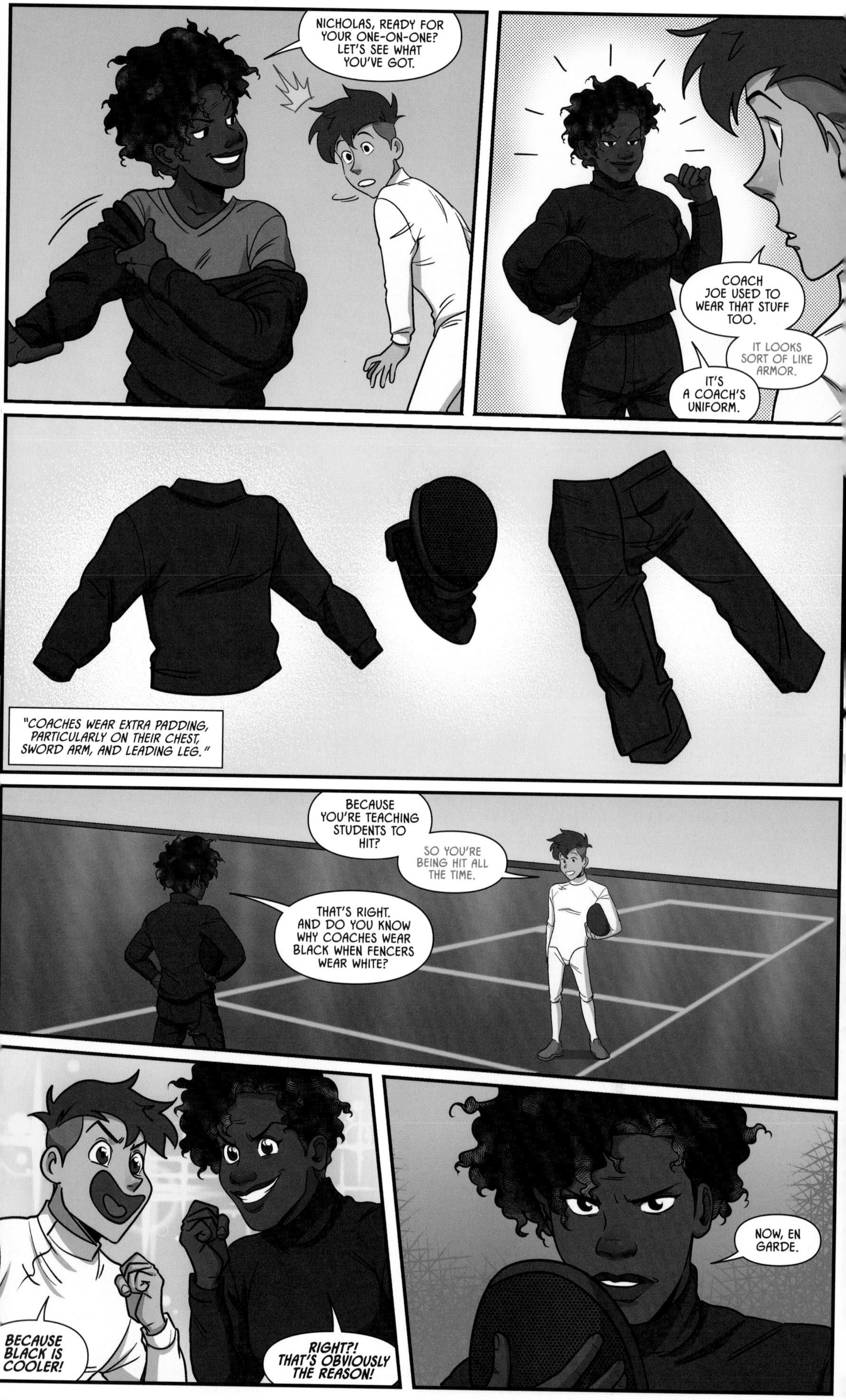
NICHOLAS, READY FOR YOUR ONE-ON-ONE? LET'S SEE WHAT YOU'VE GOT.
COACH JOE USED TO WEAR THAT STUFF TOO.
IT LOOKS SORT OF LIKE ARMOR.
IT'S A COACH'S UNIFORM.
"COACHES WEAR EXTRA PADDING, PARTICULARLY ON THEIR CHEST, SWORD ARM, AND LEADING LEG."
BECAUSE YOU'RE TEACHING STUDENTS TO HIT?
SO YOU'RE BEING HIT ALL THE TIME.
THAT'S RIGHT. AND DO YOU KNOW WHY COACHES WEAR BLACK WHEN FENCERS WEAR WHITE?
BECAUSE BLACK IS COOLER!
RIGHT?! THAT'S OBVIOUSLY THE REASON!
NOW, EN GARDE.

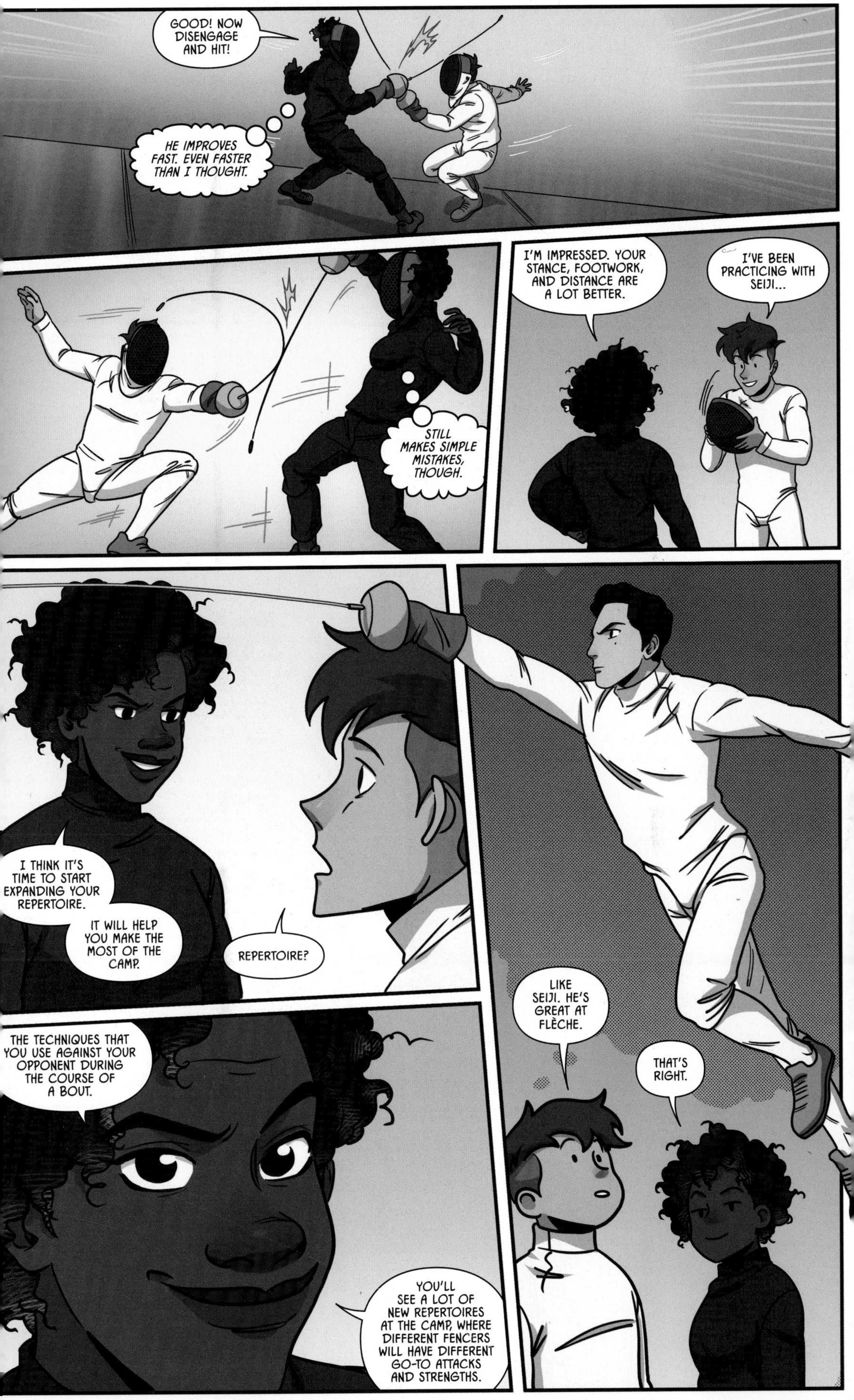
GOOD! NOW DISENGAGE AND HIT!
HE IMPROVES FAST. EVEN FASTER THAN I THOUGHT.
STILL MAKES SIMPLE MISTAKES, THOUGH.
I'M IMPRESSED. YOUR STANCE, FOOTWORK, AND DISTANCE ARE A LOT BETTER.
I'VE BEEN PRACTICING WITH SEIJI...
I THINK IT'S TIME TO START EXPANDING YOUR REPERTOIRE.
IT WILL HELP YOU MAKE THE MOST OF THE CAMP.
REPERTOIRE?
THE TECHNIQUES THAT YOU USE AGAINST YOUR OPPONENT DURING THE COURSE OF A BOUT.
YOU'LL SEE A LOT OF NEW REPERTOIRES AT THE CAMP, WHERE DIFFERENT FENCERS WILL HAVE DIFFERENT GO-TO ATTACKS AND STRENGTHS.
LIKE SEIJI. HE'S GREAT AT FLÈCHE.
THAT'S RIGHT.

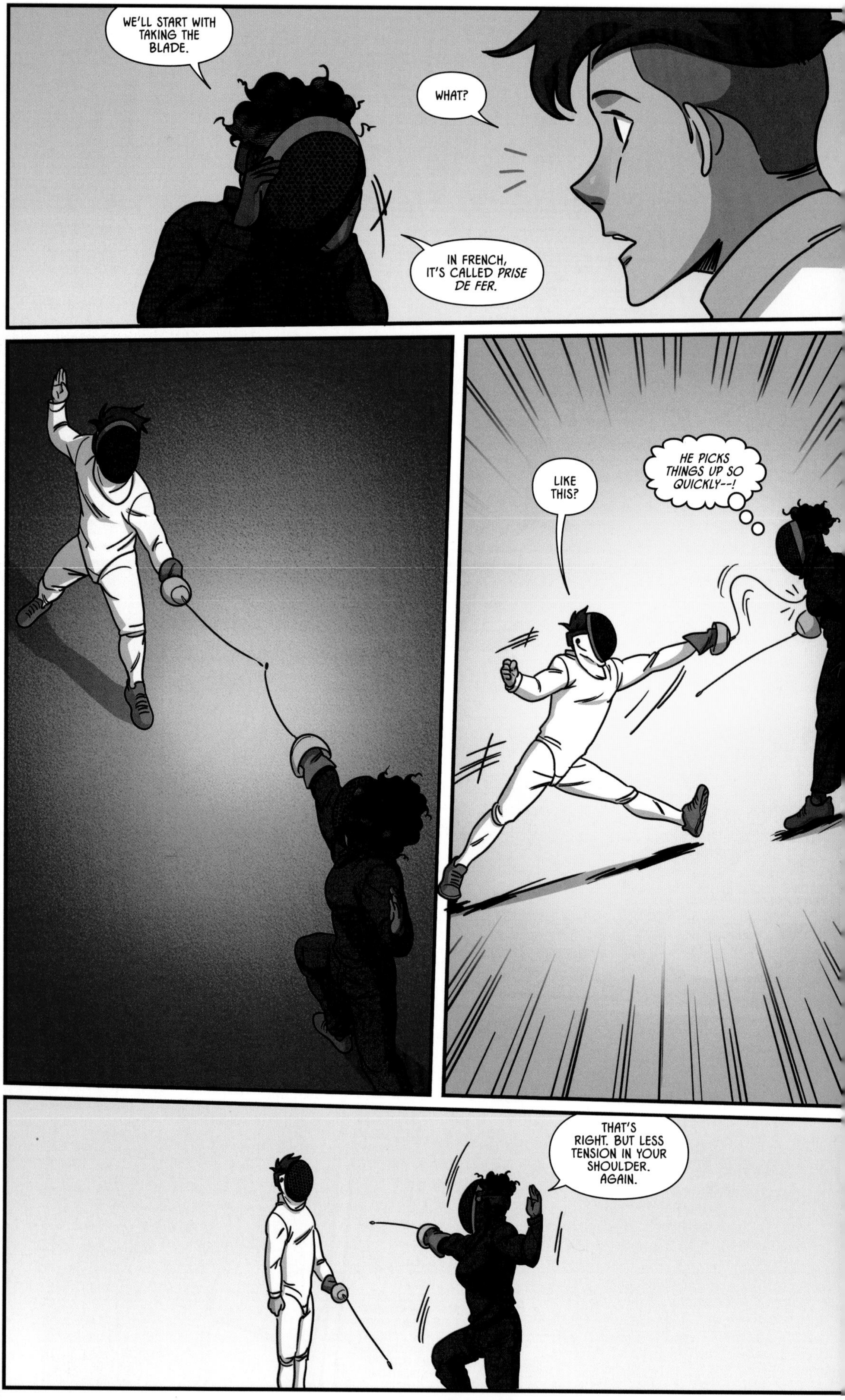
WE'LL START WITH TAKING THE BLADE.
WHAT?
IN FRENCH, IT'S CALLED *PRISE DE FER.*
LIKE THIS?
HE PICKS THINGS UP SO QUICKLY--!
THAT'S RIGHT. BUT LESS TENSION IN YOUR SHOULDER. AGAIN.

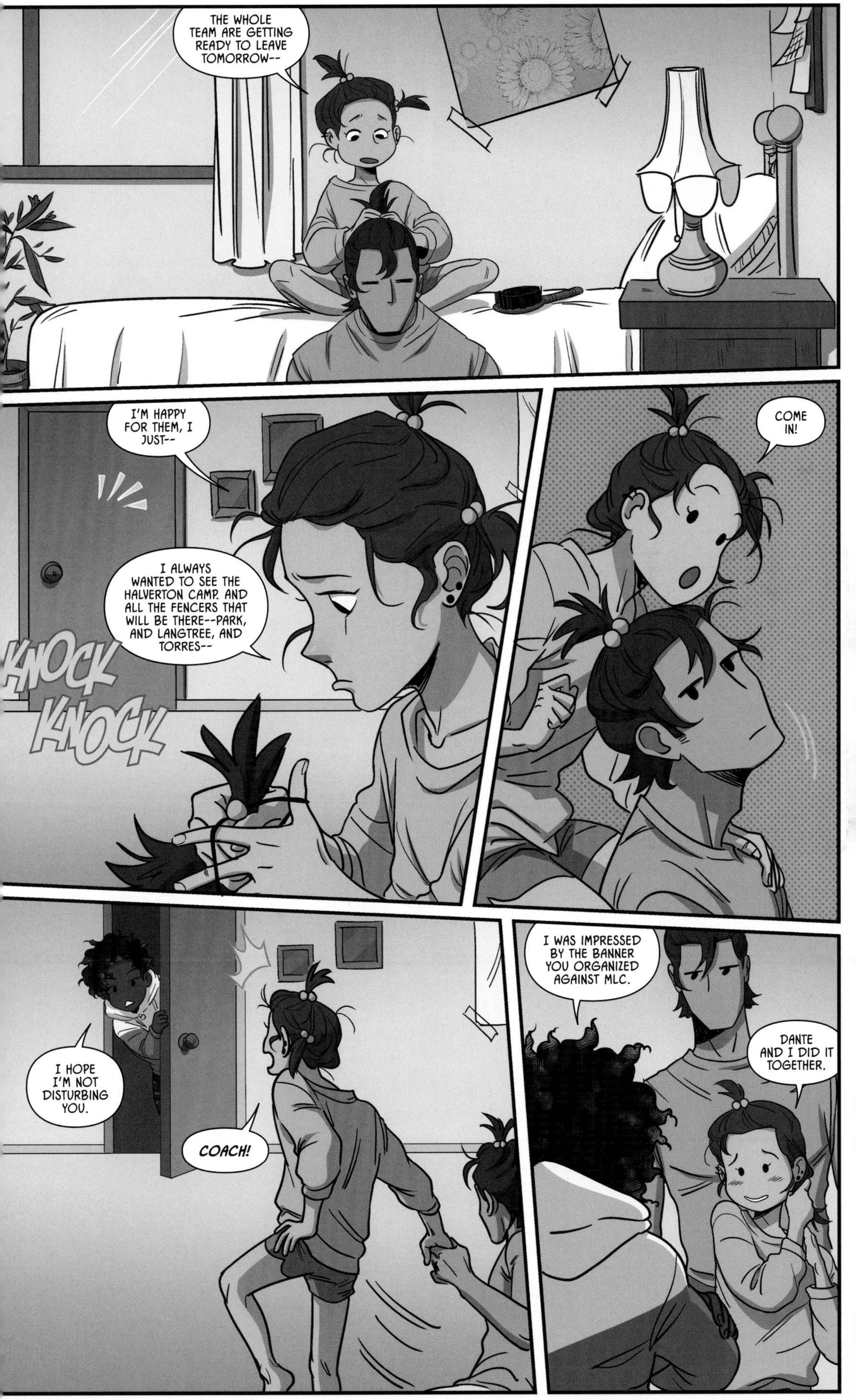
THE WHOLE TEAM ARE GETTING READY TO LEAVE TOMORROW--
I'M HAPPY FOR THEM, I JUST--
I ALWAYS WANTED TO SEE THE HALVERTON CAMP. AND ALL THE FENCERS THAT WILL BE THERE--PARK, AND LANGTREE, AND TORRES--
KNOCK KNOCK
COME IN!
I HOPE I'M NOT DISTURBING YOU.
COACH!
I WAS IMPRESSED BY THE BANNER YOU ORGANIZED AGAINST MLC.
DANTE AND I DID IT TOGETHER.

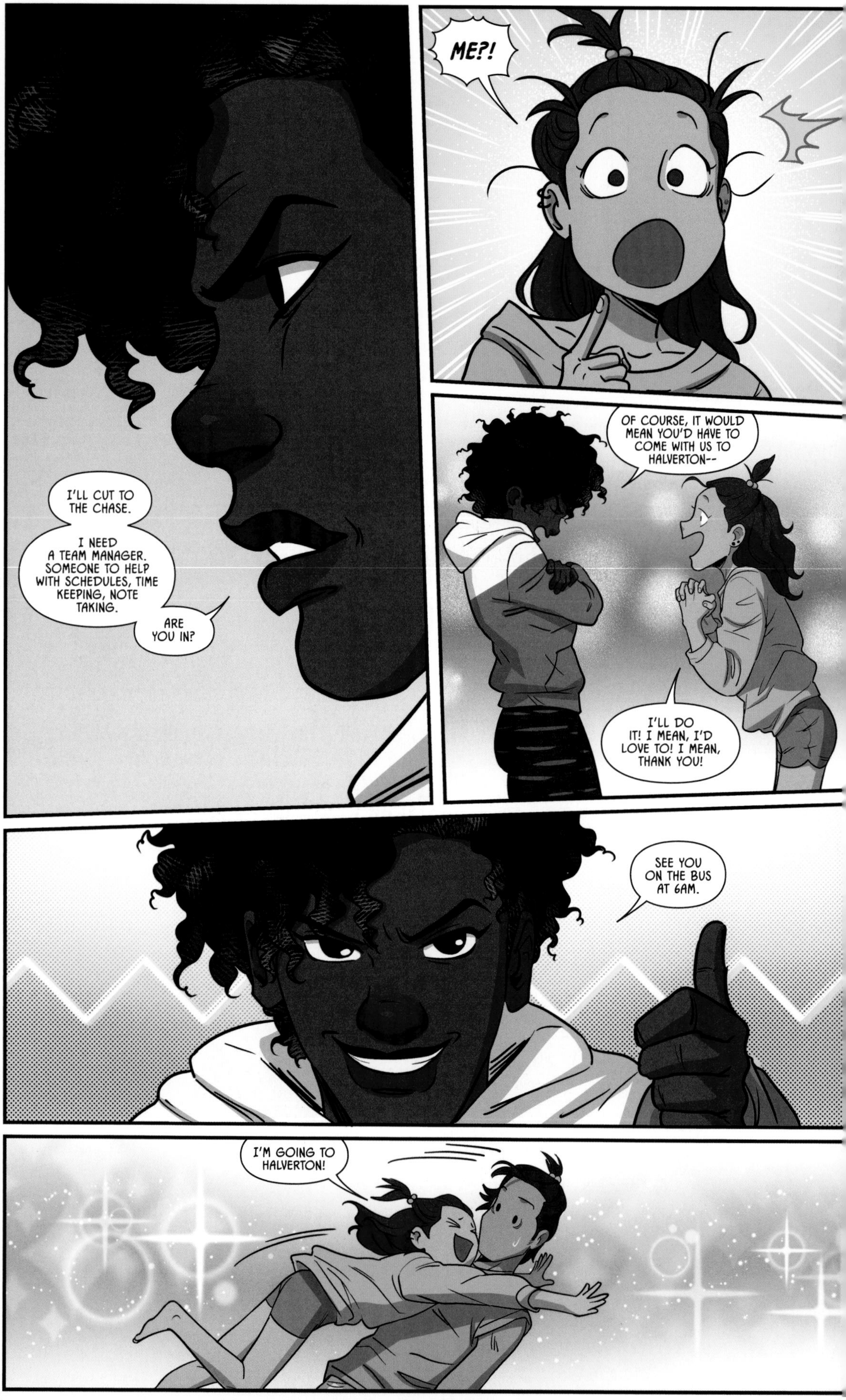
I'LL CUT TO THE CHASE.
I NEED A TEAM MANAGER. SOMEONE TO HELP WITH SCHEDULES, TIME KEEPING, NOTE TAKING.
ARE YOU IN?
ME?!
OF COURSE, IT WOULD MEAN YOU'D HAVE TO COME WITH US TO HALVERTON--
I'LL DO IT! I MEAN, I'D LOVE TO! I MEAN, THANK YOU!
SEE YOU ON THE BUS AT 6AM.
I'M GOING TO HALVERTON!

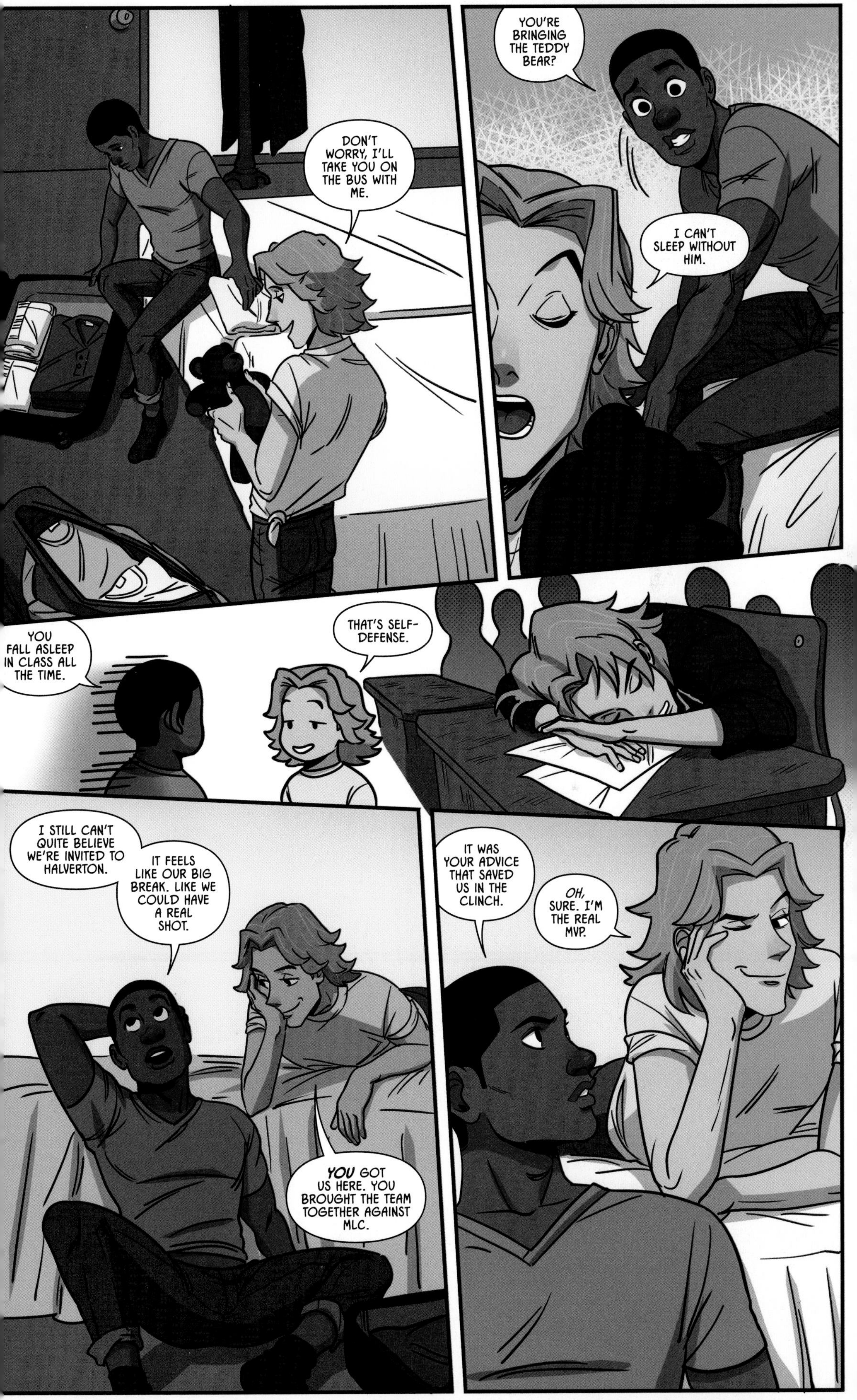
DON'T WORRY, I'LL TAKE YOU ON THE BUS WITH ME.
YOU'RE BRINGING THE TEDDY BEAR?
I CAN'T SLEEP WITHOUT HIM.
YOU FALL ASLEEP IN CLASS ALL THE TIME.
THAT'S SELF-DEFENSE.
I STILL CAN'T QUITE BELIEVE WE'RE INVITED TO HALVERTON.
IT FEELS LIKE OUR BIG BREAK. LIKE WE COULD HAVE A REAL SHOT.
YOU GOT US HERE. YOU BROUGHT THE TEAM TOGETHER AGAINST MLC.
IT WAS YOUR ADVICE THAT SAVED US IN THE CLINCH.
OH, SURE. I'M THE REAL MVP.

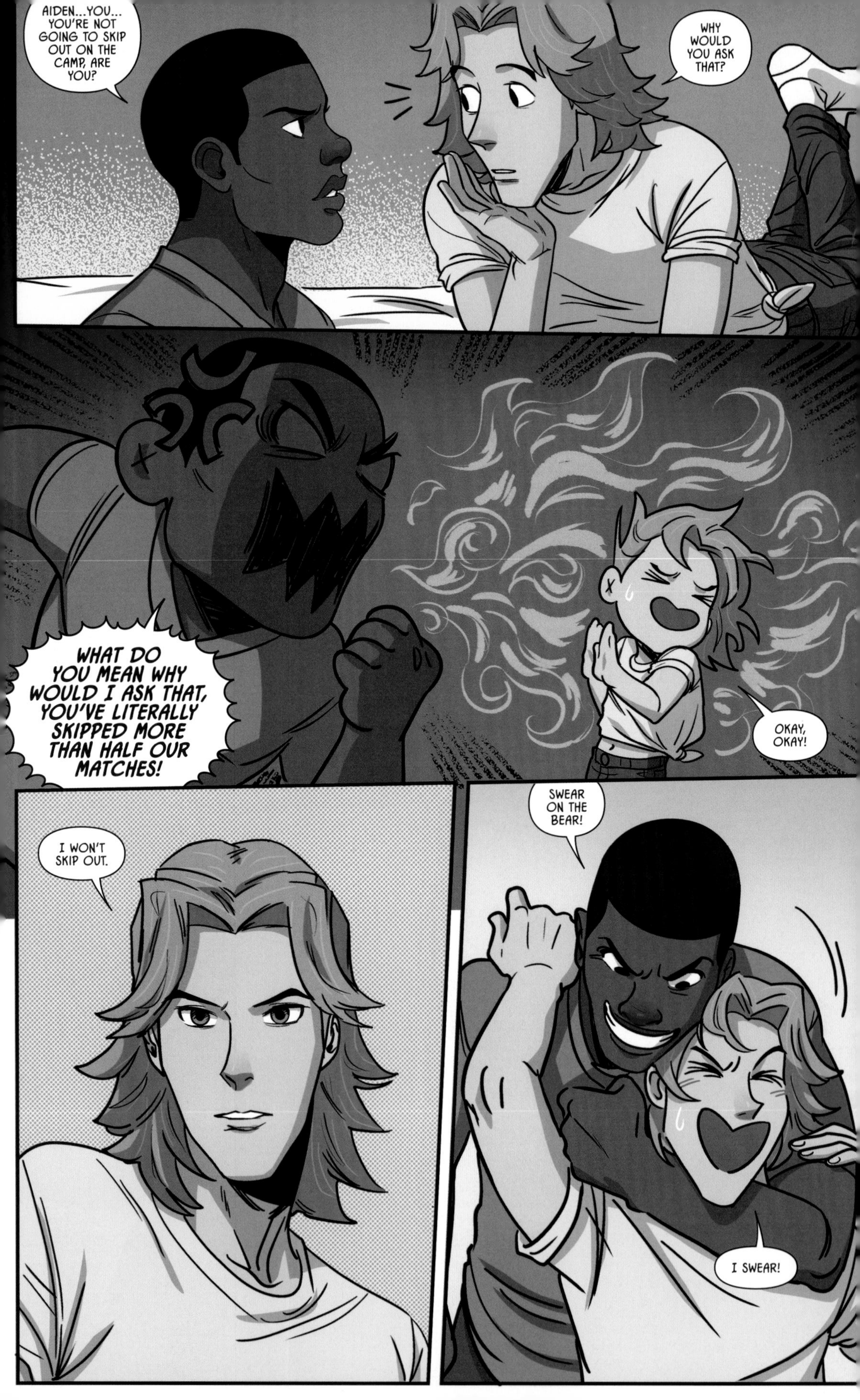
AIDEN...YOU... YOU'RE NOT GOING TO SKIP OUT ON THE CAMP, ARE YOU?
WHY WOULD YOU ASK THAT?
WHAT DO YOU MEAN WHY WOULD I ASK THAT, YOU'VE LITERALLY SKIPPED MORE THAN HALF OUR MATCHES!
OKAY, OKAY!
I WON'T SKIP OUT.
SWEAR ON THE BEAR!
I SWEAR!

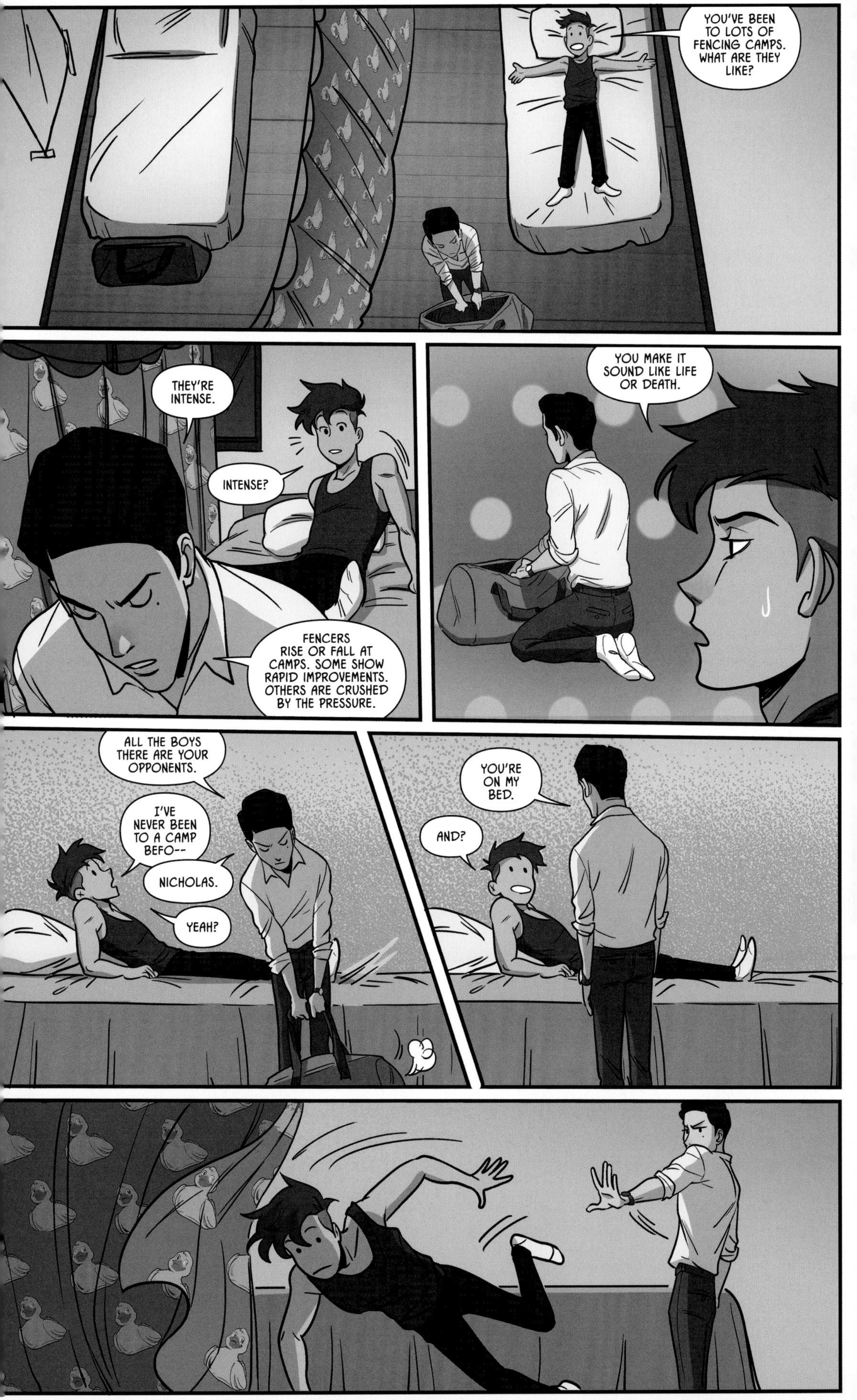
YOU'VE BEEN TO LOTS OF FENCING CAMPS. WHAT ARE THEY LIKE?
THEY'RE INTENSE.
INTENSE?
FENCERS RISE OR FALL AT CAMPS. SOME SHOW RAPID IMPROVEMENTS. OTHERS ARE CRUSHED BY THE PRESSURE.
YOU MAKE IT SOUND LIKE LIFE OR DEATH.
ALL THE BOYS THERE ARE YOUR OPPONENTS.
I'VE NEVER BEEN TO A CAMP BEFO--
NICHOLAS.
YEAH?
YOU'RE ON MY BED.
AND?

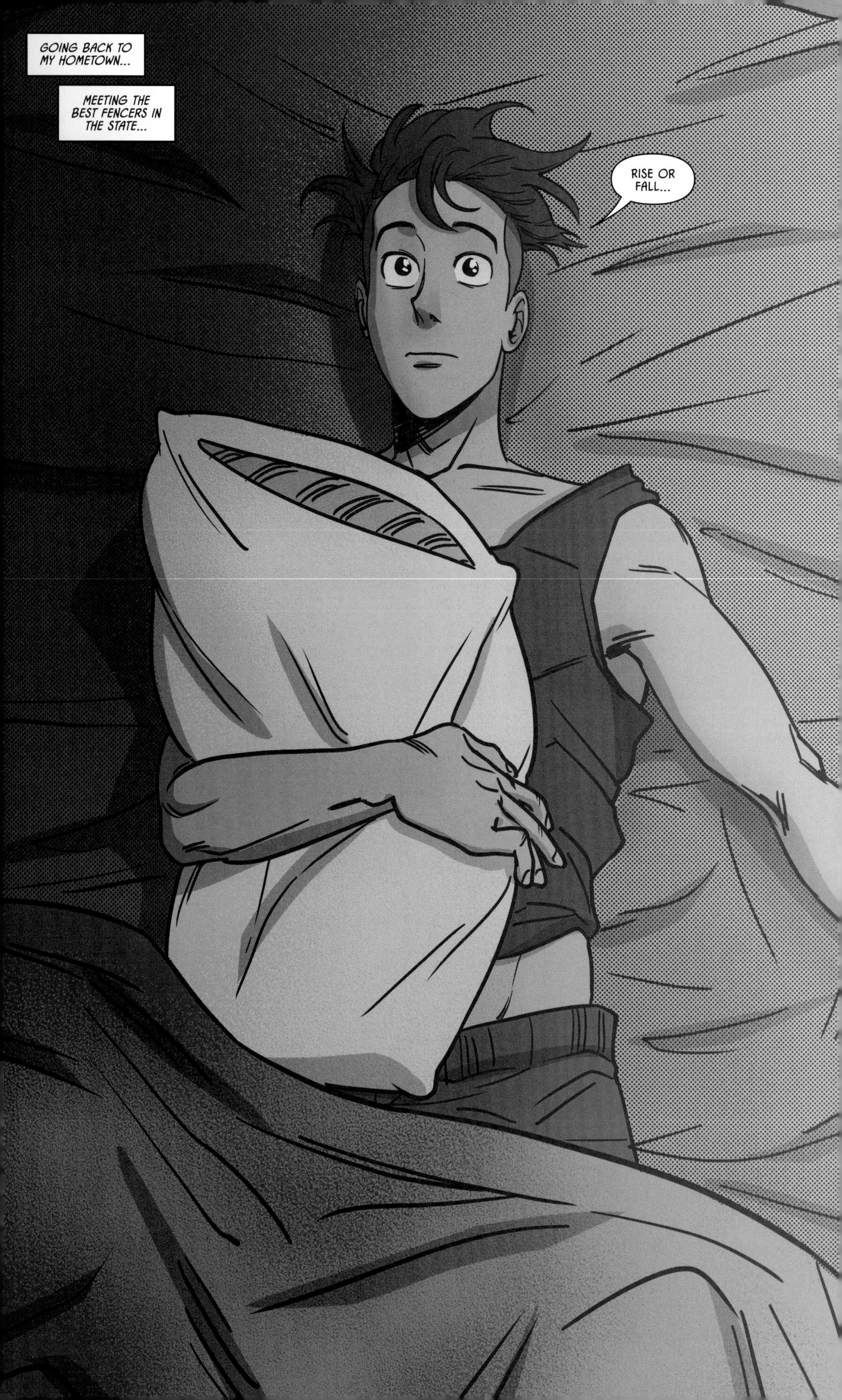
GOING BACK TO MY HOMETOWN...
MEETING THE BEST FENCERS IN THE STATE...
RISE OR FALL...

CHAPTER
EIGHTEEN

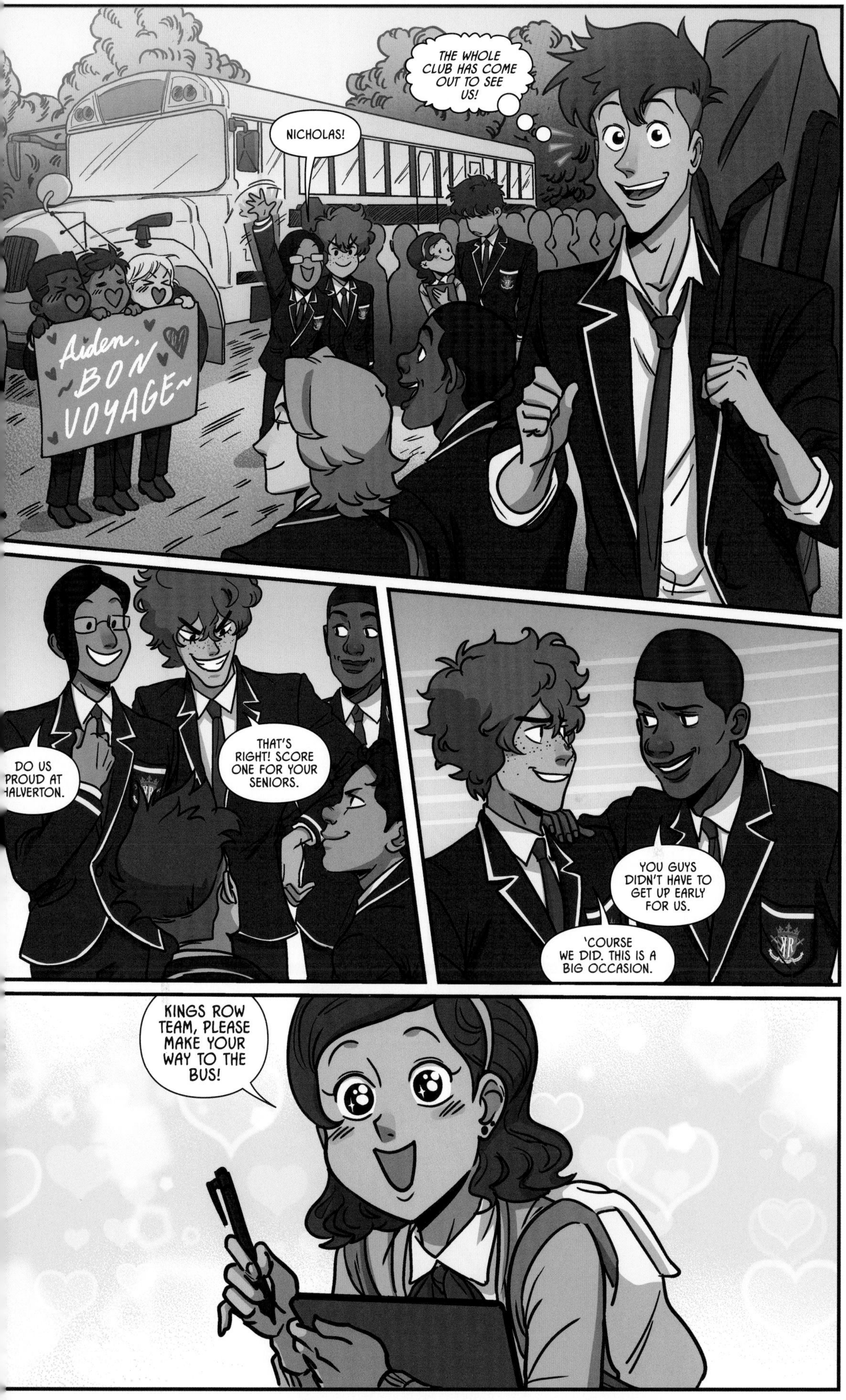
Aiden, BON VOYAGE
NICHOLAS!
THE WHOLE CLUB HAS COME OUT TO SEE US!
DO US PROUD AT HALVERTON.
THAT'S RIGHT! SCORE ONE FOR YOUR SENIORS.
YOU GUYS DIDN'T HAVE TO GET UP EARLY FOR US.
'COURSE WE DID. THIS IS A BIG OCCASION.
KINGS ROW TEAM, PLEASE MAKE YOUR WAY TO THE BUS!

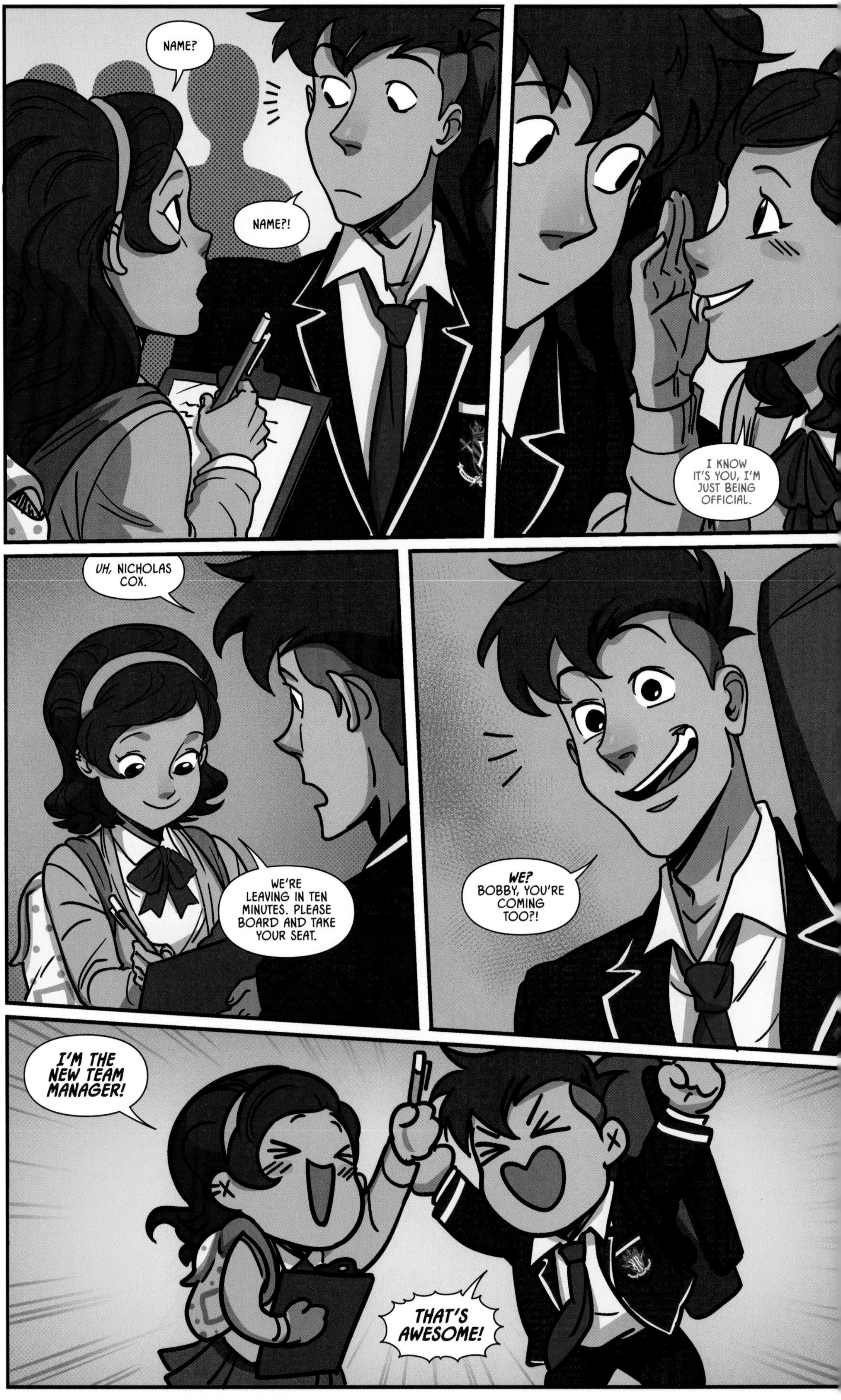
NAME?
NAME?!
I KNOW IT'S YOU, I'M JUST BEING OFFICIAL.
UH, NICHOLAS COX.
WE'RE LEAVING IN TEN MINUTES. PLEASE BOARD AND TAKE YOUR SEAT.
WE? BOBBY, YOU'RE COMING TOO?!
I'M THE NEW TEAM MANAGER!
THAT'S AWESOME!

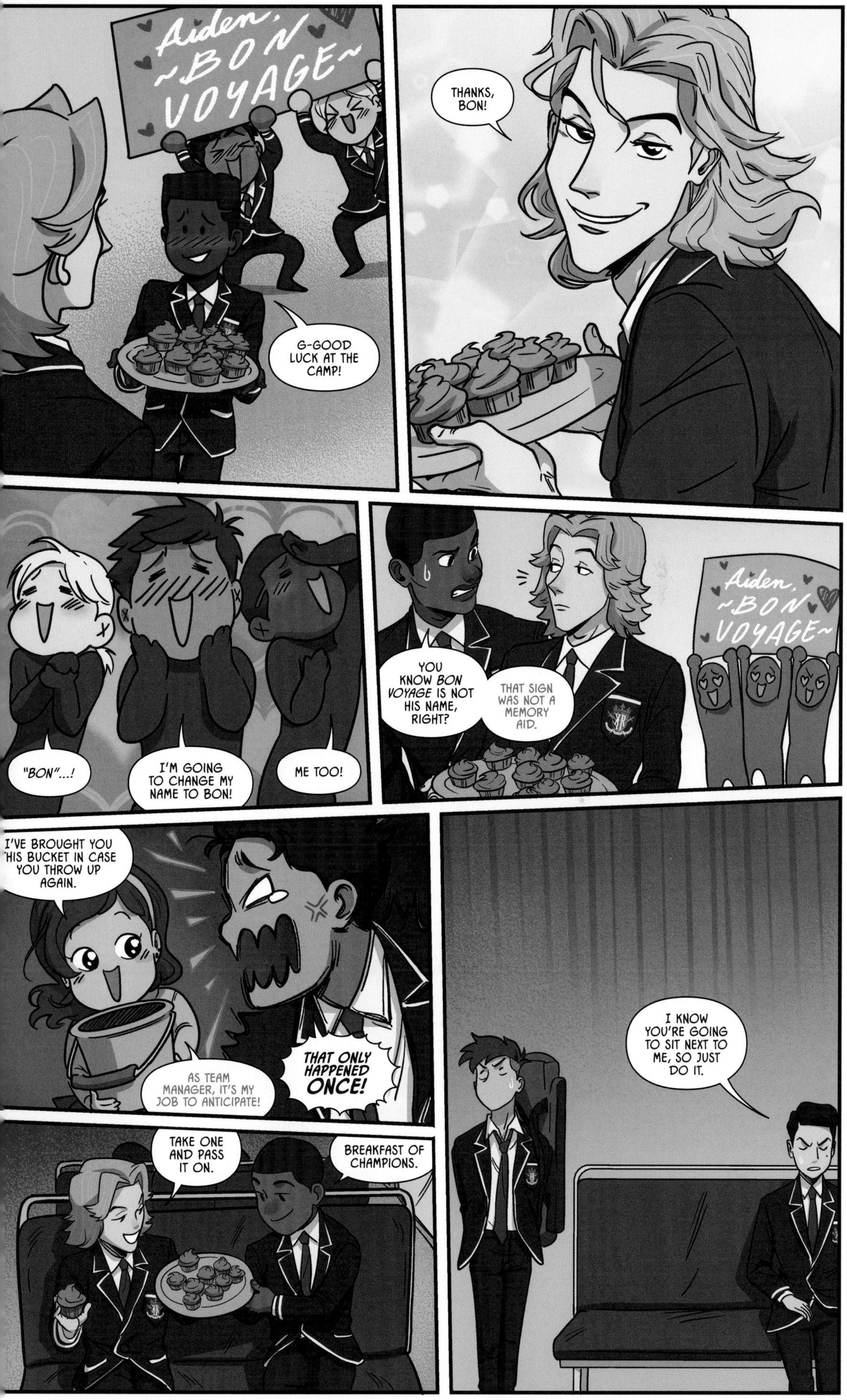
Aiden, ~BON VOYAGE~
G-GOOD LUCK AT THE CAMP!
THANKS, BON!
"BON"...!
I'M GOING TO CHANGE MY NAME TO BON!
ME TOO!
YOU KNOW *BON VOYAGE* IS NOT HIS NAME, RIGHT?
THAT SIGN WAS NOT A MEMORY AID.
Aiden, ~BON VOYAGE~
I'VE BROUGHT YOU THIS BUCKET IN CASE YOU THROW UP AGAIN.
AS TEAM MANAGER, IT'S MY JOB TO ANTICIPATE!
THAT ONLY HAPPENED ONCE!
TAKE ONE AND PASS IT ON.
BREAKFAST OF CHAMPIONS.
I KNOW YOU'RE GOING TO SIT NEXT TO ME, SO JUST DO IT.

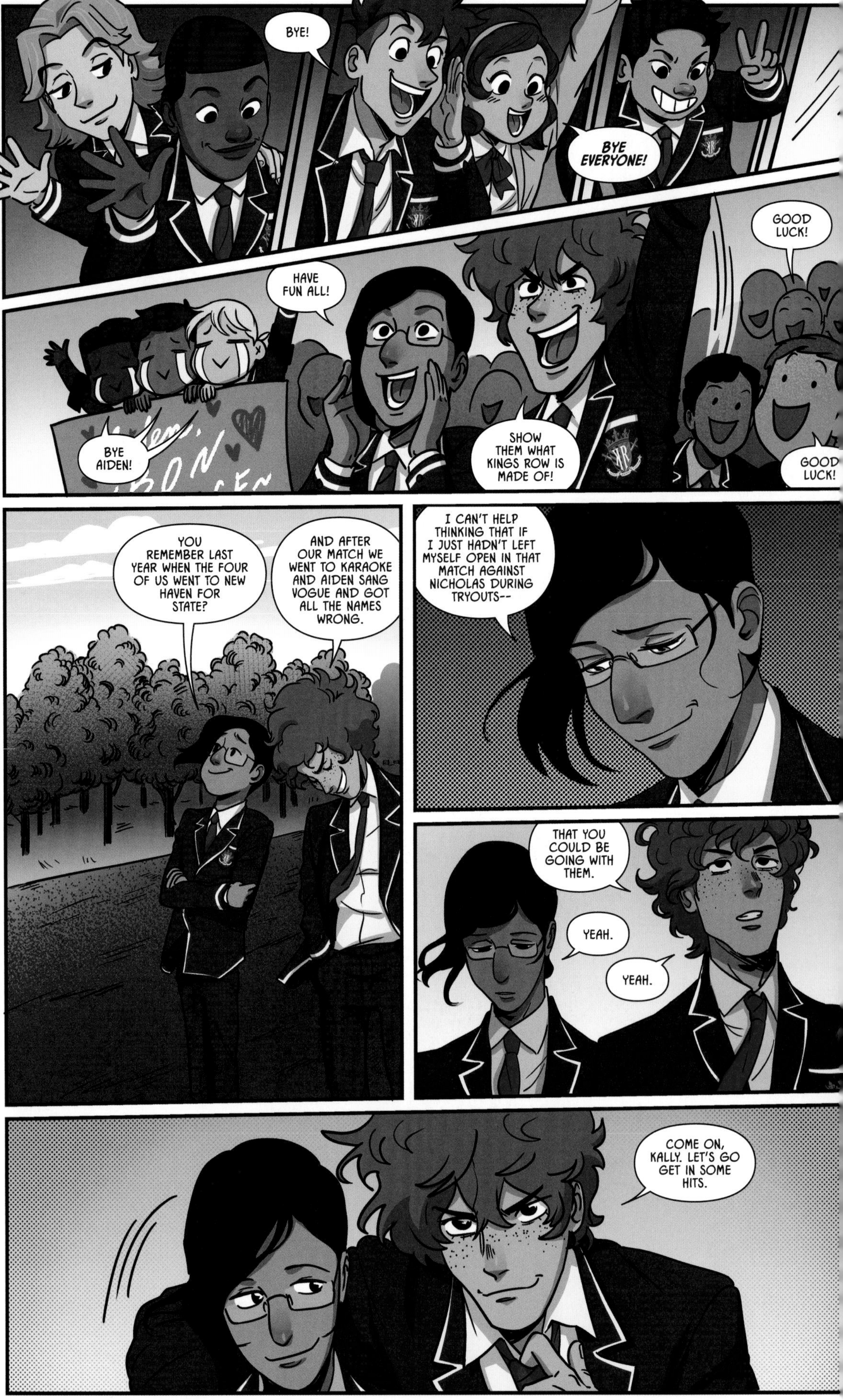
BYE!
BYE EVERYONE!
HAVE FUN ALL!
GOOD LUCK!
BYE AIDEN!
SHOW THEM WHAT KINGS ROW IS MADE OF!
GOOD LUCK!
YOU REMEMBER LAST YEAR WHEN THE FOUR OF US WENT TO NEW HAVEN FOR STATE?
AND AFTER OUR MATCH WE WENT TO KARAOKE AND AIDEN SANG VOGUE AND GOT ALL THE NAMES WRONG.
I CAN'T HELP THINKING THAT IF I JUST HADN'T LEFT MYSELF OPEN IN THAT MATCH AGAINST NICHOLAS DURING TRYOUTS--
THAT YOU COULD BE GOING WITH THEM.
YEAH.
YEAH.
COME ON, KALLY. LET'S GO GET IN SOME HITS.

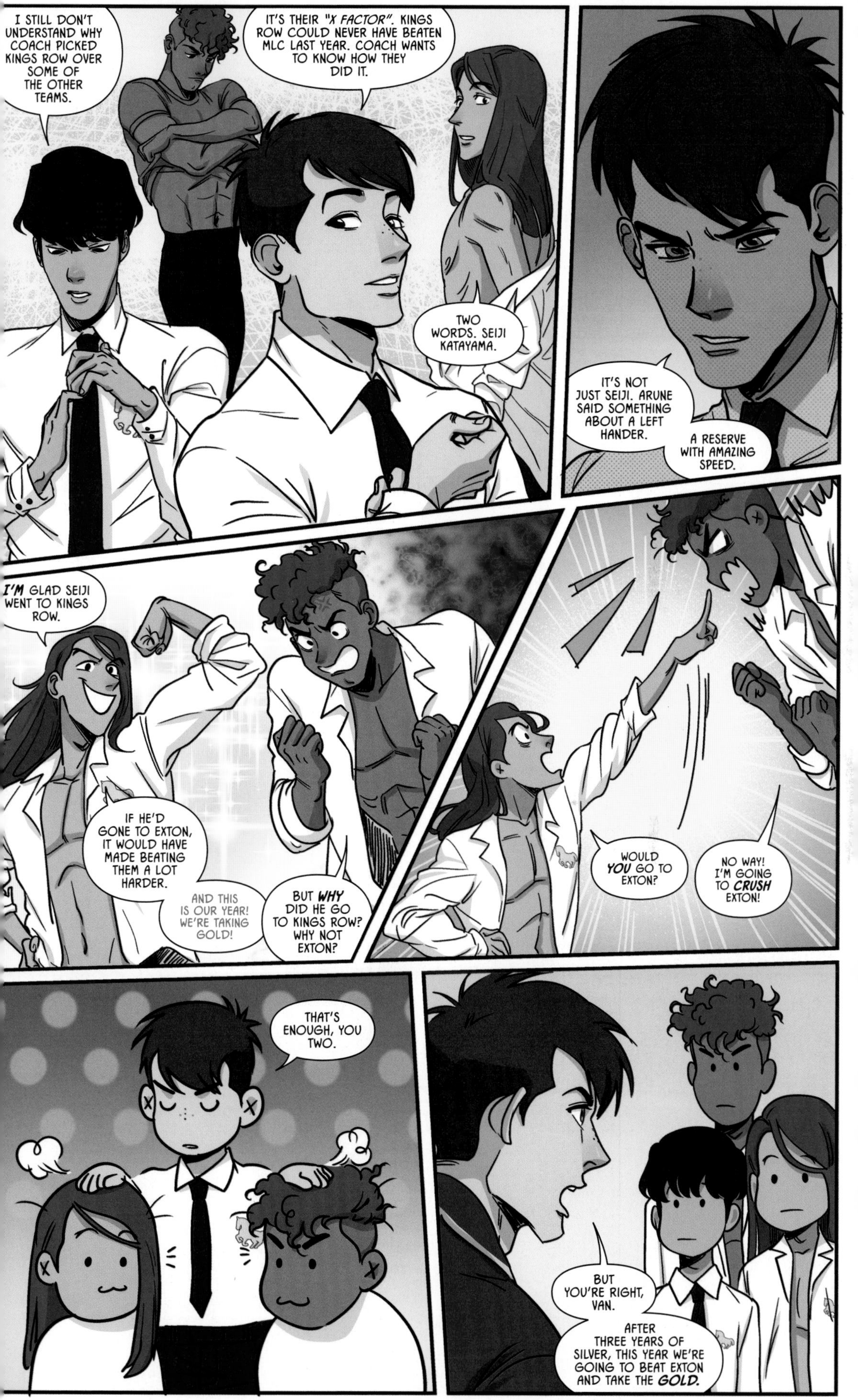
I STILL DON'T UNDERSTAND WHY COACH PICKED KINGS ROW OVER SOME OF THE OTHER TEAMS.
IT'S THEIR *"X FACTOR"*. KINGS ROW COULD NEVER HAVE BEATEN MLC LAST YEAR. COACH WANTS TO KNOW HOW THEY DID IT.
TWO WORDS. SEIJI KATAYAMA.
IT'S NOT JUST SEIJI. ARUNE SAID SOMETHING ABOUT A LEFT HANDER.
A RESERVE WITH AMAZING SPEED.
I'M GLAD SEIJI WENT TO KINGS ROW.
IF HE'D GONE TO EXTON, IT WOULD HAVE MADE BEATING THEM A LOT HARDER.
AND THIS IS OUR YEAR! WE'RE TAKING GOLD!
BUT ***WHY*** DID HE GO TO KINGS ROW? WHY NOT EXTON?
WOULD ***YOU*** GO TO EXTON?
NO WAY! I'M GOING TO ***CRUSH*** EXTON!
THAT'S ENOUGH, YOU TWO.
BUT YOU'RE RIGHT, VAN.
AFTER THREE YEARS OF SILVER, THIS YEAR WE'RE GOING TO BEAT EXTON AND TAKE THE ***GOLD.***

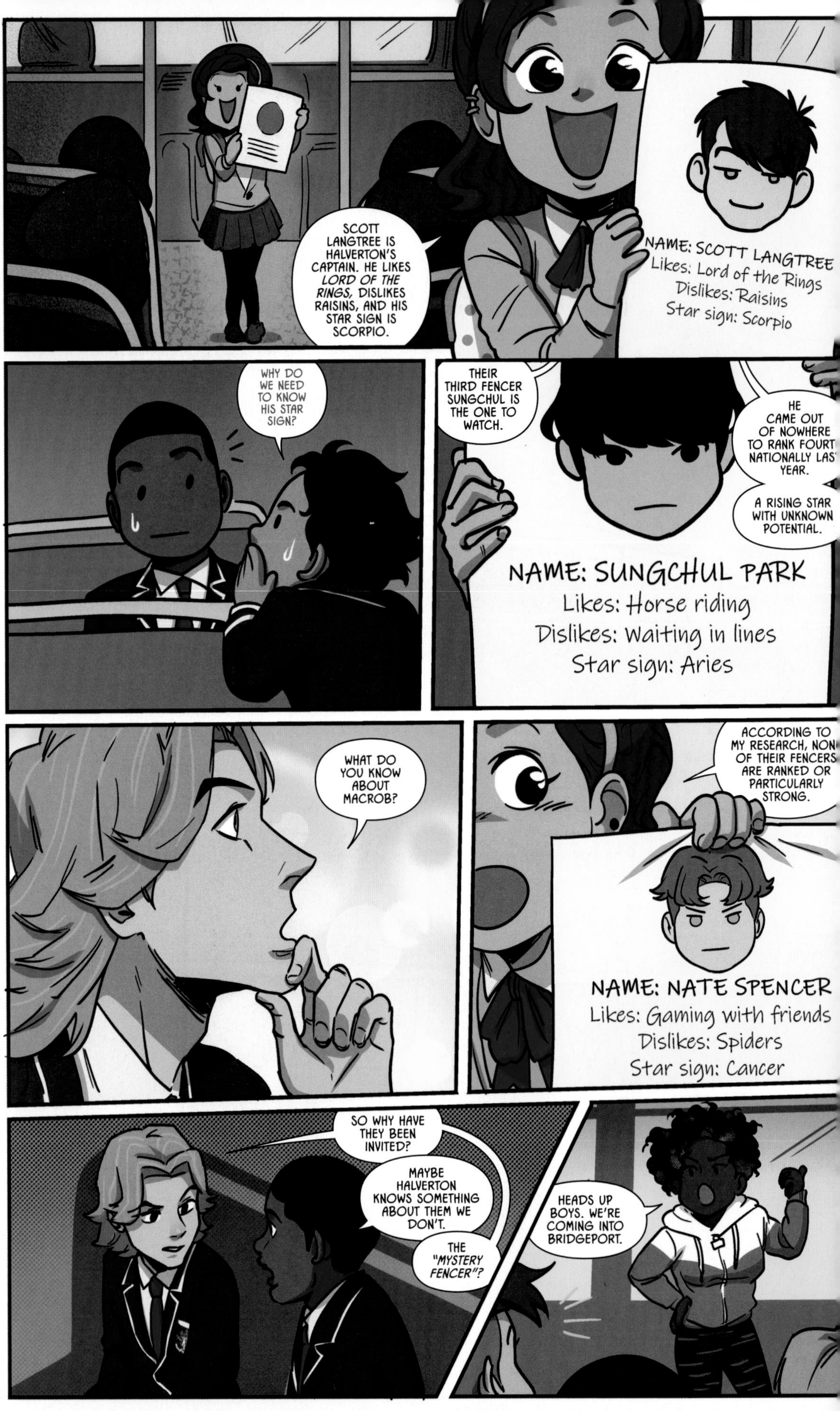
SCOTT LANGTREE IS HALVERTON'S CAPTAIN. HE LIKES *LORD OF THE RINGS*, DISLIKES RAISINS, AND HIS STAR SIGN IS SCORPIO.
NAME: SCOTT LANGTREE
Likes: Lord of the Rings
Dislikes: Raisins
Star sign: Scorpio
WHY DO WE NEED TO KNOW HIS STAR SIGN?
THEIR THIRD FENCER SUNGCHUL IS THE ONE TO WATCH.
HE CAME OUT OF NOWHERE TO RANK FOURT NATIONALLY LAS YEAR.
A RISING STAR WITH UNKNOWN POTENTIAL.
NAME: SUNGCHUL PARK
Likes: Horse riding
Dislikes: Waiting in lines
Star sign: Aries
WHAT DO YOU KNOW ABOUT MACROB?
ACCORDING TO MY RESEARCH, NON OF THEIR FENCERS ARE RANKED OR PARTICULARLY STRONG.
NAME: NATE SPENCER
Likes: Gaming with friends
Dislikes: Spiders
Star sign: Cancer
SO WHY HAVE THEY BEEN INVITED?
MAYBE HALVERTON KNOWS SOMETHING ABOUT THEM WE DON'T.
THE "*MYSTERY FENCER*"?
HEADS UP BOYS. WE'RE COMING INTO BRIDGEPORT.

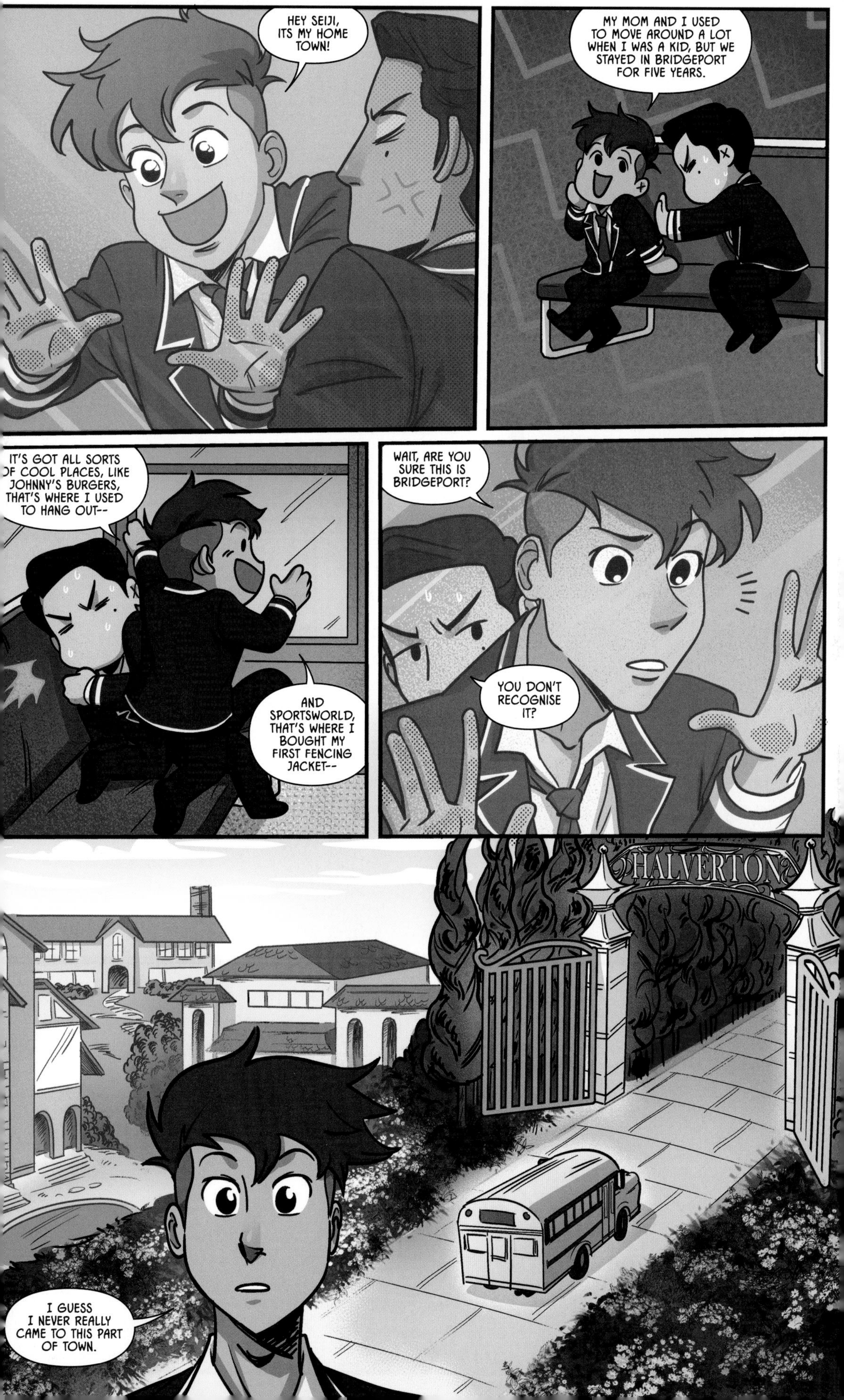
HEY SEIJI, ITS MY HOME TOWN!
MY MOM AND I USED TO MOVE AROUND A LOT WHEN I WAS A KID, BUT WE STAYED IN BRIDGEPORT FOR FIVE YEARS.
IT'S GOT ALL SORTS OF COOL PLACES, LIKE JOHNNY'S BURGERS, THAT'S WHERE I USED TO HANG OUT--
AND SPORTSWORLD, THAT'S WHERE I BOUGHT MY FIRST FENCING JACKET--
WAIT, ARE YOU SURE THIS IS BRIDGEPORT?
YOU DON'T RECOGNISE IT?
HALVERTON
I GUESS I NEVER REALLY CAME TO THIS PART OF TOWN.

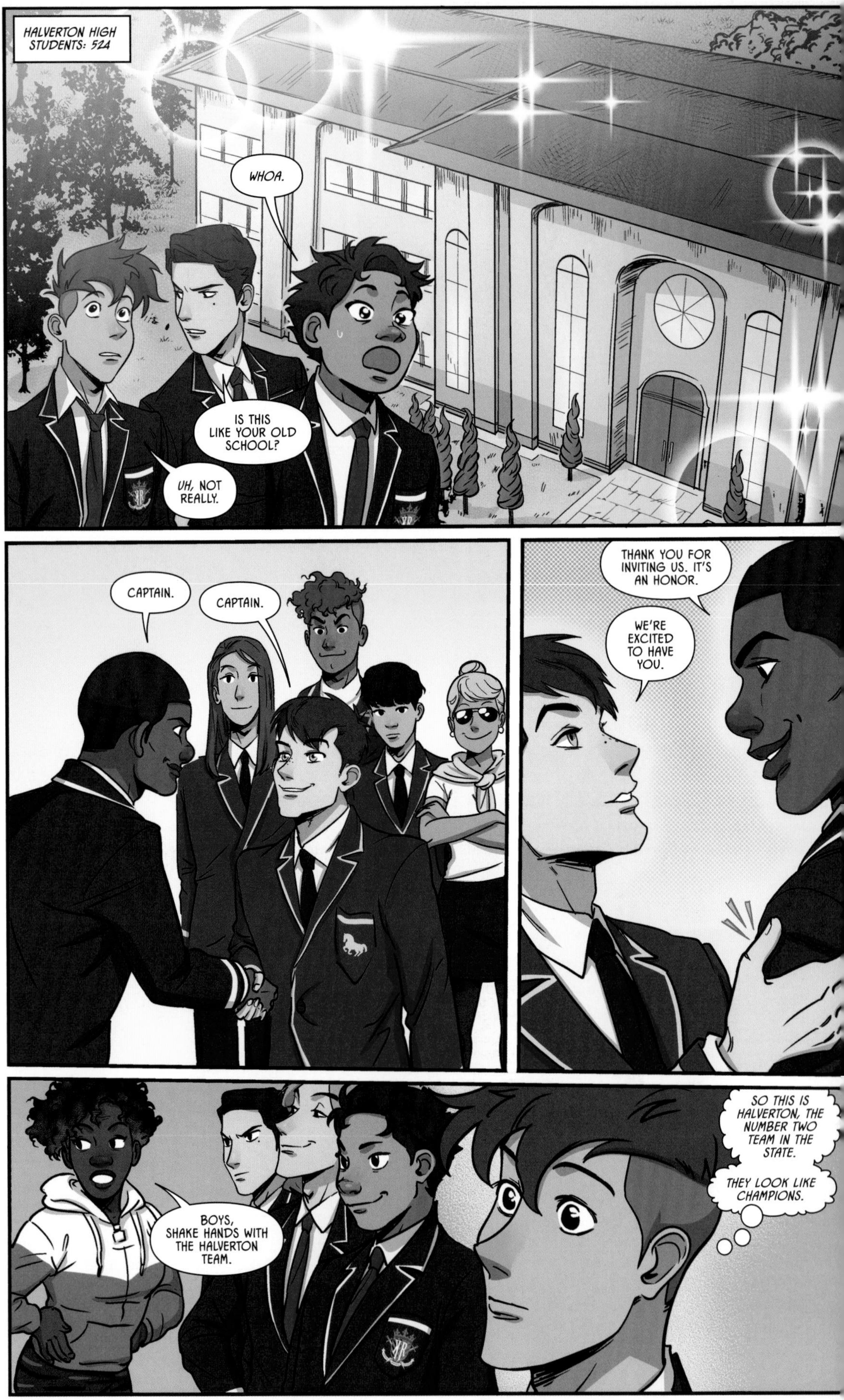
HALVERTON HIGH STUDENTS: 524
WHOA.
IS THIS LIKE YOUR OLD SCHOOL?
UH, NOT REALLY.
CAPTAIN.
CAPTAIN.
THANK YOU FOR INVITING US. IT'S AN HONOR.
WE'RE EXCITED TO HAVE YOU.
BOYS, SHAKE HANDS WITH THE HALVERTON TEAM.
SO THIS IS HALVERTON, THE NUMBER TWO TEAM IN THE STATE.
THEY LOOK LIKE CHAMPIONS.

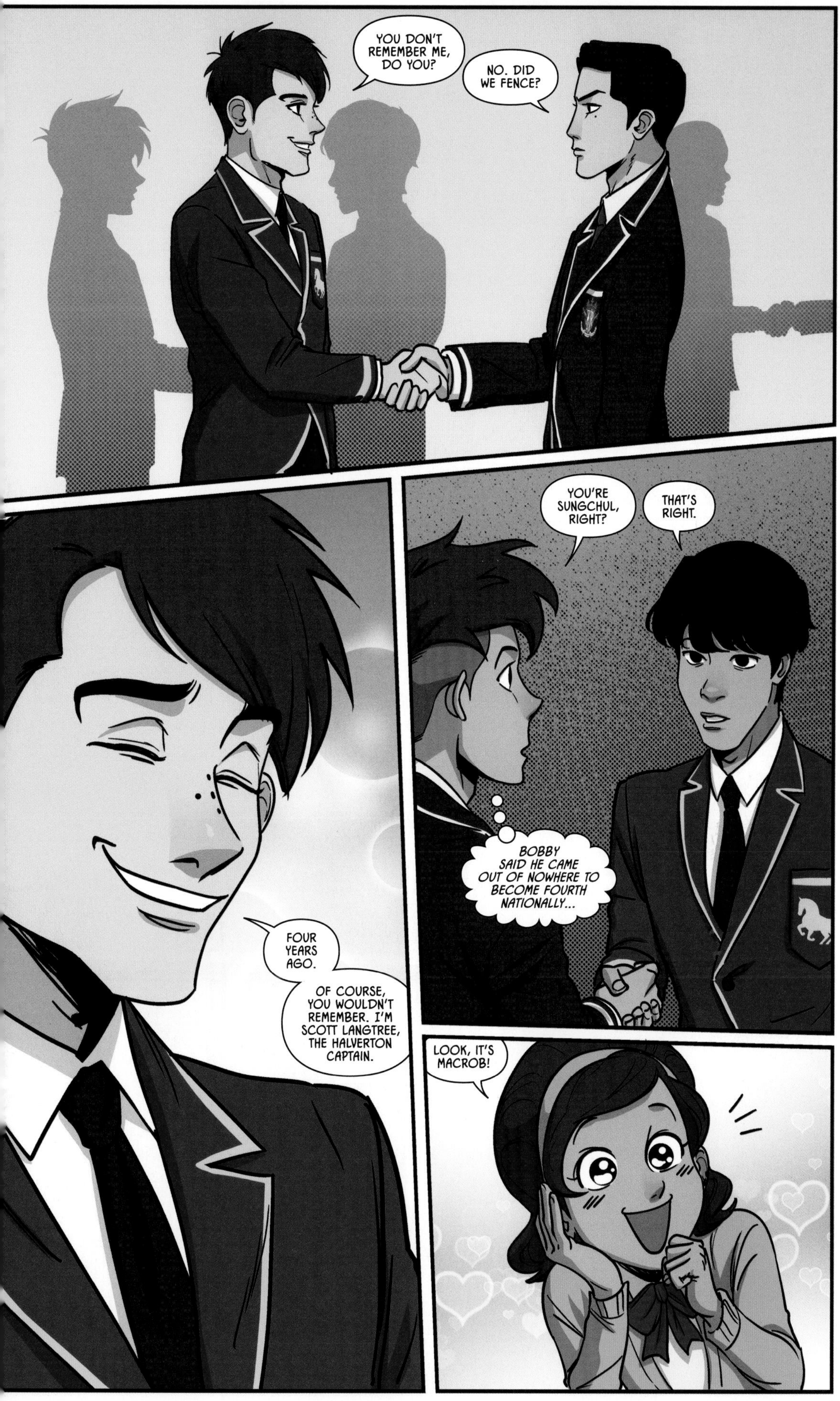
YOU DON'T REMEMBER ME, DO YOU?
NO. DID WE FENCE?
FOUR YEARS AGO.
OF COURSE, YOU WOULDN'T REMEMBER. I'M SCOTT LANGTREE, THE HALVERTON CAPTAIN.
YOU'RE SUNGCHUL, RIGHT?
THAT'S RIGHT.
BOBBY SAID HE CAME OUT OF NOWHERE TO BECOME FOURTH NATIONALLY...
LOOK, IT'S MACROB!

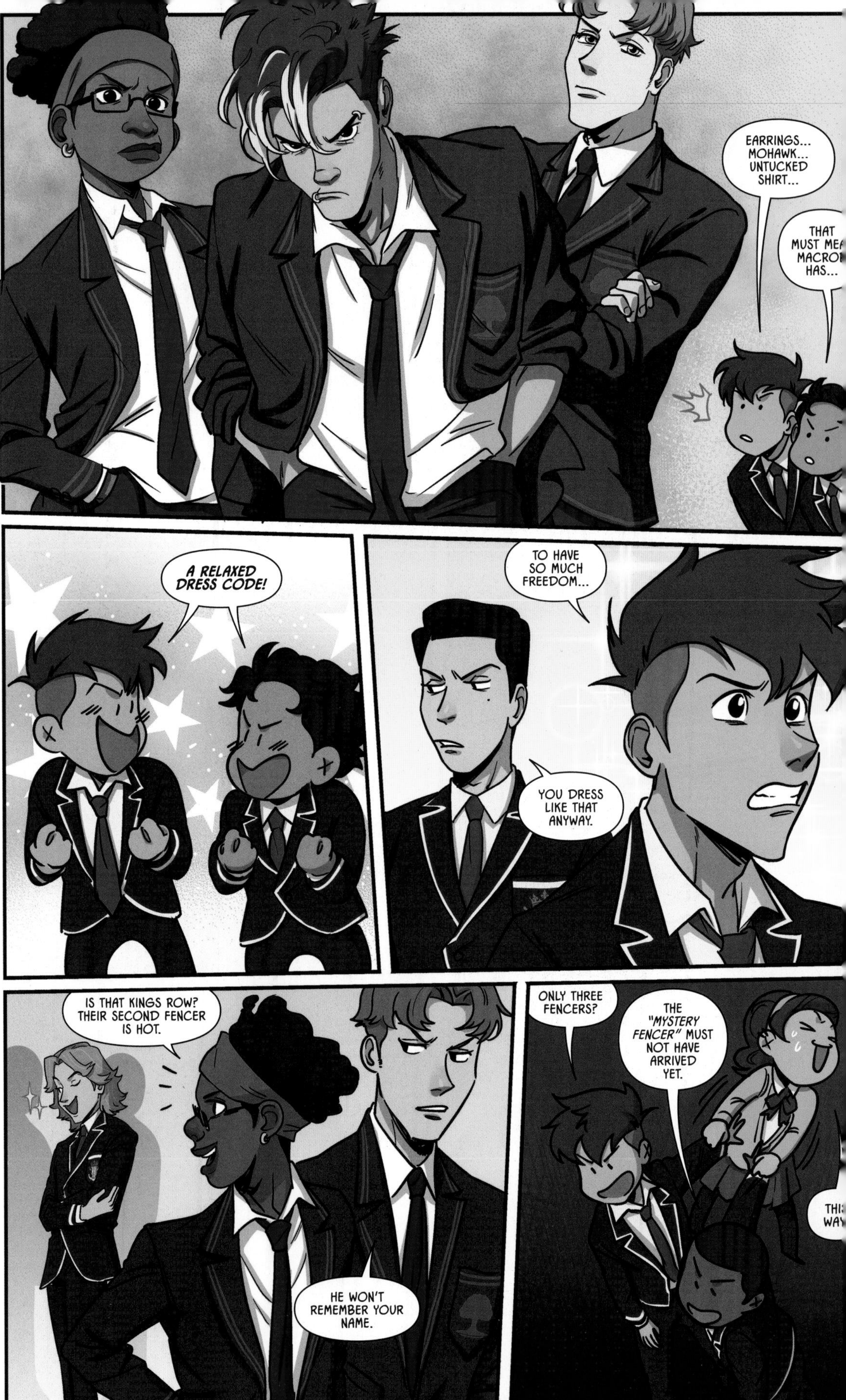
EARRINGS... MOHAWK... UNTUCKED SHIRT...
THAT MUST MEA MACRO HAS...
A RELAXED DRESS CODE!
TO HAVE SO MUCH FREEDOM...
YOU DRESS LIKE THAT ANYWAY.
IS THAT KINGS ROW? THEIR SECOND FENCER IS HOT.
HE WON'T REMEMBER YOUR NAME.
ONLY THREE FENCERS?
THE "MYSTERY FENCER" MUST NOT HAVE ARRIVED YET.
THI WA

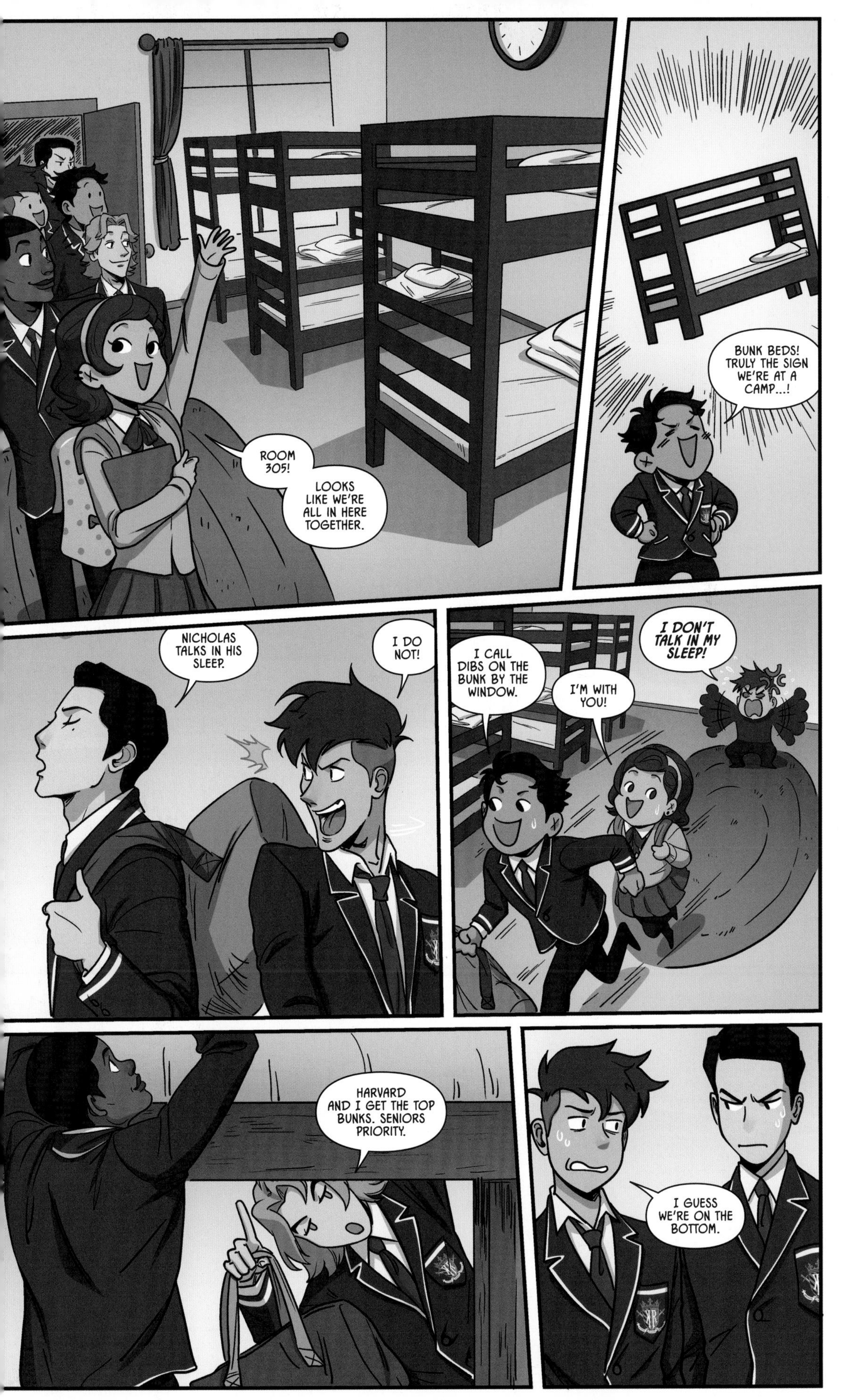
ROOM 305!
LOOKS LIKE WE'RE ALL IN HERE TOGETHER.
BUNK BEDS! TRULY THE SIGN WE'RE AT A CAMP...!
NICHOLAS TALKS IN HIS SLEEP.
I DO NOT!
I CALL DIBS ON THE BUNK BY THE WINDOW.
I'M WITH YOU!
I DON'T TALK IN MY SLEEP!
HARVARD AND I GET THE TOP BUNKS. SENIORS PRIORITY.
I GUESS WE'RE ON THE BOTTOM.

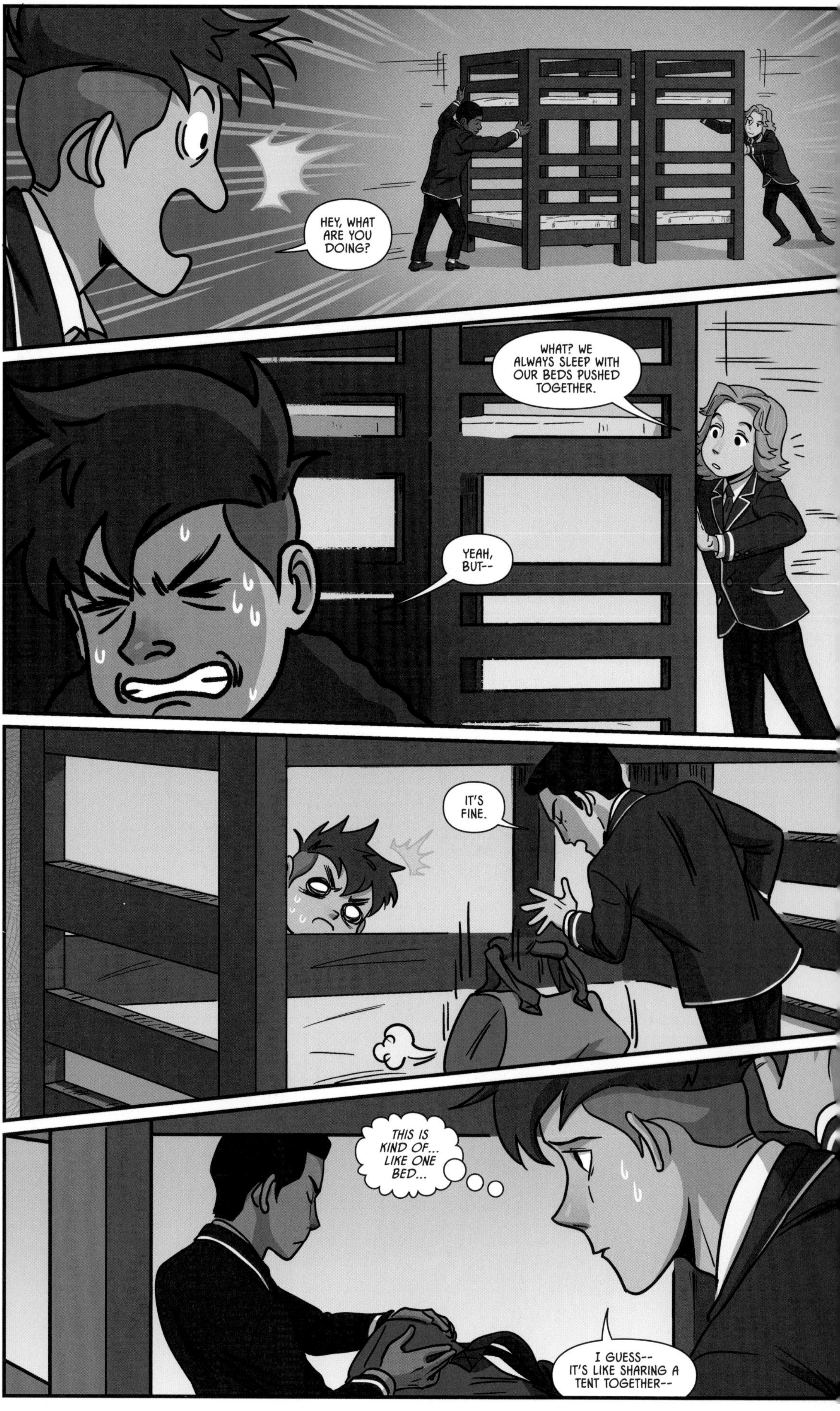
HEY, WHAT ARE YOU DOING?
WHAT? WE ALWAYS SLEEP WITH OUR BEDS PUSHED TOGETHER.
YEAH, BUT--
IT'S FINE.
THIS IS KIND OF... LIKE ONE BED...
I GUESS-- IT'S LIKE SHARING A TENT TOGETHER--

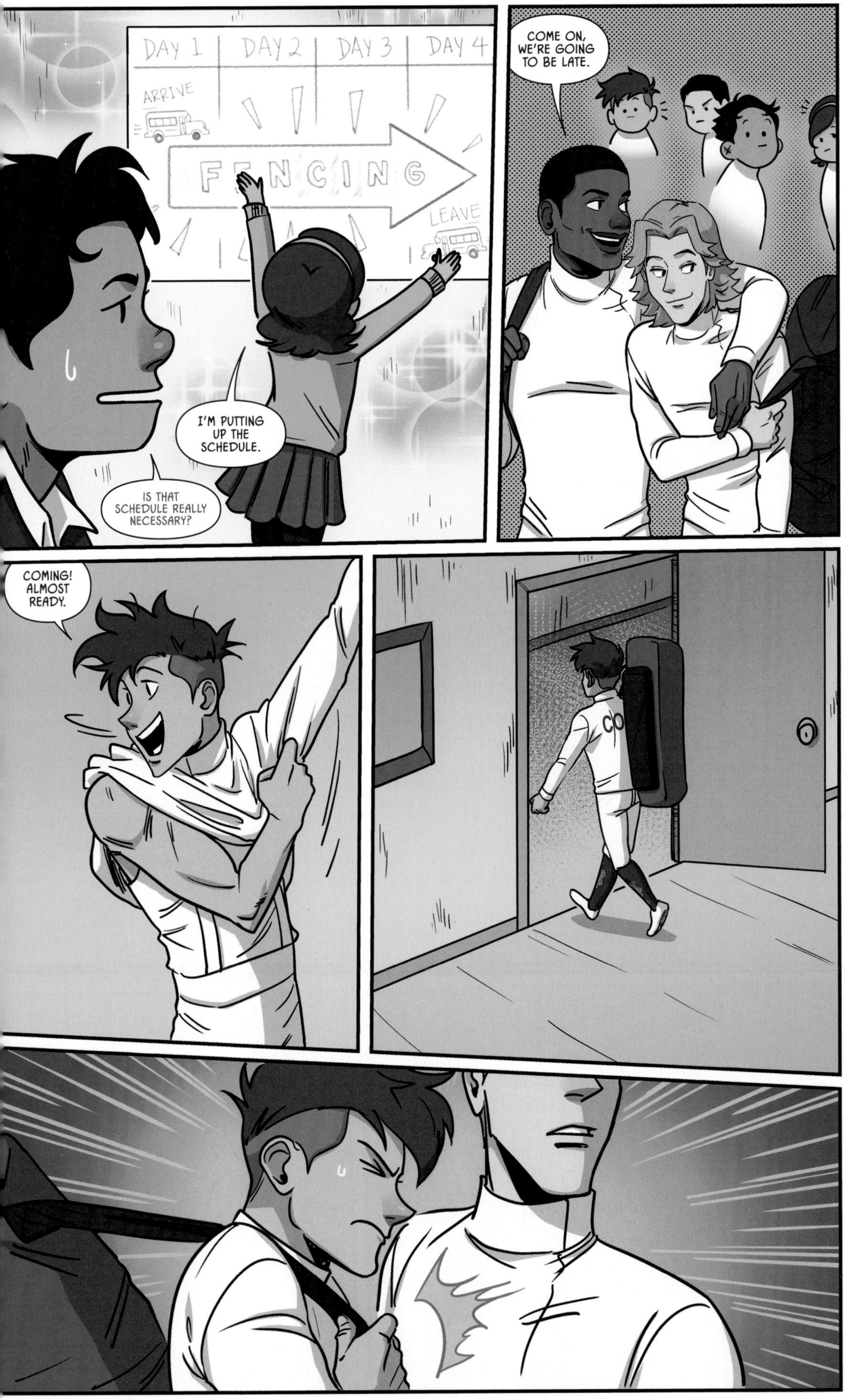
DAY 1
DAY 2
DAY 3
DAY 4
ARRIVE
FENCING
LEAVE
I'M PUTTING UP THE SCHEDULE.
IS THAT SCHEDULE REALLY NECESSARY?
COME ON, WE'RE GOING TO BE LATE.
COMING! ALMOST READY.

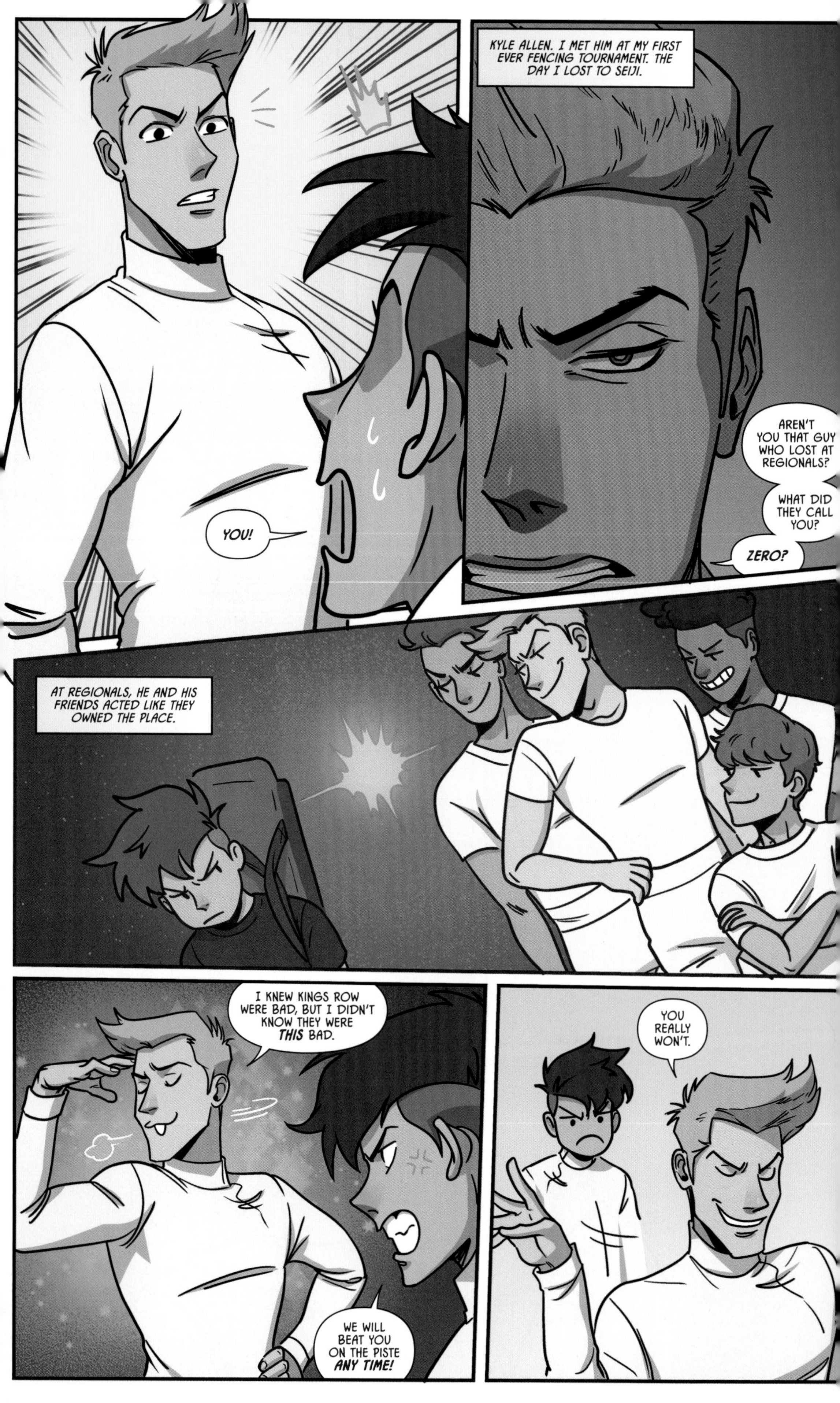
YOU!
KYLE ALLEN. I MET HIM AT MY FIRST EVER FENCING TOURNAMENT. THE DAY I LOST TO SEIJI.
AREN'T YOU THAT GUY WHO LOST AT REGIONALS?
WHAT DID THEY CALL YOU?
ZERO?
AT REGIONALS, HE AND HIS FRIENDS ACTED LIKE THEY OWNED THE PLACE.
I KNEW KINGS ROW WERE BAD, BUT I DIDN'T KNOW THEY WERE THIS BAD.
WE WILL BEAT YOU ON THE PISTE ANY TIME!
YOU REALLY WON'T.

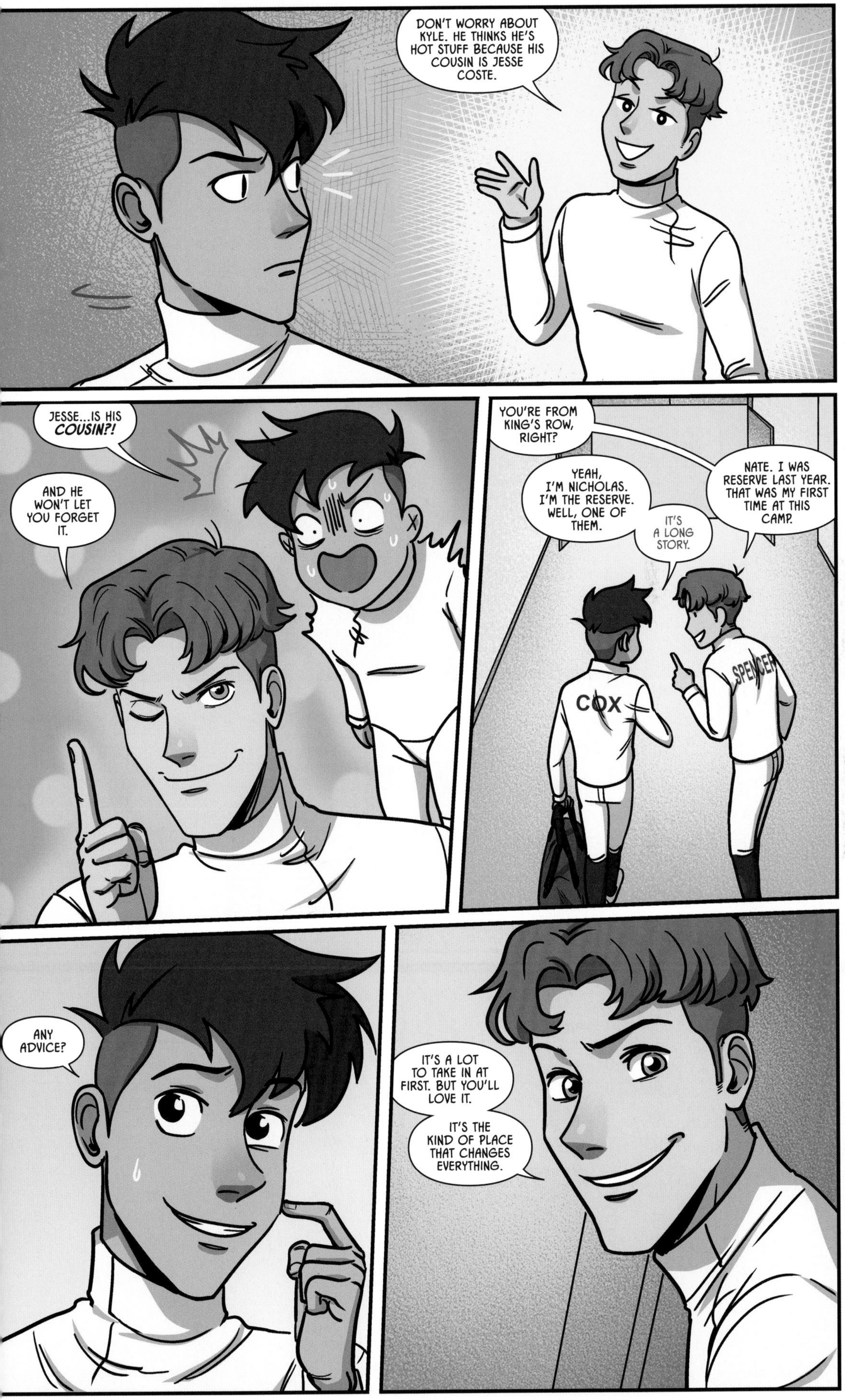
DON'T WORRY ABOUT KYLE. HE THINKS HE'S HOT STUFF BECAUSE HIS COUSIN IS JESSE COSTE.
JESSE...IS HIS *COUSIN?!*
AND HE WON'T LET YOU FORGET IT.
YOU'RE FROM KING'S ROW, RIGHT?
YEAH, I'M NICHOLAS. I'M THE RESERVE. WELL, ONE OF THEM.
IT'S A LONG STORY.
NATE. I WAS RESERVE LAST YEAR. THAT WAS MY FIRST TIME AT THIS CAMP.
COX
ANY ADVICE?
IT'S A LOT TO TAKE IN AT FIRST. BUT YOU'LL LOVE IT.
IT'S THE KIND OF PLACE THAT CHANGES EVERYTHING.

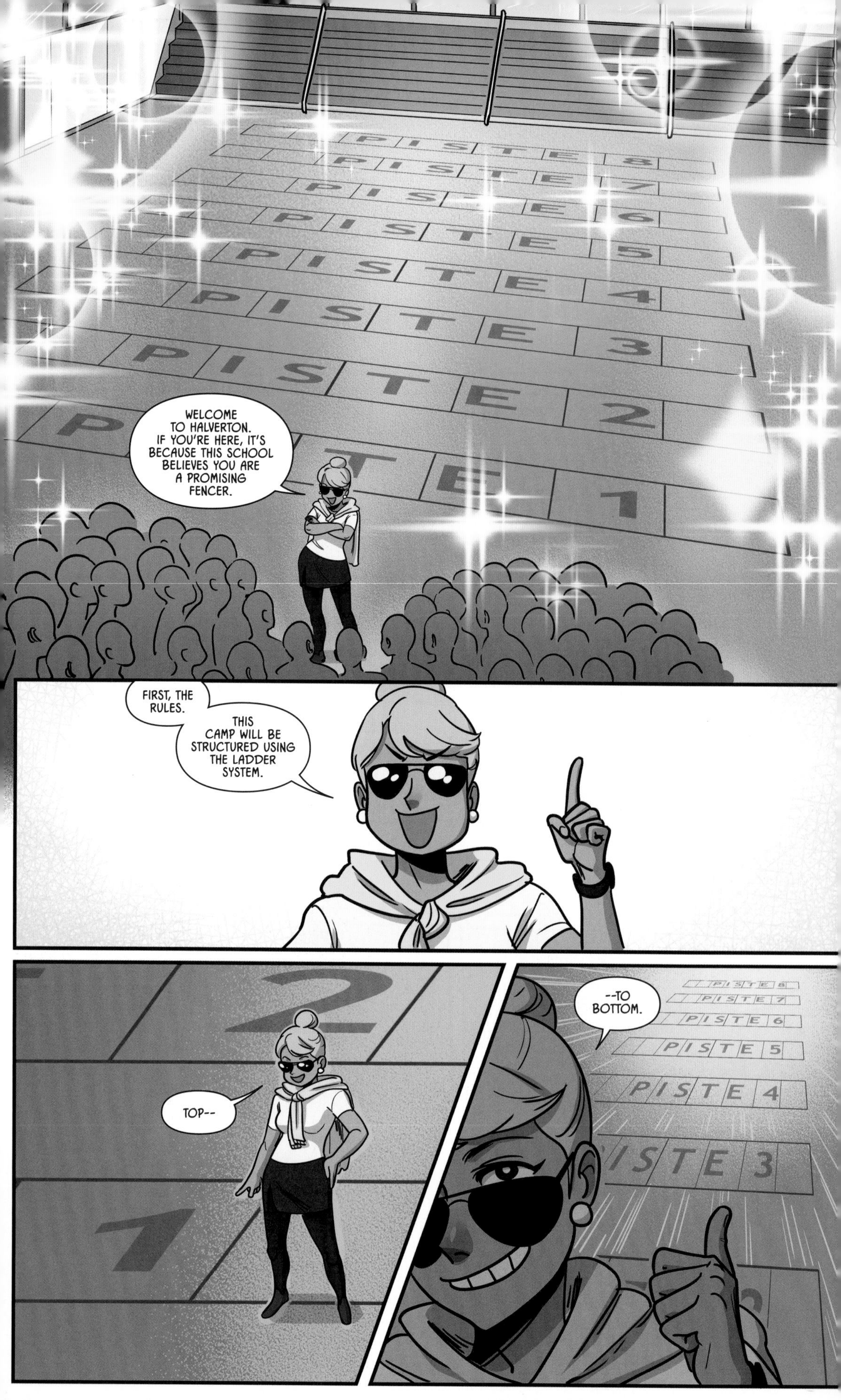
WELCOME TO HALVERTON. IF YOU'RE HERE, IT'S BECAUSE THIS SCHOOL BELIEVES YOU ARE A PROMISING FENCER.
FIRST, THE RULES.
THIS CAMP WILL BE STRUCTURED USING THE LADDER SYSTEM.
TOP--
--TO BOTTOM.

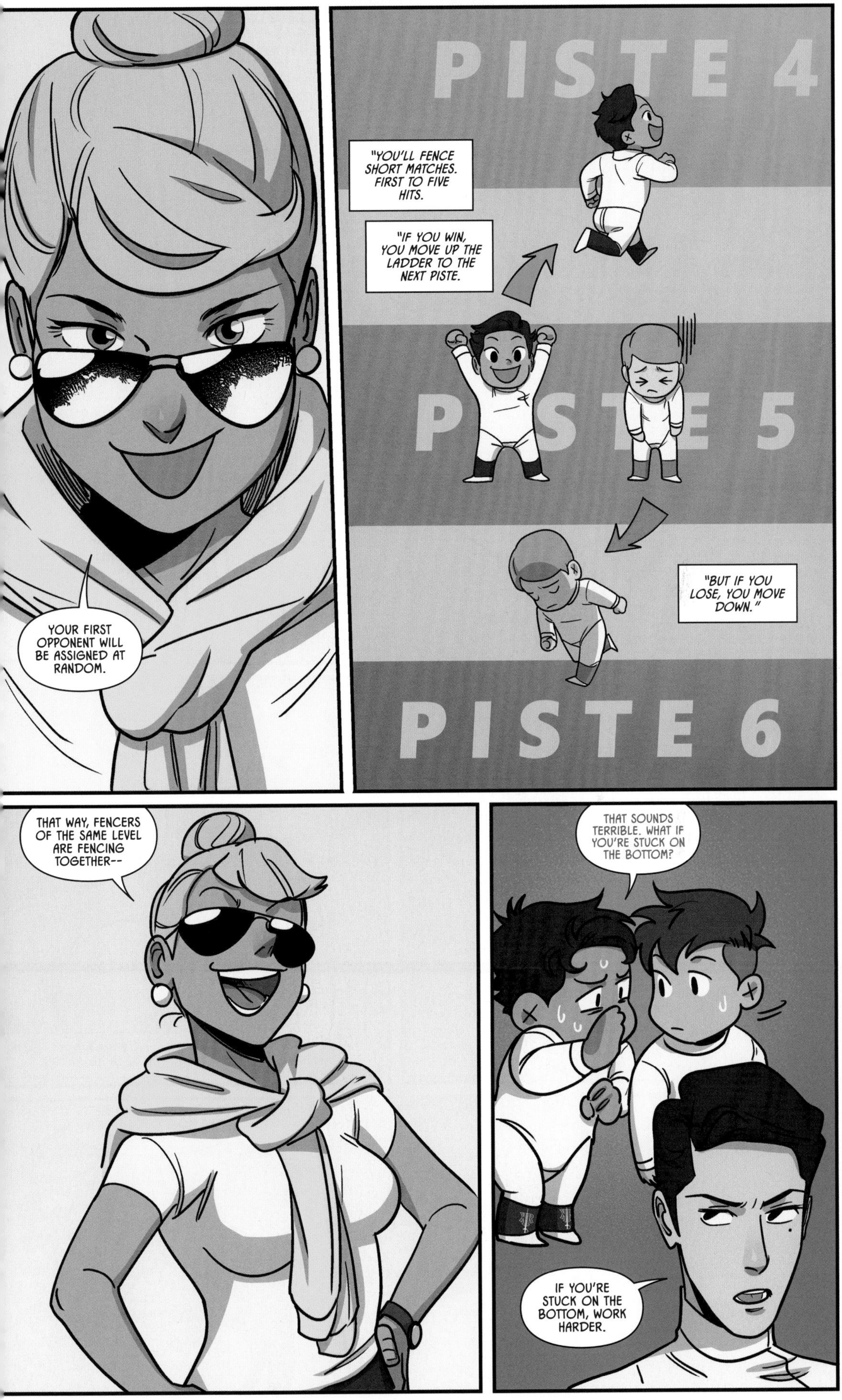
YOUR FIRST OPPONENT WILL BE ASSIGNED AT RANDOM.
PISTE 4
"YOU'LL FENCE SHORT MATCHES. FIRST TO FIVE HITS.
"IF YOU WIN, YOU MOVE UP THE LADDER TO THE NEXT PISTE.
PISTE 5
"BUT IF YOU LOSE, YOU MOVE DOWN."
PISTE 6
THAT WAY, FENCERS OF THE SAME LEVEL ARE FENCING TOGETHER--
THAT SOUNDS TERRIBLE. WHAT IF YOU'RE STUCK ON THE BOTTOM?
IF YOU'RE STUCK ON THE BOTTOM, WORK HARDER.

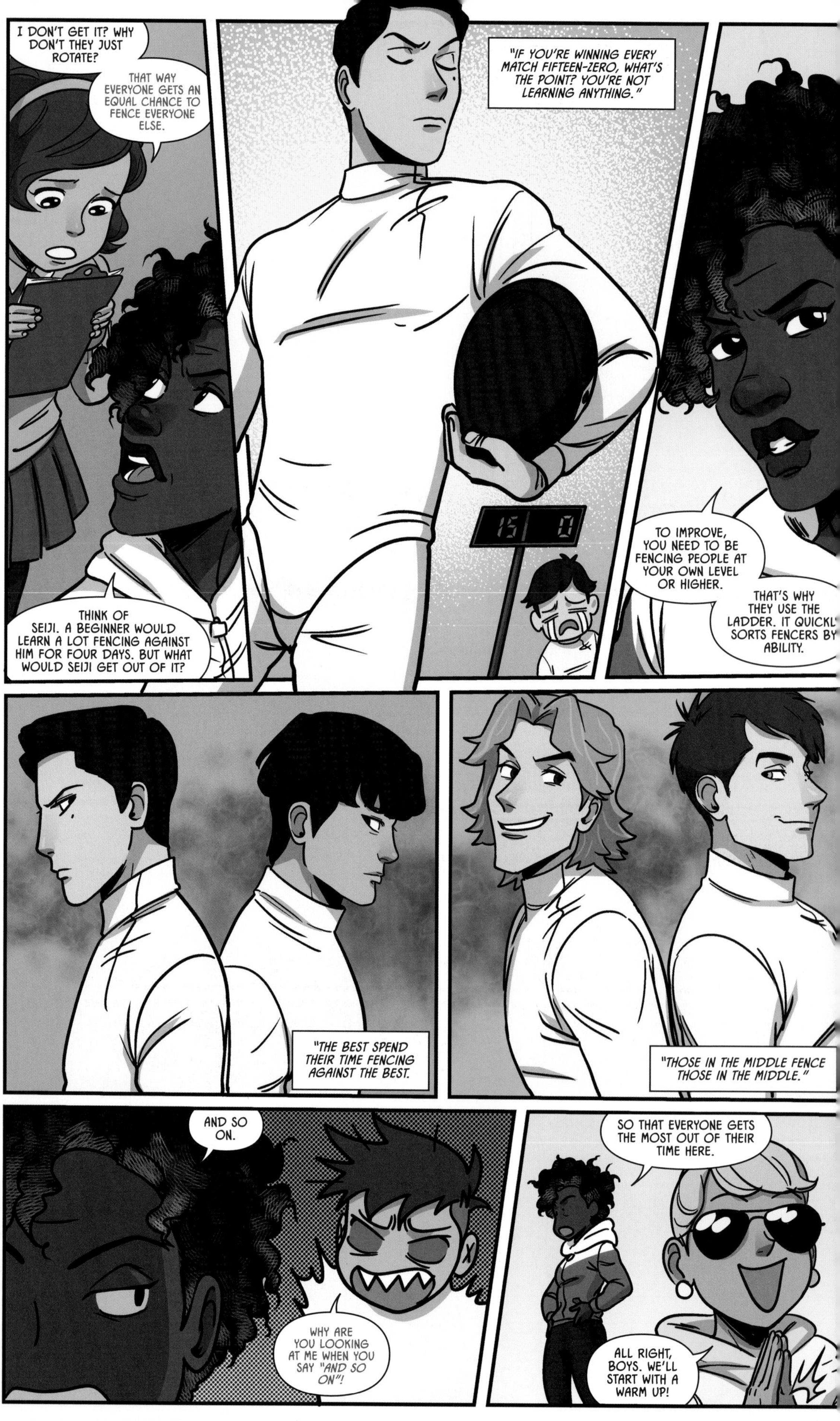
I DON'T GET IT? WHY DON'T THEY JUST ROTATE?
THAT WAY EVERYONE GETS AN EQUAL CHANCE TO FENCE EVERYONE ELSE.
THINK OF SEIJI. A BEGINNER WOULD LEARN A LOT FENCING AGAINST HIM FOR FOUR DAYS. BUT WHAT WOULD SEIJI GET OUT OF IT?
"IF YOU'RE WINNING EVERY MATCH FIFTEEN-ZERO, WHAT'S THE POINT? YOU'RE NOT LEARNING ANYTHING."
15 0
TO IMPROVE, YOU NEED TO BE FENCING PEOPLE AT YOUR OWN LEVEL OR HIGHER.
THAT'S WHY THEY USE THE LADDER. IT QUICKL SORTS FENCERS BY ABILITY.
"THE BEST SPEND THEIR TIME FENCING AGAINST THE BEST.
"THOSE IN THE MIDDLE FENCE THOSE IN THE MIDDLE."
AND SO ON.
WHY ARE YOU LOOKING AT ME WHEN YOU SAY "AND SO ON"!
SO THAT EVERYONE GETS THE MOST OUT OF THEIR TIME HERE.
ALL RIGHT, BOYS. WE'LL START WITH A WARM UP!

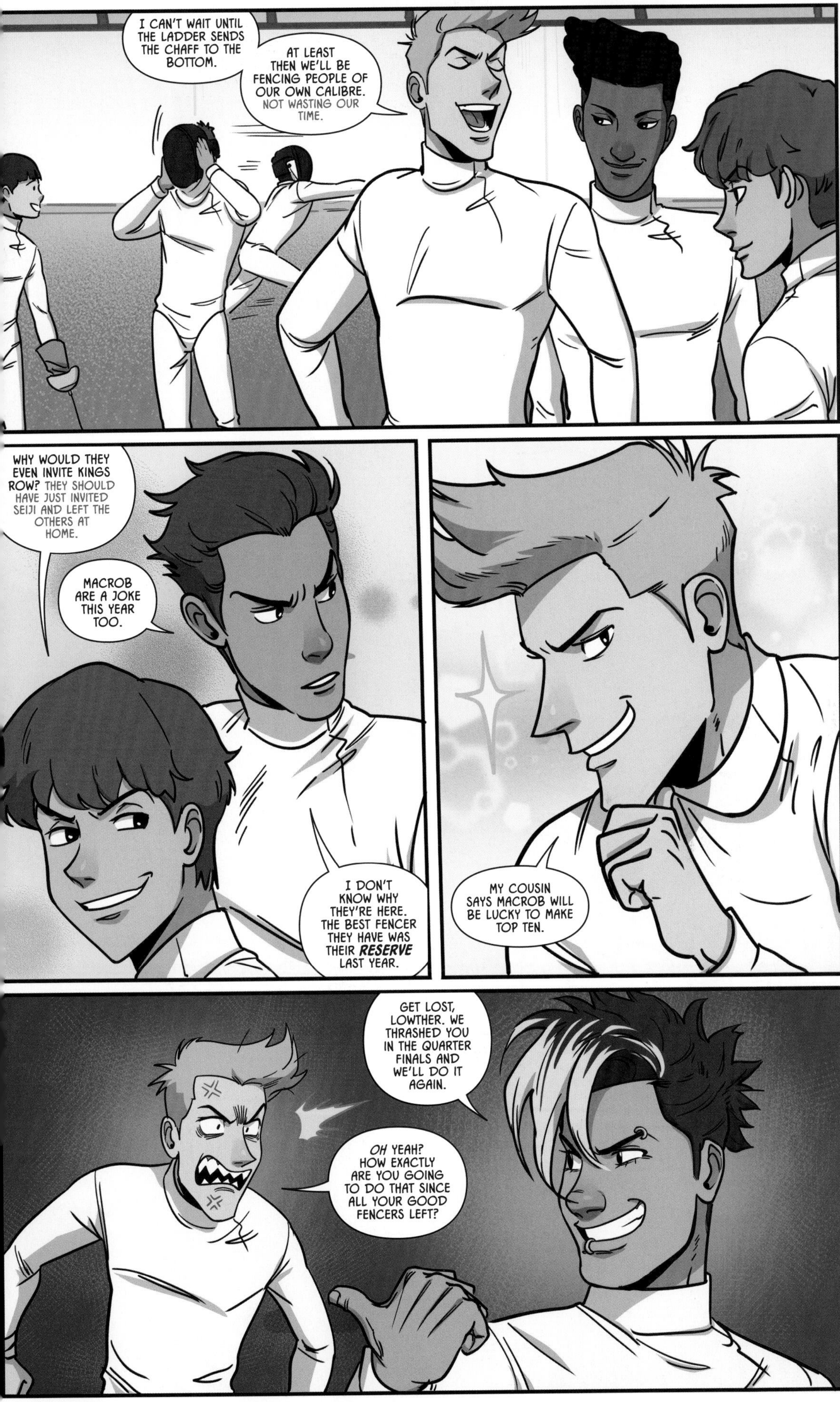
I CAN'T WAIT UNTIL THE LADDER SENDS THE CHAFF TO THE BOTTOM.
AT LEAST THEN WE'LL BE FENCING PEOPLE OF OUR OWN CALIBRE. NOT WASTING OUR TIME.
WHY WOULD THEY EVEN INVITE KINGS ROW? THEY SHOULD HAVE JUST INVITED SEIJI AND LEFT THE OTHERS AT HOME.
MACROB ARE A JOKE THIS YEAR TOO.
I DON'T KNOW WHY THEY'RE HERE. THE BEST FENCER THEY HAVE WAS THEIR *RESERVE* LAST YEAR.
MY COUSIN SAYS MACROB WILL BE LUCKY TO MAKE TOP TEN.
GET LOST, LOWTHER. WE THRASHED YOU IN THE QUARTER FINALS AND WE'LL DO IT AGAIN.
OH YEAH? HOW EXACTLY ARE YOU GOING TO DO THAT SINCE ALL YOUR GOOD FENCERS LEFT?

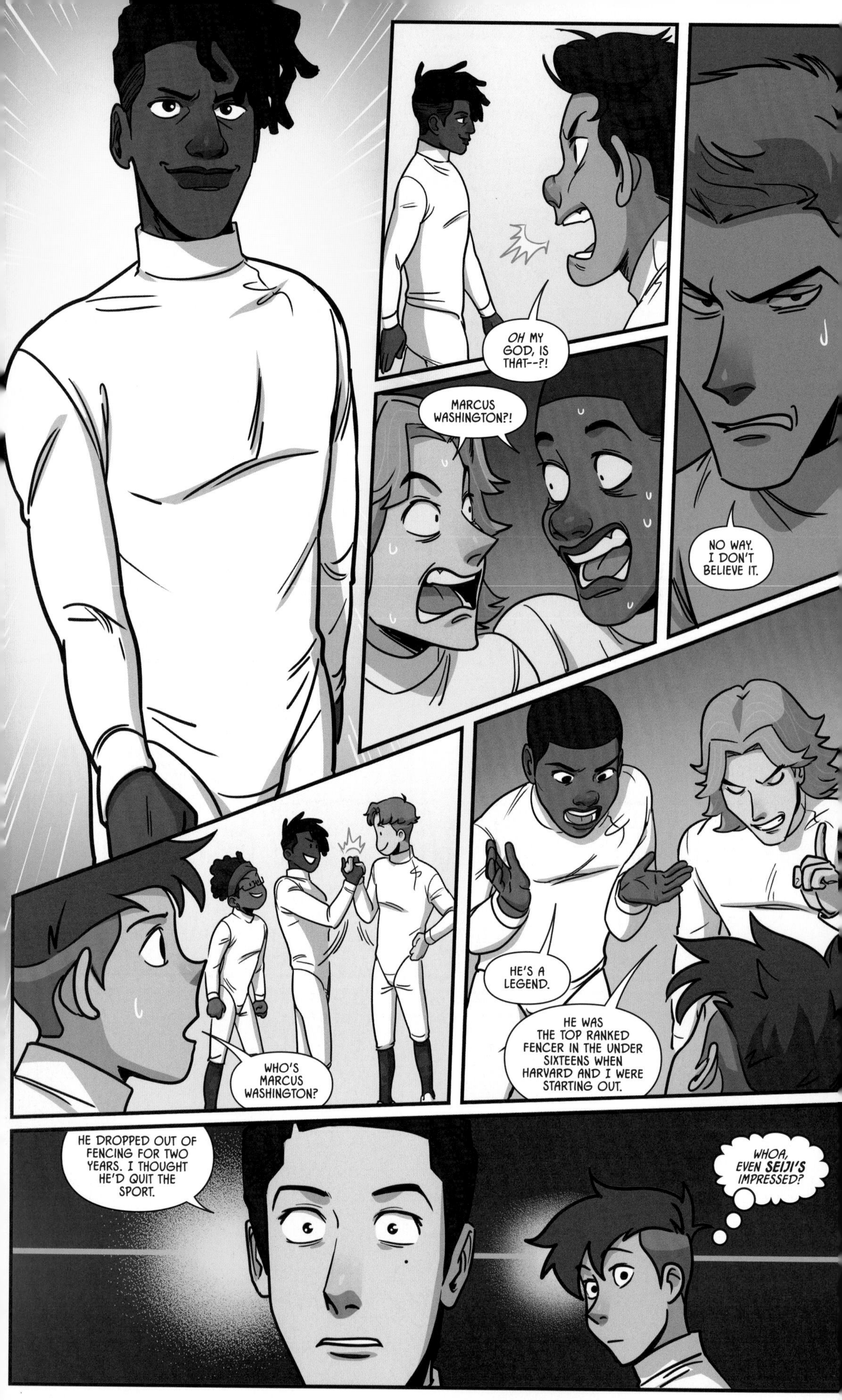
OH MY GOD, IS THAT--?!
MARCUS WASHINGTON?!
NO WAY. I DON'T BELIEVE IT.
WHO'S MARCUS WASHINGTON?
HE'S A LEGEND.
HE WAS THE TOP RANKED FENCER IN THE UNDER SIXTEENS WHEN HARVARD AND I WERE STARTING OUT.
HE DROPPED OUT OF FENCING FOR TWO YEARS. I THOUGHT HE'D QUIT THE SPORT.
WHOA, EVEN **SEIJI'S** IMPRESSED?

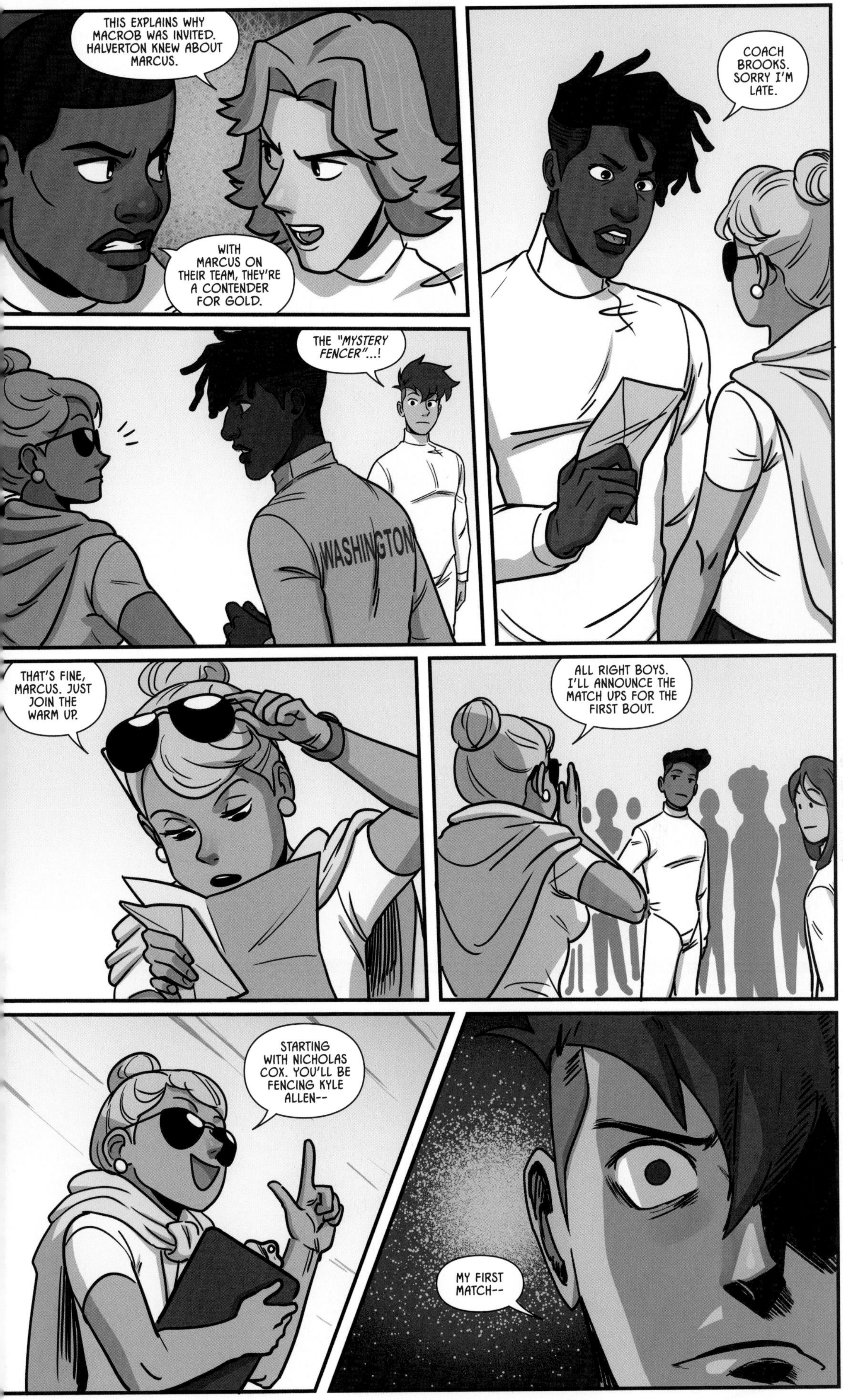

THIS EXPLAINS WHY MACROB WAS INVITED. HALVERTON KNEW ABOUT MARCUS.
WITH MARCUS ON THEIR TEAM, THEY'RE A CONTENDER FOR GOLD.
COACH BROOKS. SORRY I'M LATE.
THE *"MYSTERY FENCER"*...!
WASHINGTON
THAT'S FINE, MARCUS. JUST JOIN THE WARM UP.
ALL RIGHT BOYS. I'LL ANNOUNCE THE MATCH UPS FOR THE FIRST BOUT.
STARTING WITH NICHOLAS COX. YOU'LL BE FENCING KYLE ALLEN--
MY FIRST MATCH--

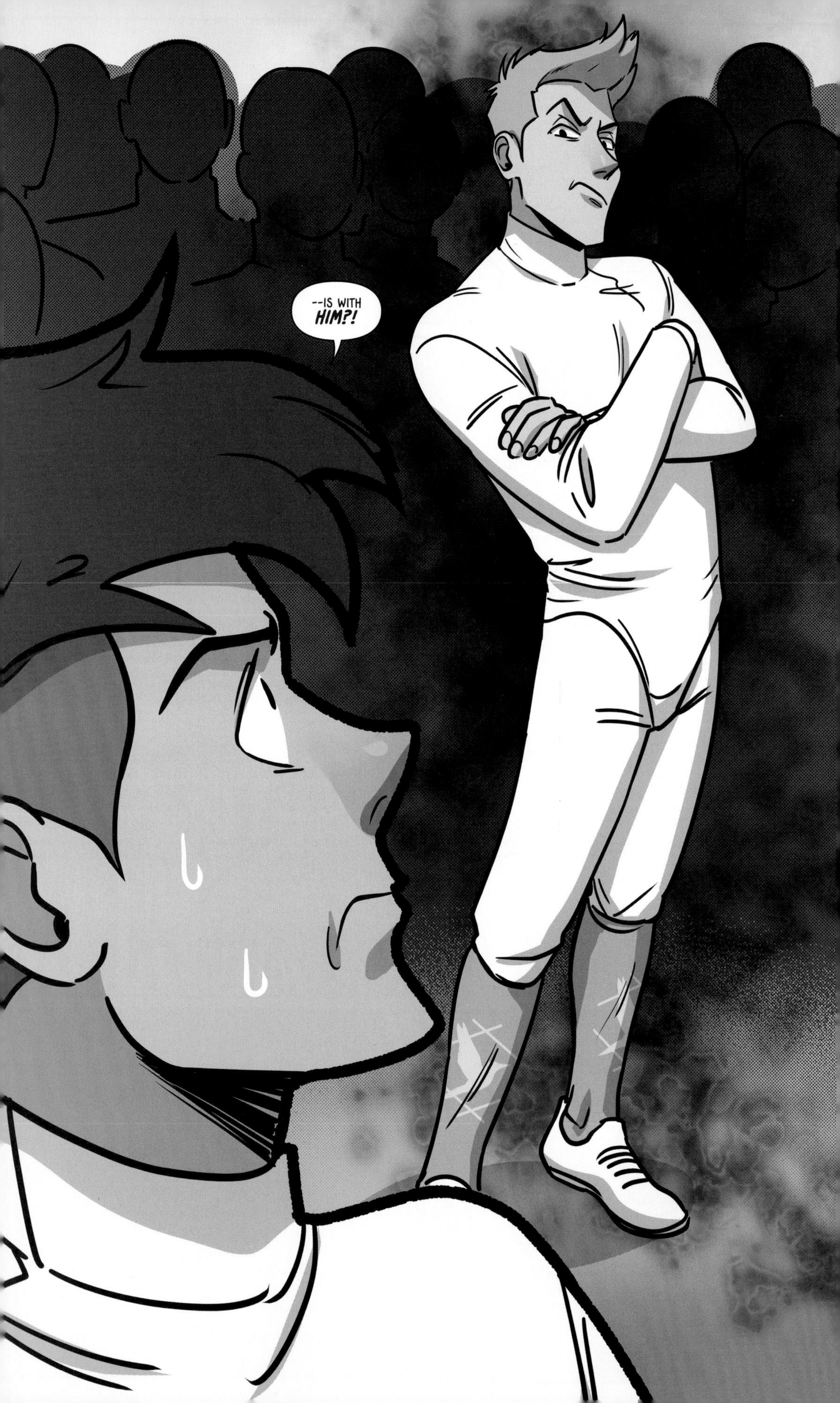
--IS WITH HIM?!

CHAPTER
NINETEEN

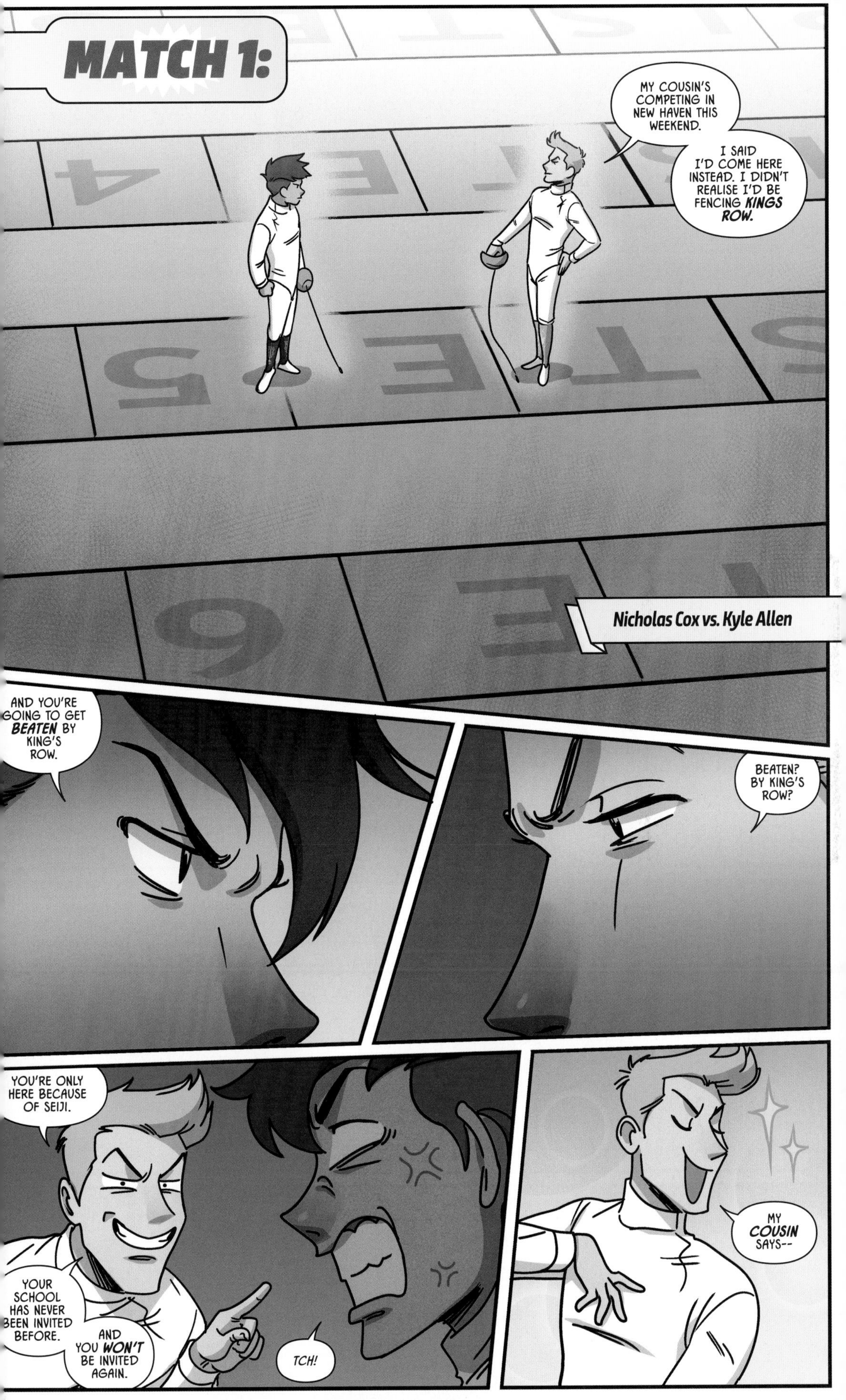
MATCH 1:
MY COUSIN'S COMPETING IN NEW HAVEN THIS WEEKEND.
I SAID I'D COME HERE INSTEAD. I DIDN'T REALISE I'D BE FENCING KINGS ROW.
Nicholas Cox vs. Kyle Allen
AND YOU'RE GOING TO GET BEATEN BY KING'S ROW.
BEATEN? BY KING'S ROW?
YOU'RE ONLY HERE BECAUSE OF SEIJI.
YOUR SCHOOL HAS NEVER BEEN INVITED BEFORE.
AND YOU WON'T BE INVITED AGAIN.
TCH!
MY COUSIN SAYS--

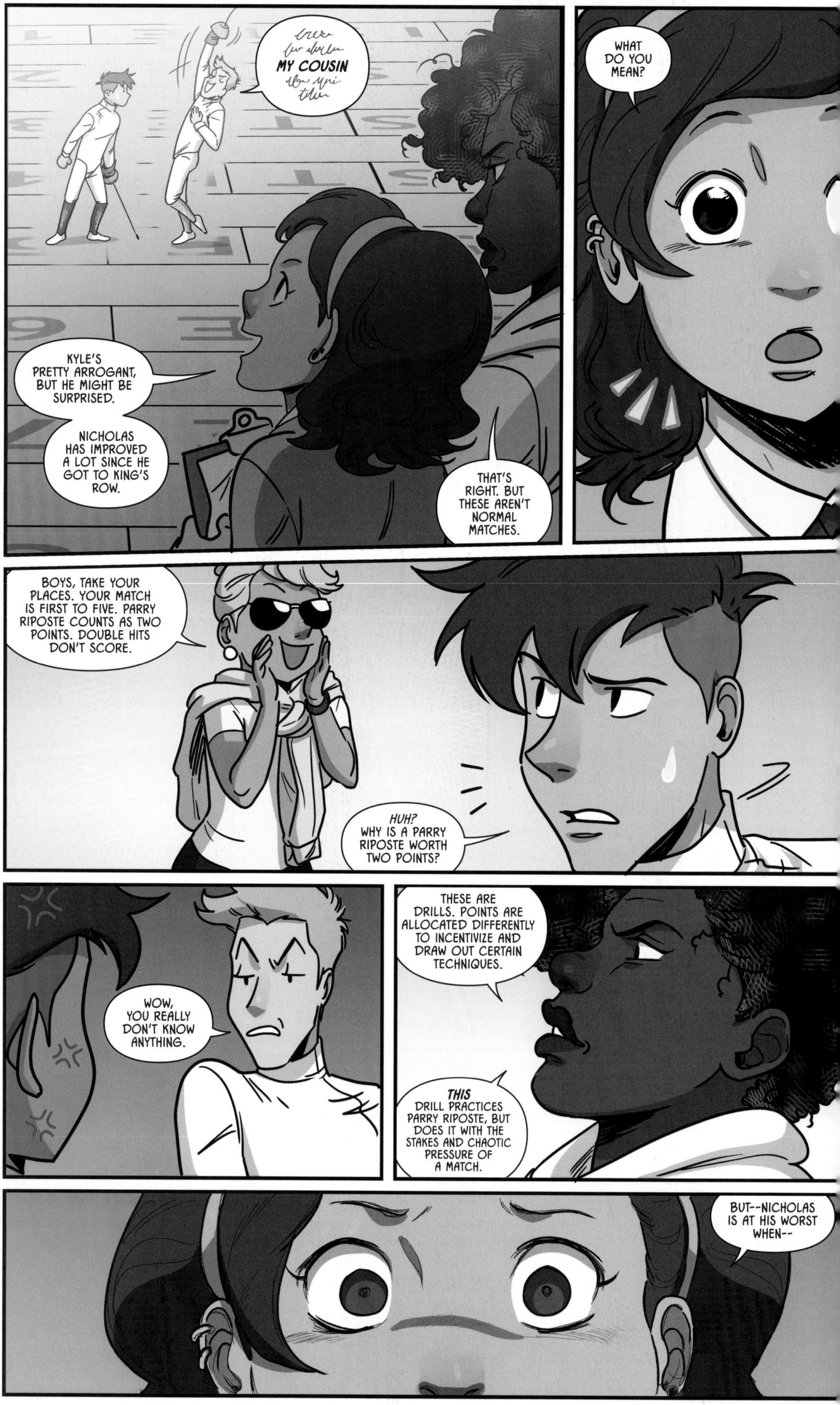
MY COUSIN
KYLE'S PRETTY ARROGANT, BUT HE MIGHT BE SURPRISED.
NICHOLAS HAS IMPROVED A LOT SINCE HE GOT TO KING'S ROW.
THAT'S RIGHT. BUT THESE AREN'T NORMAL MATCHES.
WHAT DO YOU MEAN?
BOYS, TAKE YOUR PLACES. YOUR MATCH IS FIRST TO FIVE. PARRY RIPOSTE COUNTS AS TWO POINTS. DOUBLE HITS DON'T SCORE.
HUH? WHY IS A PARRY RIPOSTE WORTH TWO POINTS?
WOW, YOU REALLY DON'T KNOW ANYTHING.
THESE ARE DRILLS. POINTS ARE ALLOCATED DIFFERENTLY TO INCENTIVIZE AND DRAW OUT CERTAIN TECHNIQUES.
THIS DRILL PRACTICES PARRY RIPOSTE, BUT DOES IT WITH THE STAKES AND CHAOTIC PRESSURE OF A MATCH.
BUT--NICHOLAS IS AT HIS WORST WHEN--

THERE, HE'S OPEN--!

WAIT, I NEED TO PARRY RIPOSTE TO SCORE DOUBLE POINTS--

--HE'S OVERTHINKING!

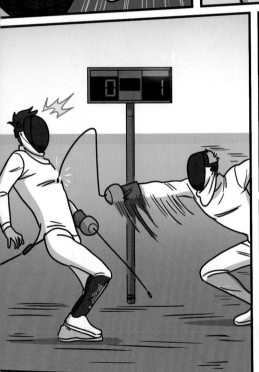

IT WAS LIKE KYLE KNEW THAT WAS COMING!

OF COURSE. IF A PARRY RIPOSTE IS WORTH TWO POINTS, YOU CAN EXPECT YOUR OPPONENT TO TRY TO USE IT.

THESE DRILLS PRACTICE THE TECHNIQUE *AND* ITS DEFENSE.

THAT HIT WAS WORTH TWO POINTS--! THE MATCH IS ALMOST OVER!

THESE SHORT FIVE-POINT MATCHES ARE BRUTALLY FAST. YOU BARELY HAVE TIME TO GET YOUR BEARINGS BEFORE--

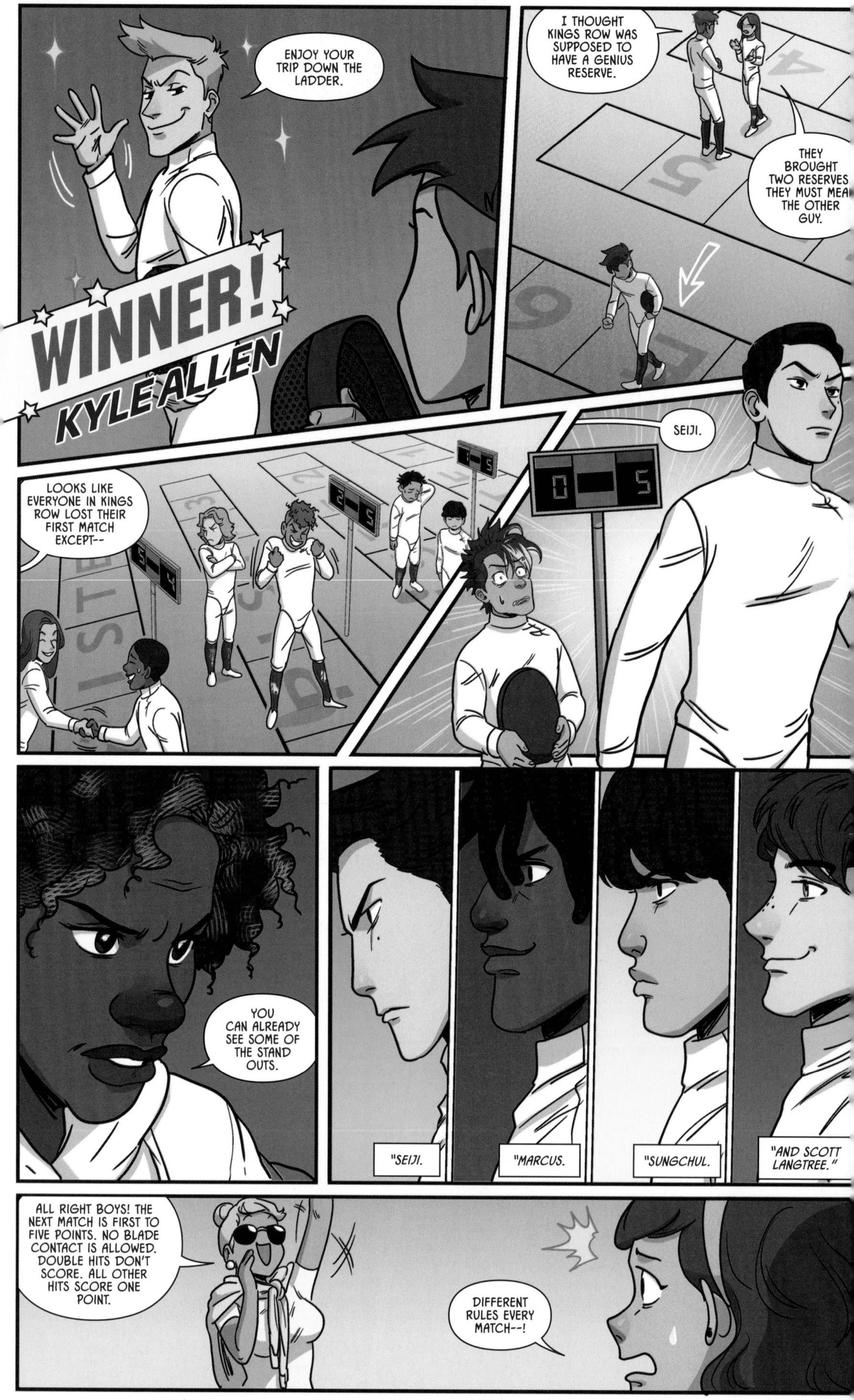
ENJOY YOUR TRIP DOWN THE LADDER.
WINNER!
KYLE ALLEN
I THOUGHT KINGS ROW WAS SUPPOSED TO HAVE A GENIUS RESERVE.
THEY BROUGHT TWO RESERVES THEY MUST MEA THE OTHER GUY.
LOOKS LIKE EVERYONE IN KINGS ROW LOST THEIR FIRST MATCH EXCEPT--
SEIJI.
YOU CAN ALREADY SEE SOME OF THE STAND OUTS.
"SEIJI.
"MARCUS.
"SUNGCHUL.
"AND SCOTT LANGTREE."
ALL RIGHT BOYS! THE NEXT MATCH IS FIRST TO FIVE POINTS. NO BLADE CONTACT IS ALLOWED. DOUBLE HITS DON'T SCORE. ALL OTHER HITS SCORE ONE POINT.
DIFFERENT RULES EVERY MATCH--!

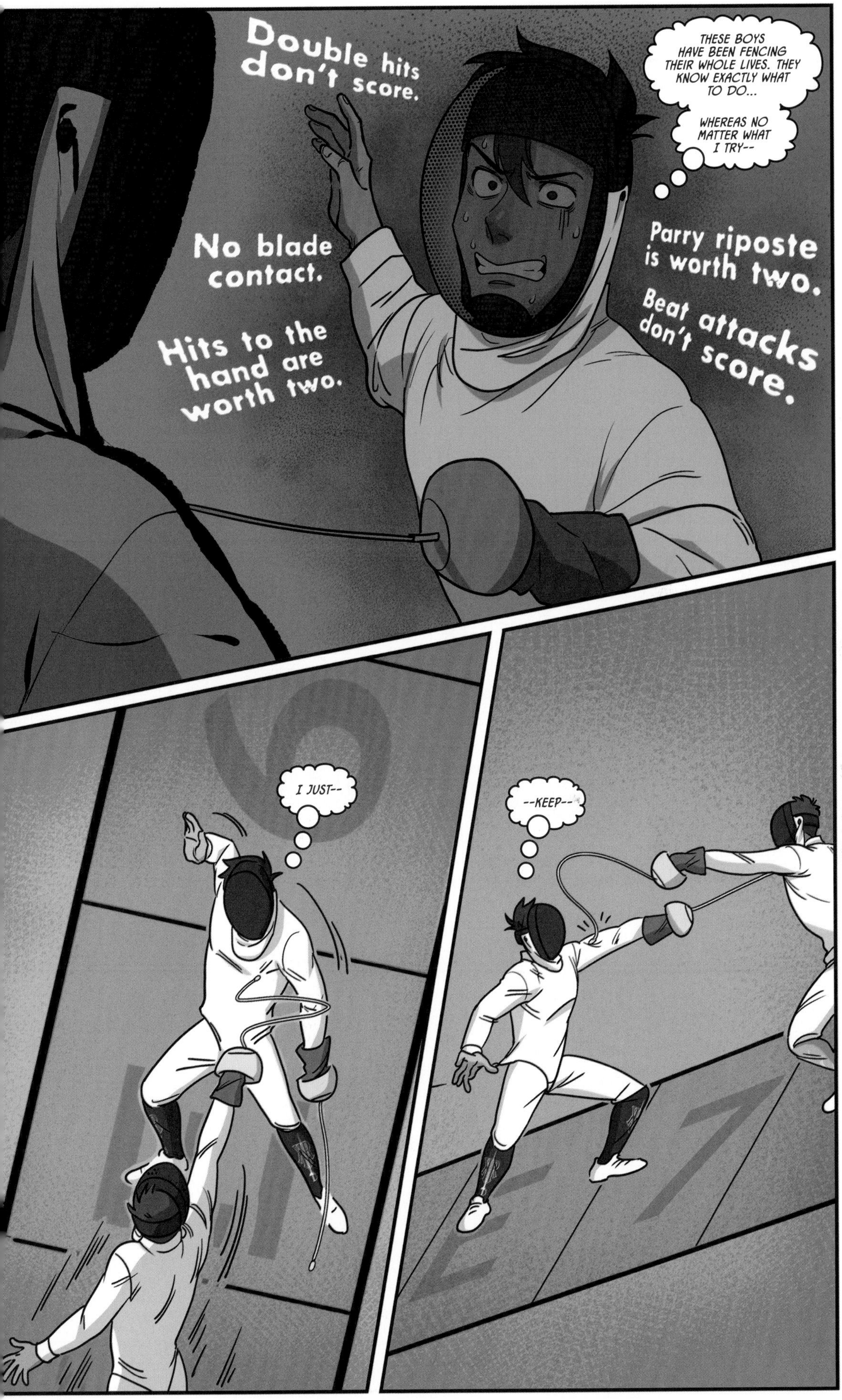
Double hits don't score.
THESE BOYS HAVE BEEN FENCING THEIR WHOLE LIVES. THEY KNOW EXACTLY WHAT TO DO...
WHEREAS NO MATTER WHAT I TRY--
No blade contact.
Parry riposte is worth two.
Hits to the hand are worth two.
Beat attacks don't score.
I JUST--
--KEEP--

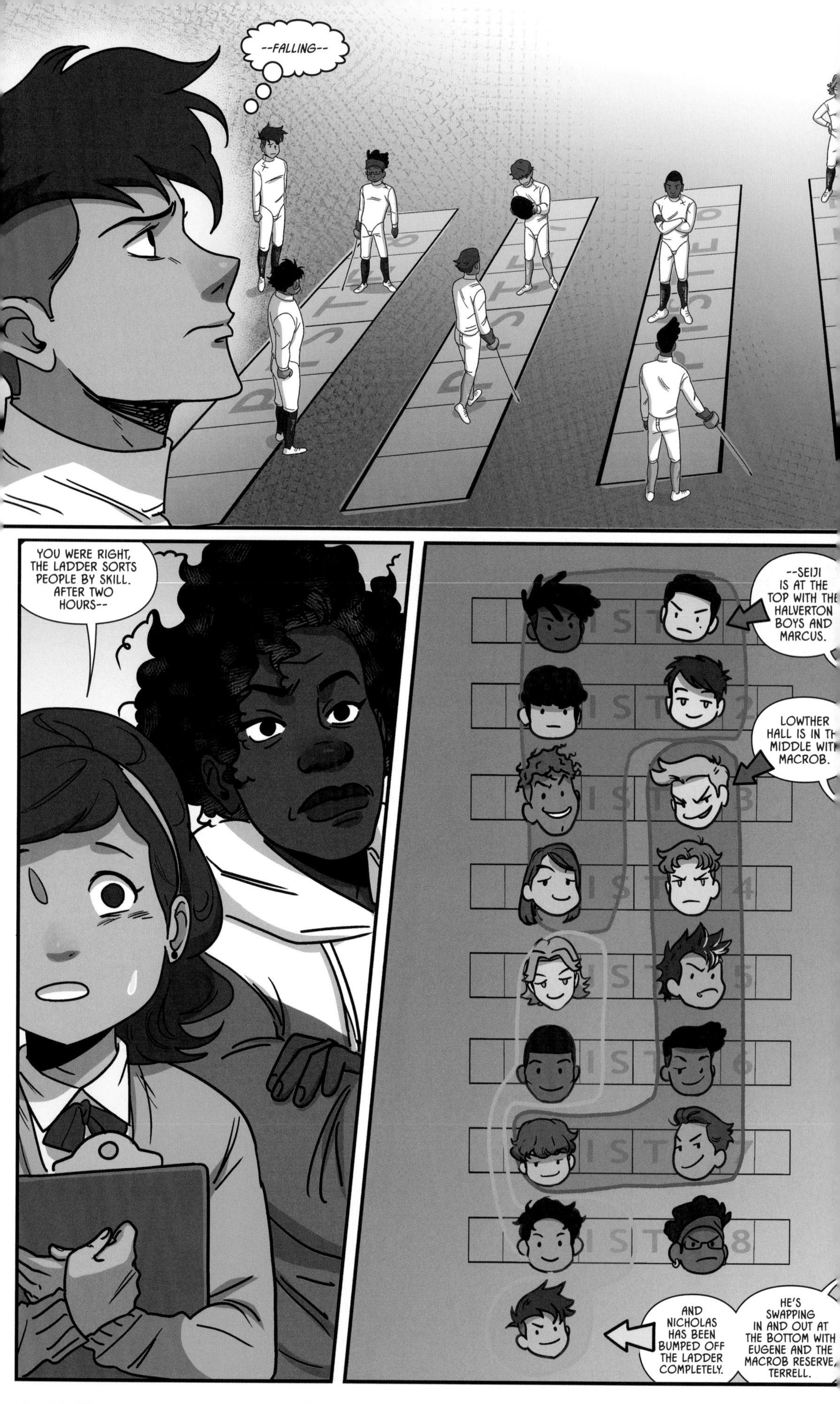
--FALLING--
YOU WERE RIGHT, THE LADDER SORTS PEOPLE BY SKILL. AFTER TWO HOURS--
--SEIJI IS AT THE TOP WITH THE HALVERTON BOYS AND MARCUS.
LOWTHER HALL IS IN THE MIDDLE WITH MACROB.
HE'S SWAPPING IN AND OUT AT THE BOTTOM WITH EUGENE AND THE MACROB RESERVE, TERRELL.
AND NICHOLAS HAS BEEN BUMPED OFF THE LADDER COMPLETELY.

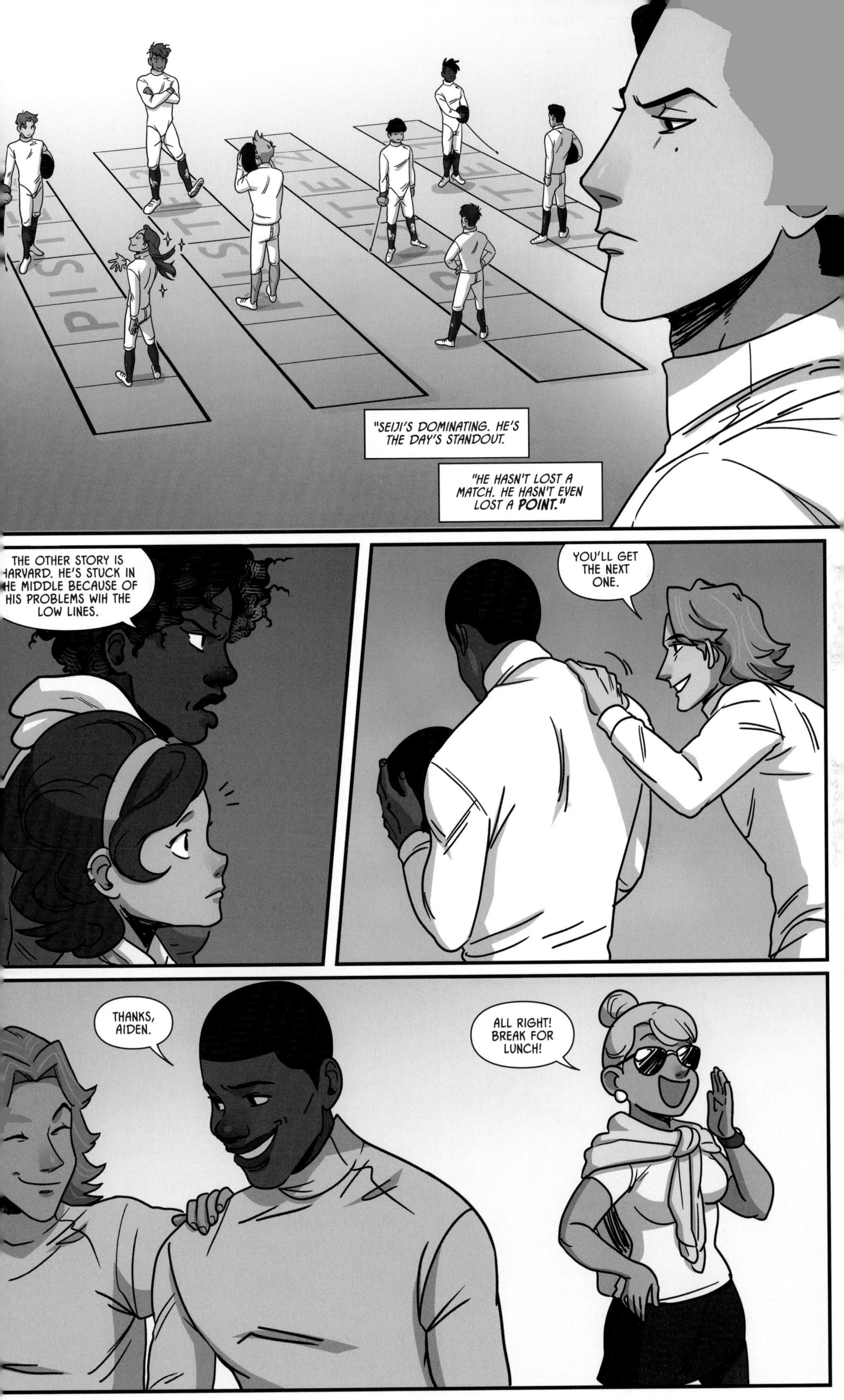

PISTE 1
PISTE 2
PISTE 3
"SEIJI'S DOMINATING. HE'S THE DAY'S STANDOUT.
"HE HASN'T LOST A MATCH. HE HASN'T EVEN LOST A POINT."
THE OTHER STORY IS HARVARD. HE'S STUCK IN THE MIDDLE BECAUSE OF HIS PROBLEMS WIH THE LOW LINES.
YOU'LL GET THE NEXT ONE.
THANKS, AIDEN.
ALL RIGHT! BREAK FOR LUNCH!

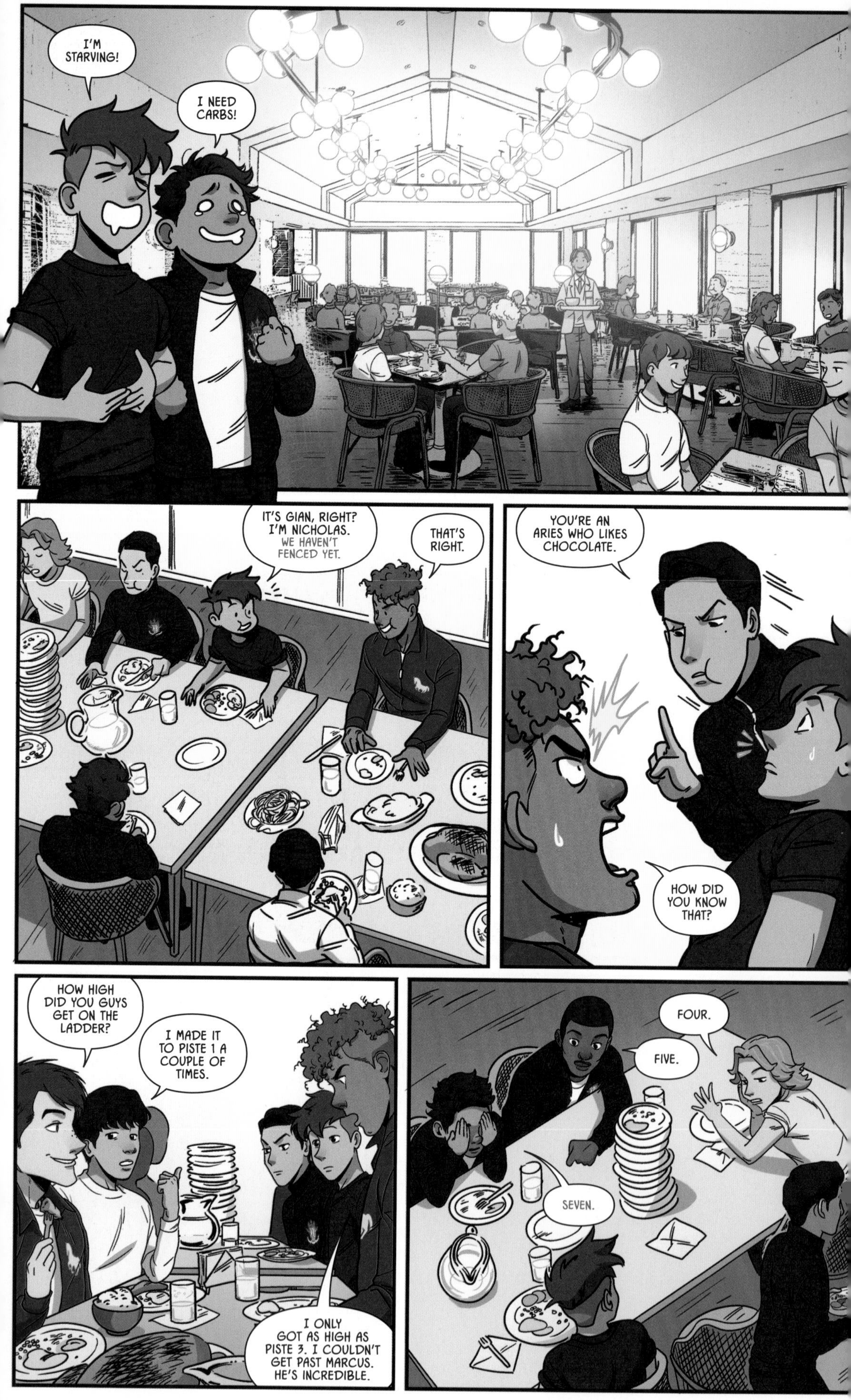
I'M STARVING!
I NEED CARBS!
IT'S GIAN, RIGHT? I'M NICHOLAS. WE HAVEN'T FENCED YET.
THAT'S RIGHT.
YOU'RE AN ARIES WHO LIKES CHOCOLATE.
HOW DID YOU KNOW THAT?
HOW HIGH DID YOU GUYS GET ON THE LADDER?
I MADE IT TO PISTE 1 A COUPLE OF TIMES.
I ONLY GOT AS HIGH AS PISTE 3. I COULDN'T GET PAST MARCUS. HE'S INCREDIBLE.
FOUR.
FIVE.
SEVEN.

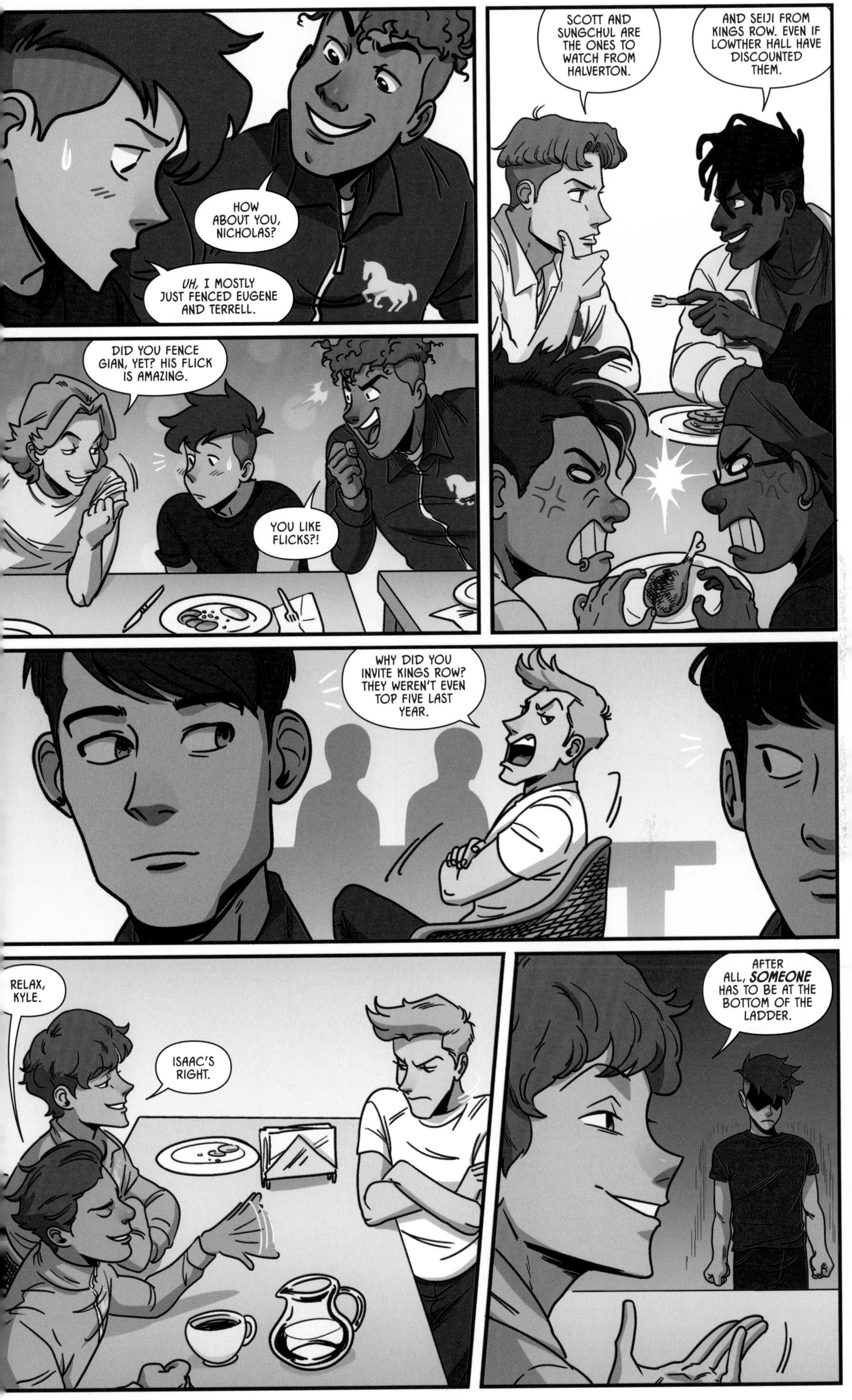
HOW ABOUT YOU, NICHOLAS?
UH, I MOSTLY JUST FENCED EUGENE AND TERRELL.
DID YOU FENCE GIAN, YET? HIS FLICK IS AMAZING.
YOU LIKE FLICKS?!
SCOTT AND SUNGCHUL ARE THE ONES TO WATCH FROM HALVERTON.
AND SEIJI FROM KINGS ROW. EVEN IF LOWTHER HALL HAVE DISCOUNTED THEM.
WHY DID YOU INVITE KINGS ROW? THEY WEREN'T EVEN TOP FIVE LAST YEAR.
RELAX, KYLE.
ISAAC'S RIGHT.
AFTER ALL, ***SOMEONE*** HAS TO BE AT THE BOTTOM OF THE LADDER.

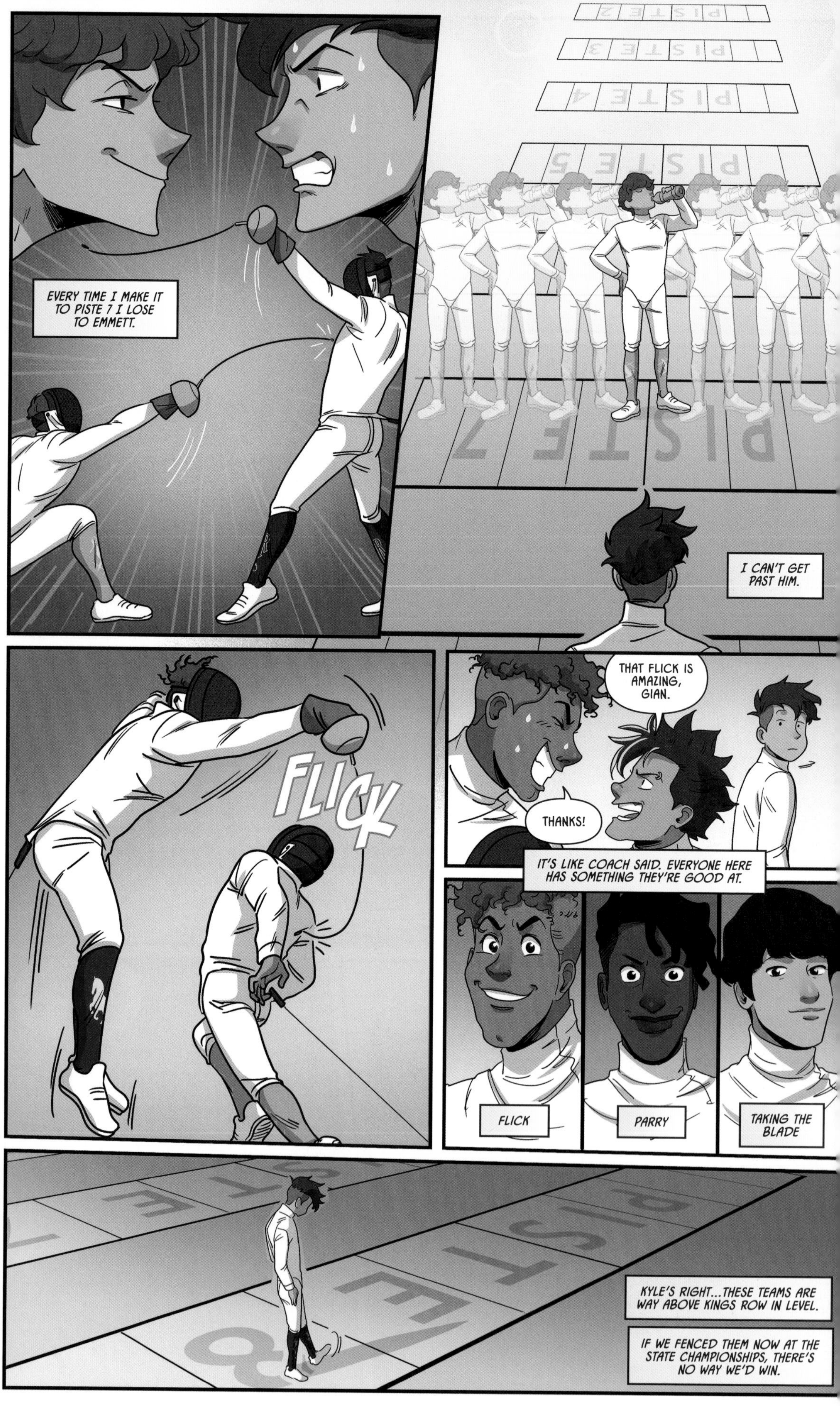
EVERY TIME I MAKE IT TO PISTE 7 I LOSE TO EMMETT.
PISTE 2
PISTE 3
PISTE 4
PISTE 5
PISTE 7
I CAN'T GET PAST HIM.
FLICK
THAT FLICK IS AMAZING, GIAN.
THANKS!
IT'S LIKE COACH SAID. EVERYONE HERE HAS SOMETHING THEY'RE GOOD AT.
FLICK
PARRY
TAKING THE BLADE
KYLE'S RIGHT...THESE TEAMS ARE WAY ABOVE KINGS ROW IN LEVEL.
IF WE FENCED THEM NOW AT THE STATE CHAMPIONSHIPS, THERE'S NO WAY WE'D WIN.

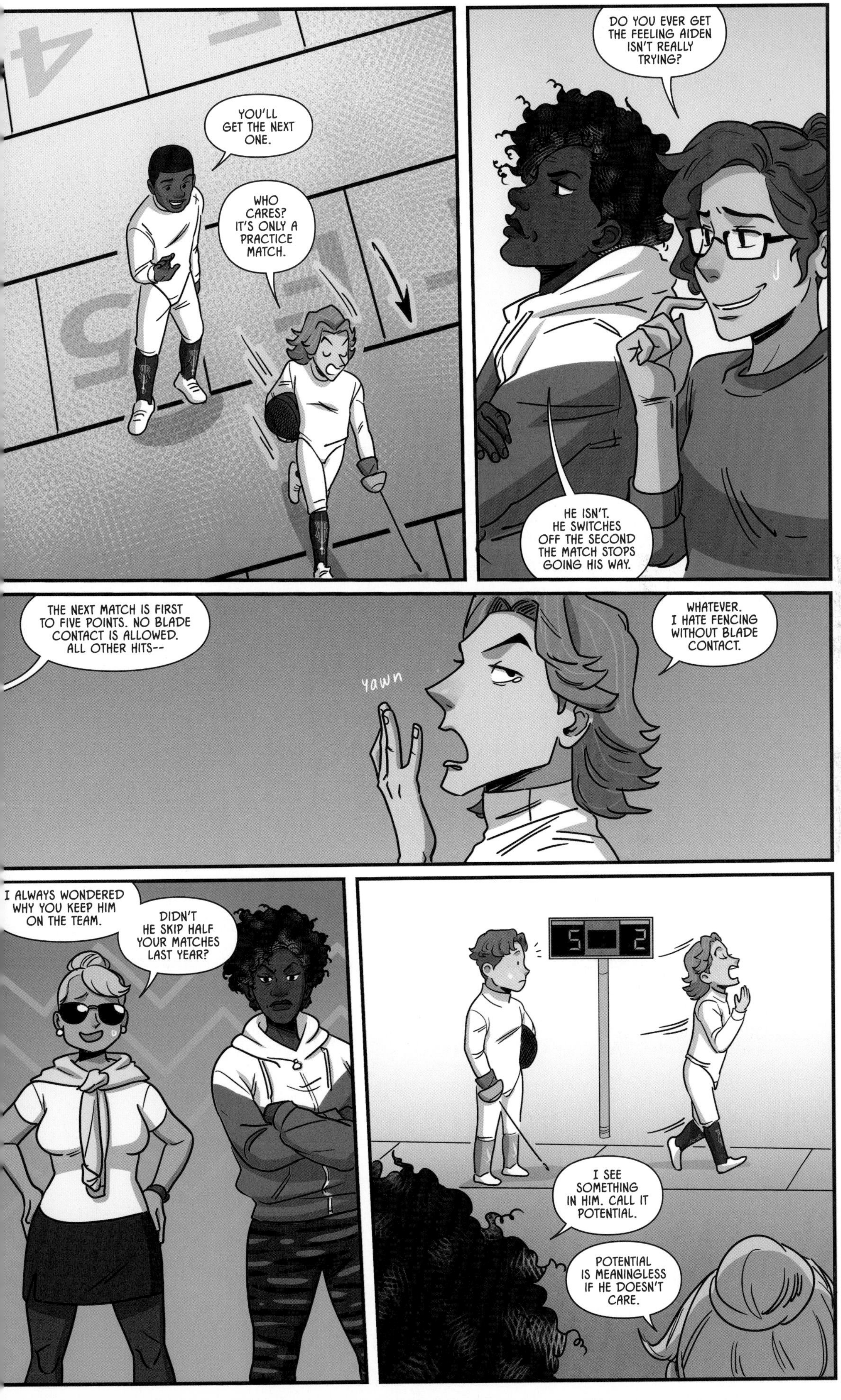
YOU'LL GET THE NEXT ONE.
WHO CARES? IT'S ONLY A PRACTICE MATCH.
DO YOU EVER GET THE FEELING AIDEN ISN'T REALLY TRYING?
HE ISN'T. HE SWITCHES OFF THE SECOND THE MATCH STOPS GOING HIS WAY.
THE NEXT MATCH IS FIRST TO FIVE POINTS. NO BLADE CONTACT IS ALLOWED. ALL OTHER HITS--
yawn
WHATEVER. I HATE FENCING WITHOUT BLADE CONTACT.
I ALWAYS WONDERED WHY YOU KEEP HIM ON THE TEAM.
DIDN'T HE SKIP HALF YOUR MATCHES LAST YEAR?
5 2
I SEE SOMETHING IN HIM. CALL IT POTENTIAL.
POTENTIAL IS MEANINGLESS IF HE DOESN'T CARE.

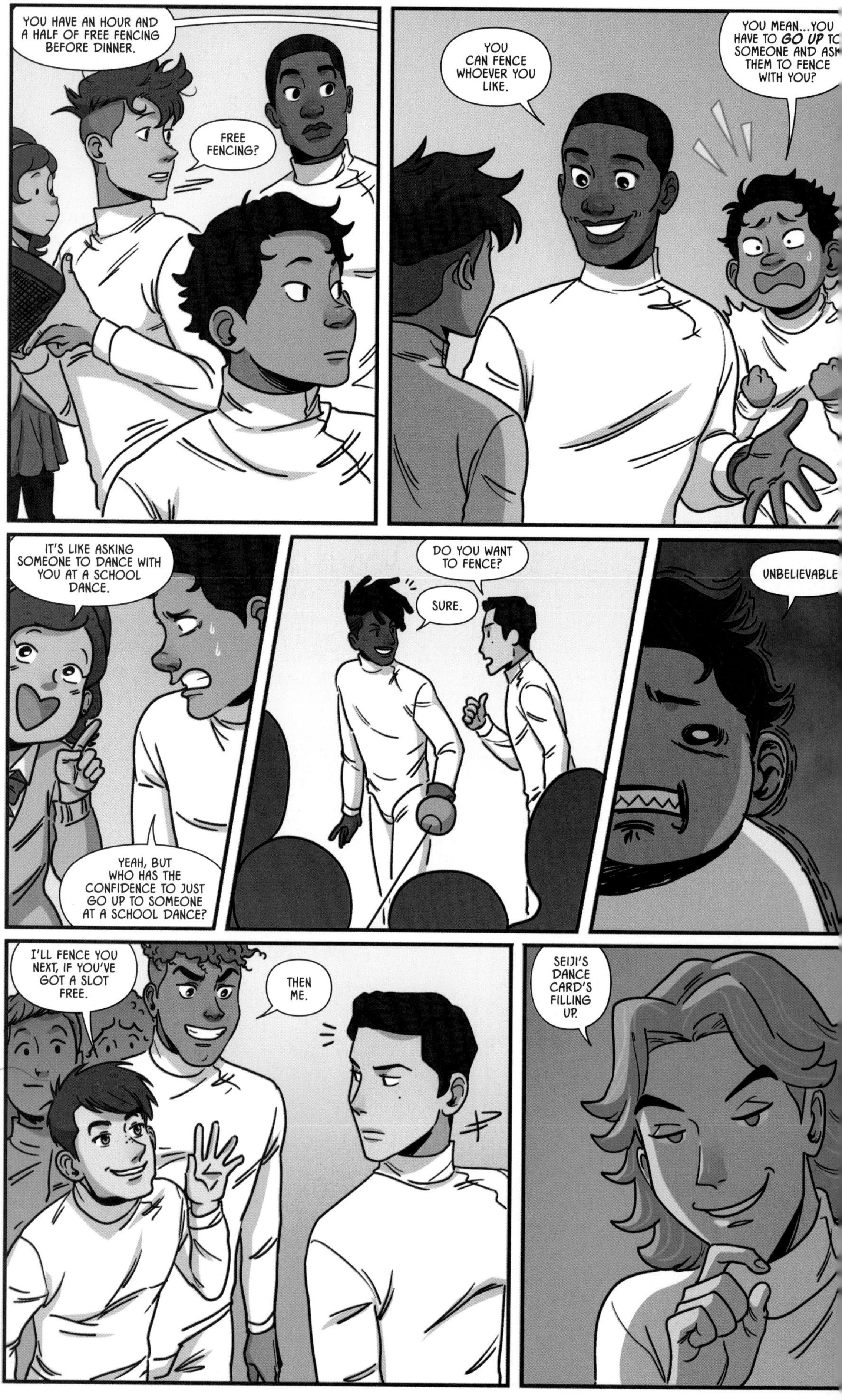

YOU HAVE AN HOUR AND A HALF OF FREE FENCING BEFORE DINNER.
FREE FENCING?
YOU CAN FENCE WHOEVER YOU LIKE.
YOU MEAN...YOU HAVE TO GO UP TO SOMEONE AND ASK THEM TO FENCE WITH YOU?
IT'S LIKE ASKING SOMEONE TO DANCE WITH YOU AT A SCHOOL DANCE.
YEAH, BUT WHO HAS THE CONFIDENCE TO JUST GO UP TO SOMEONE AT A SCHOOL DANCE?
DO YOU WANT TO FENCE?
SURE.
UNBELIEVABLE
I'LL FENCE YOU NEXT, IF YOU'VE GOT A SLOT FREE.
THEN ME.
SEIJI'S DANCE CARD'S FILLING UP.

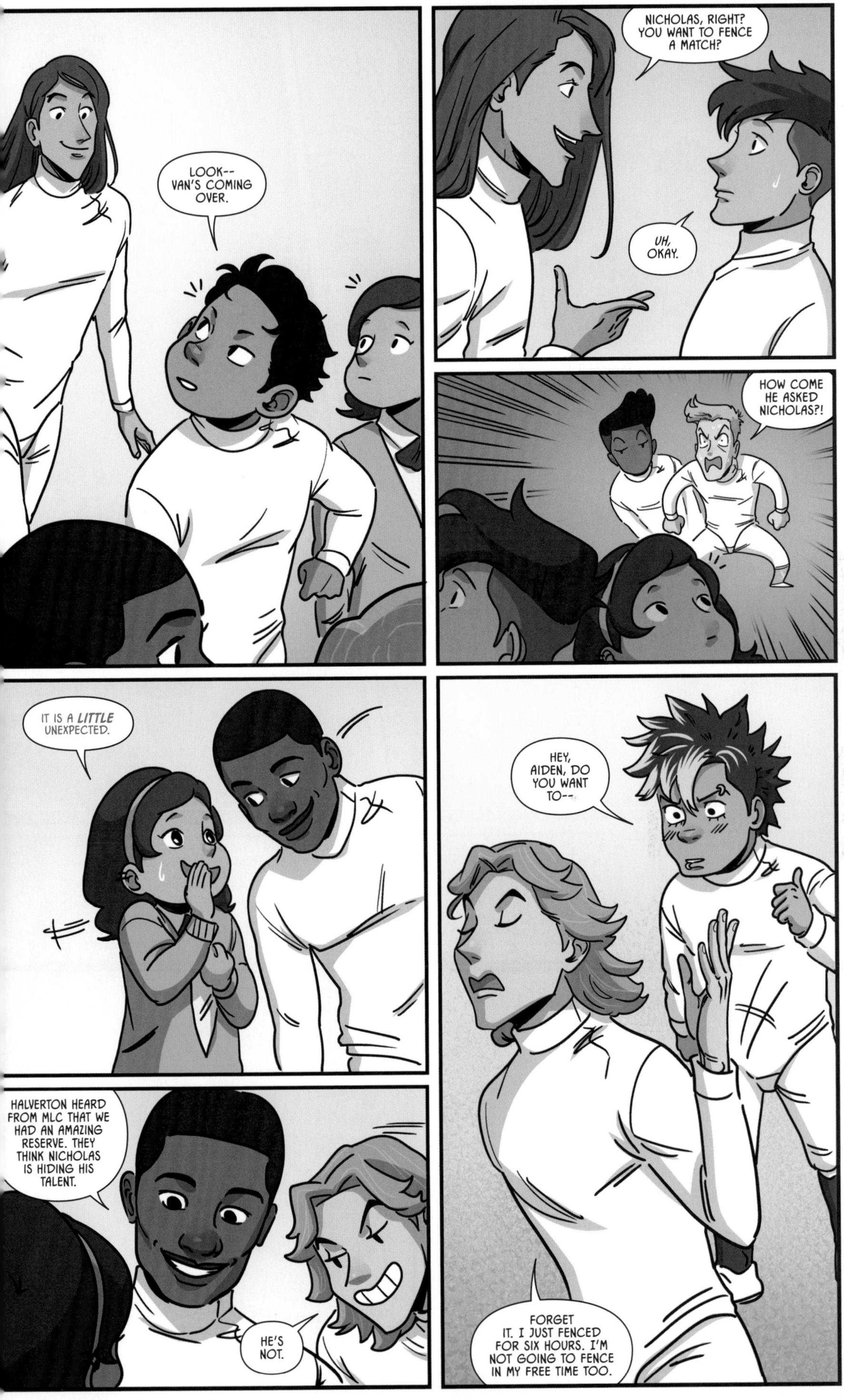
LOOK-- VAN'S COMING OVER.
NICHOLAS, RIGHT? YOU WANT TO FENCE A MATCH?
UH, OKAY.
HOW COME HE ASKED NICHOLAS?!
IT IS A *LITTLE* UNEXPECTED.
HALVERTON HEARD FROM MLC THAT WE HAD AN AMAZING RESERVE. THEY THINK NICHOLAS IS HIDING HIS TALENT.
HE'S NOT.
HEY, AIDEN, DO YOU WANT TO--
FORGET IT. I JUST FENCED FOR SIX HOURS. I'M NOT GOING TO FENCE IN MY FREE TIME TOO.

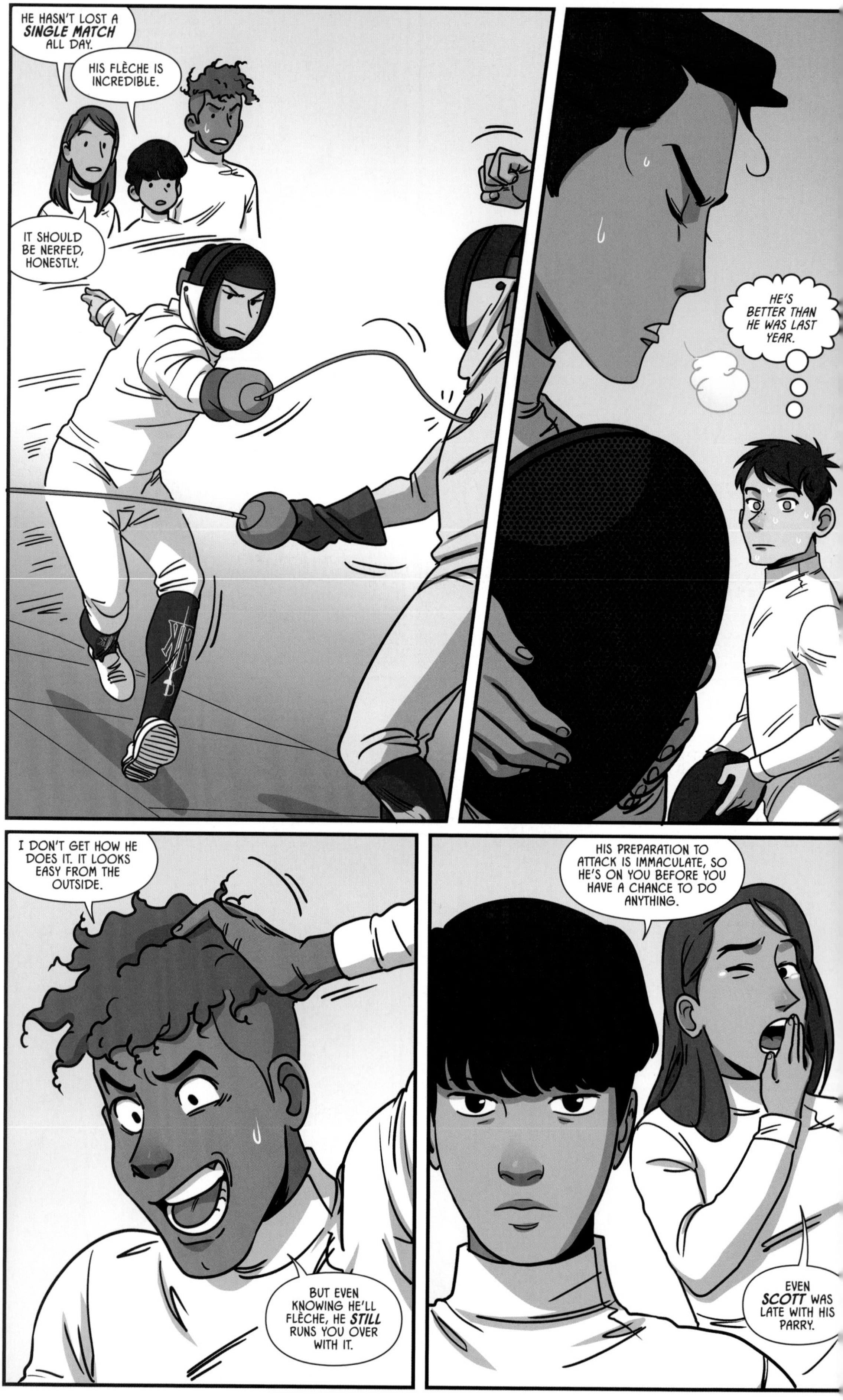
HE HASN'T LOST A **SINGLE MATCH** ALL DAY.
HIS FLÈCHE IS INCREDIBLE.
IT SHOULD BE NERFED, HONESTLY.
HE'S BETTER THAN HE WAS LAST YEAR.
I DON'T GET HOW HE DOES IT. IT LOOKS EASY FROM THE OUTSIDE.
BUT EVEN KNOWING HE'LL FLÈCHE, HE **STILL** RUNS YOU OVER WITH IT.
HIS PREPARATION TO ATTACK IS IMMACULATE, SO HE'S ON YOU BEFORE YOU HAVE A CHANCE TO DO ANYTHING.
EVEN **SCOTT** WAS LATE WITH HIS PARRY.

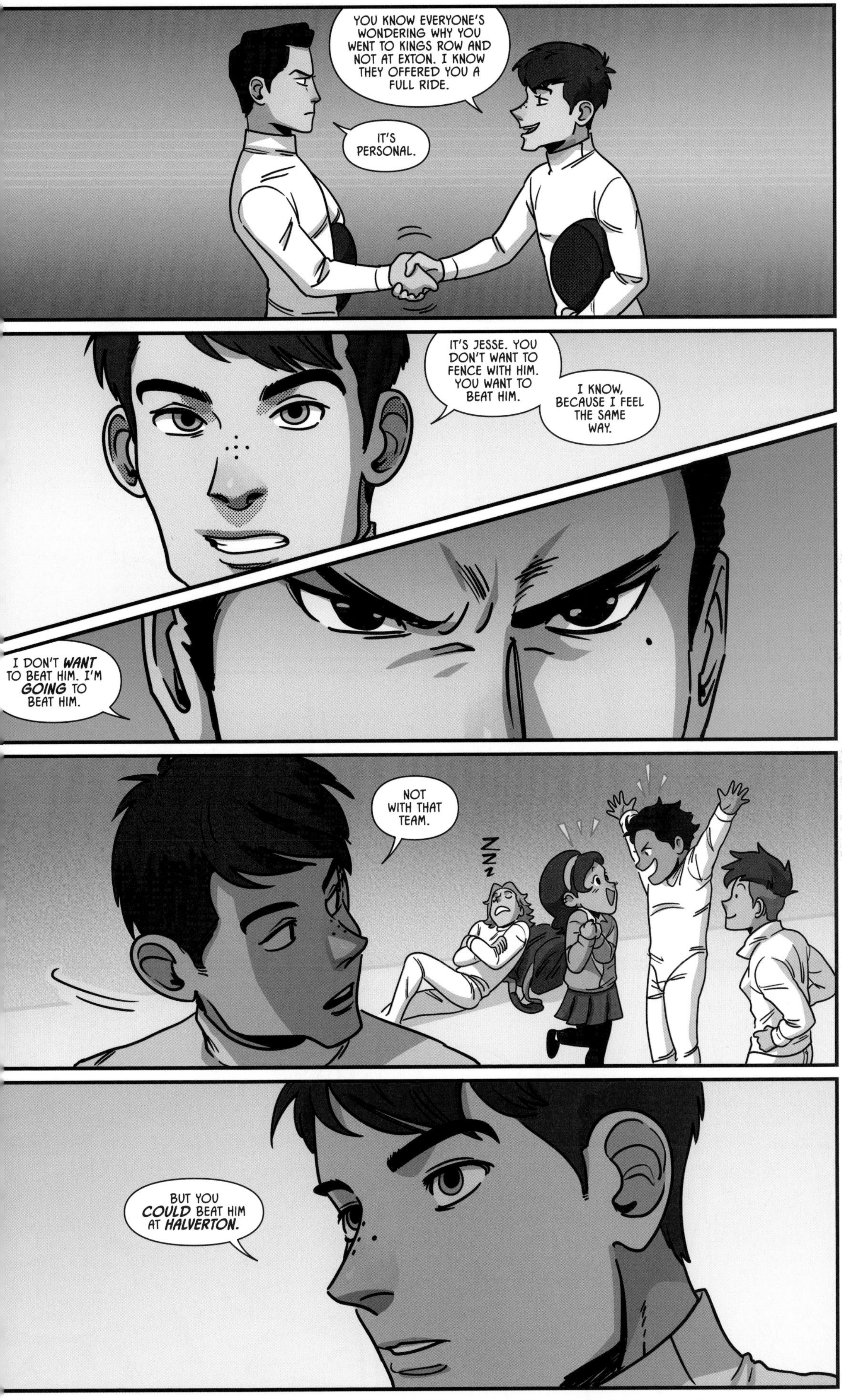

YOU KNOW EVERYONE'S WONDERING WHY YOU WENT TO KINGS ROW AND NOT AT EXTON. I KNOW THEY OFFERED YOU A FULL RIDE.
IT'S PERSONAL.
IT'S JESSE. YOU DON'T WANT TO FENCE WITH HIM. YOU WANT TO BEAT HIM.
I KNOW, BECAUSE I FEEL THE SAME WAY.
I DON'T *WANT* TO BEAT HIM. I'M *GOING* TO BEAT HIM.
NOT WITH THAT TEAM.
ZZZ
BUT YOU *COULD* BEAT HIM AT *HALVERTON.*

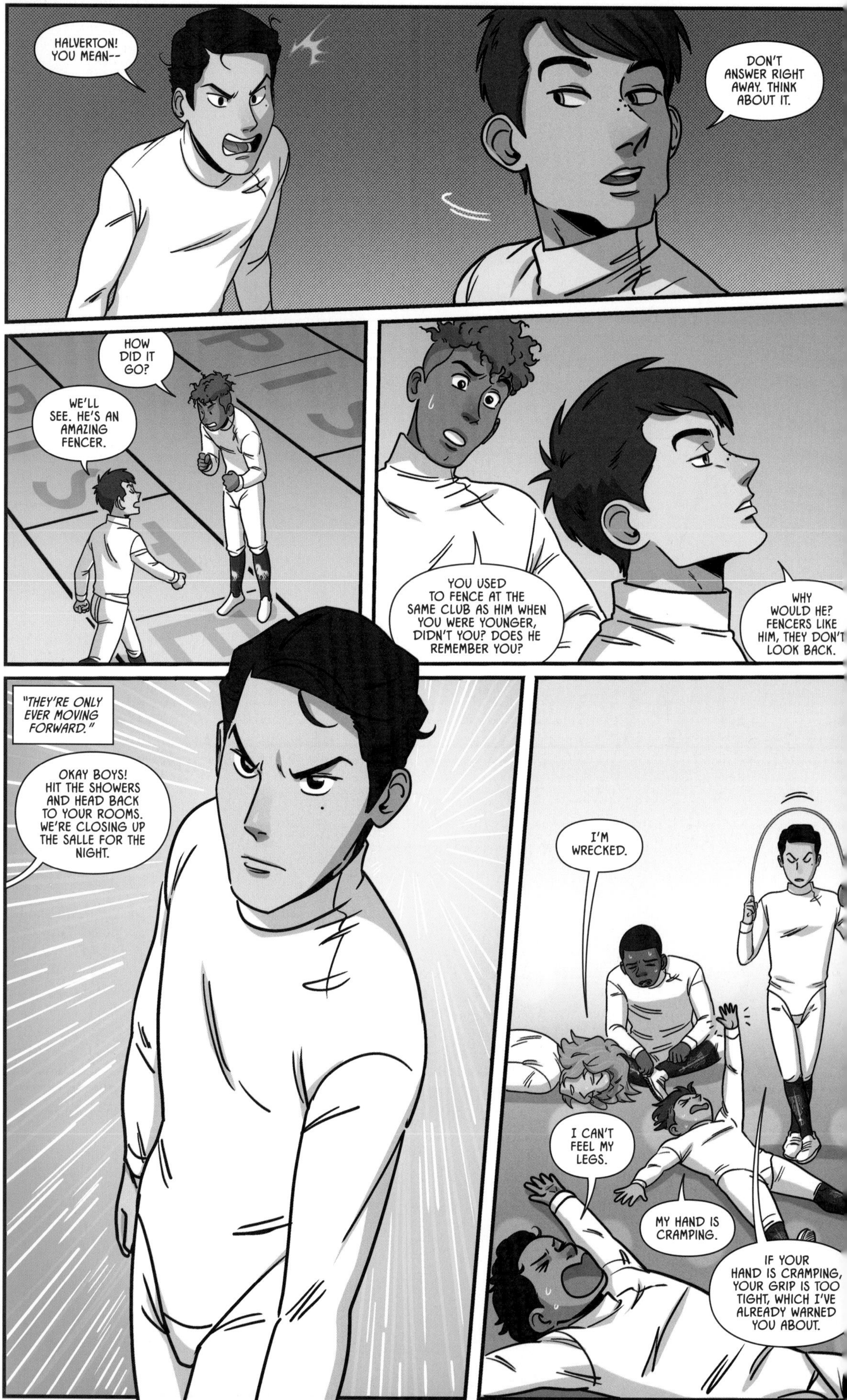
HALVERTON! YOU MEAN--
DON'T ANSWER RIGHT AWAY. THINK ABOUT IT.
HOW DID IT GO?
WE'LL SEE. HE'S AN AMAZING FENCER.
YOU USED TO FENCE AT THE SAME CLUB AS HIM WHEN YOU WERE YOUNGER, DIDN'T YOU? DOES HE REMEMBER YOU?
WHY WOULD HE? FENCERS LIKE HIM, THEY DON'T LOOK BACK.
"THEY'RE ONLY EVER MOVING FORWARD."
OKAY BOYS! HIT THE SHOWERS AND HEAD BACK TO YOUR ROOMS. WE'RE CLOSING UP THE SALLE FOR THE NIGHT.
I'M WRECKED.
I CAN'T FEEL MY LEGS.
MY HAND IS CRAMPING.
IF YOUR HAND IS CRAMPING, YOUR GRIP IS TOO TIGHT, WHICH I'VE ALREADY WARNED YOU ABOUT.

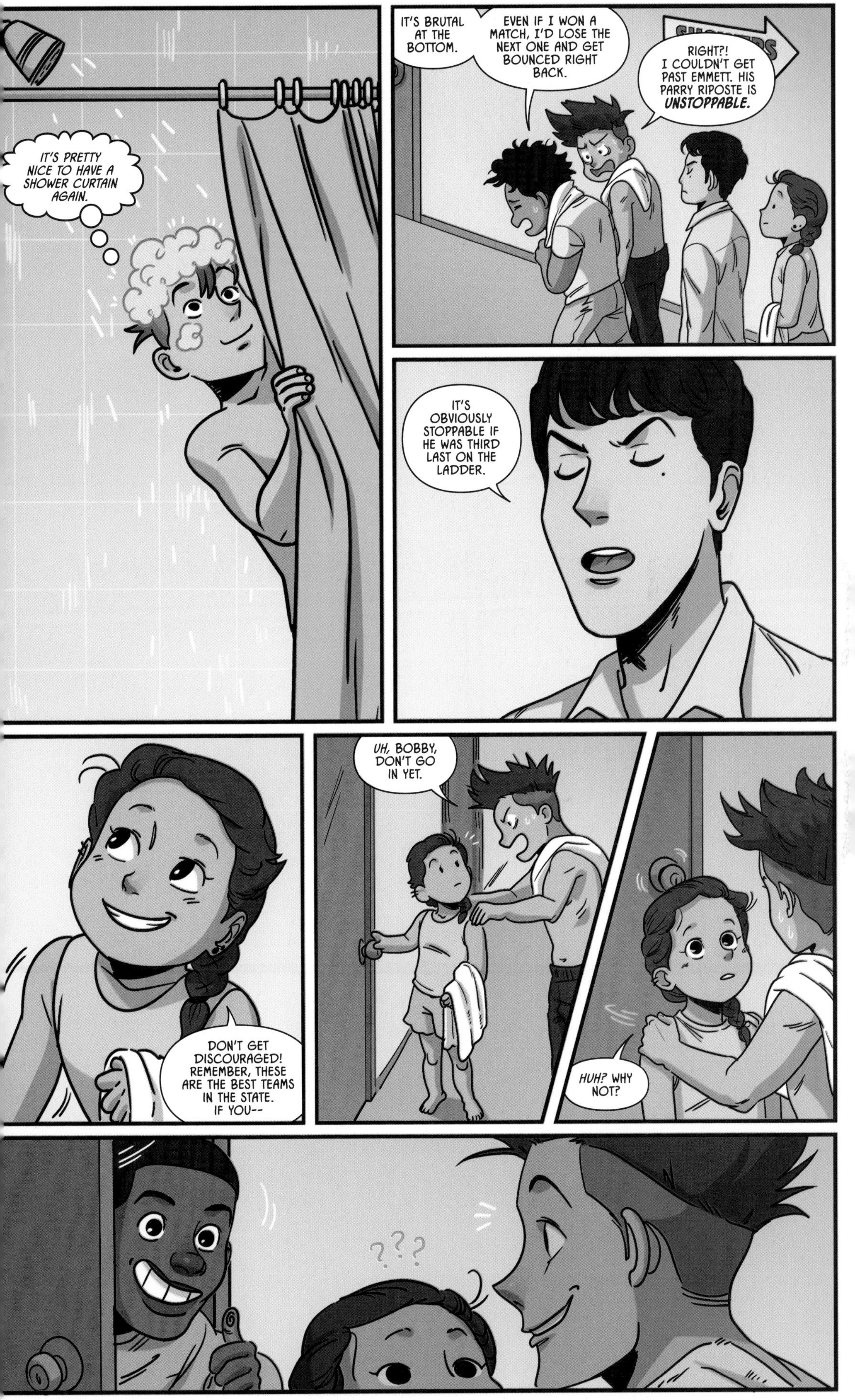
IT'S PRETTY NICE TO HAVE A SHOWER CURTAIN AGAIN.
IT'S BRUTAL AT THE BOTTOM.
EVEN IF I WON A MATCH, I'D LOSE THE NEXT ONE AND GET BOUNCED RIGHT BACK.
RIGHT?! I COULDN'T GET PAST EMMETT. HIS PARRY RIPOSTE IS UNSTOPPABLE.
IT'S OBVIOUSLY STOPPABLE IF HE WAS THIRD LAST ON THE LADDER.
DON'T GET DISCOURAGED! REMEMBER, THESE ARE THE BEST TEAMS IN THE STATE. IF YOU--
UH, BOBBY, DON'T GO IN YET.
HUH? WHY NOT?
???

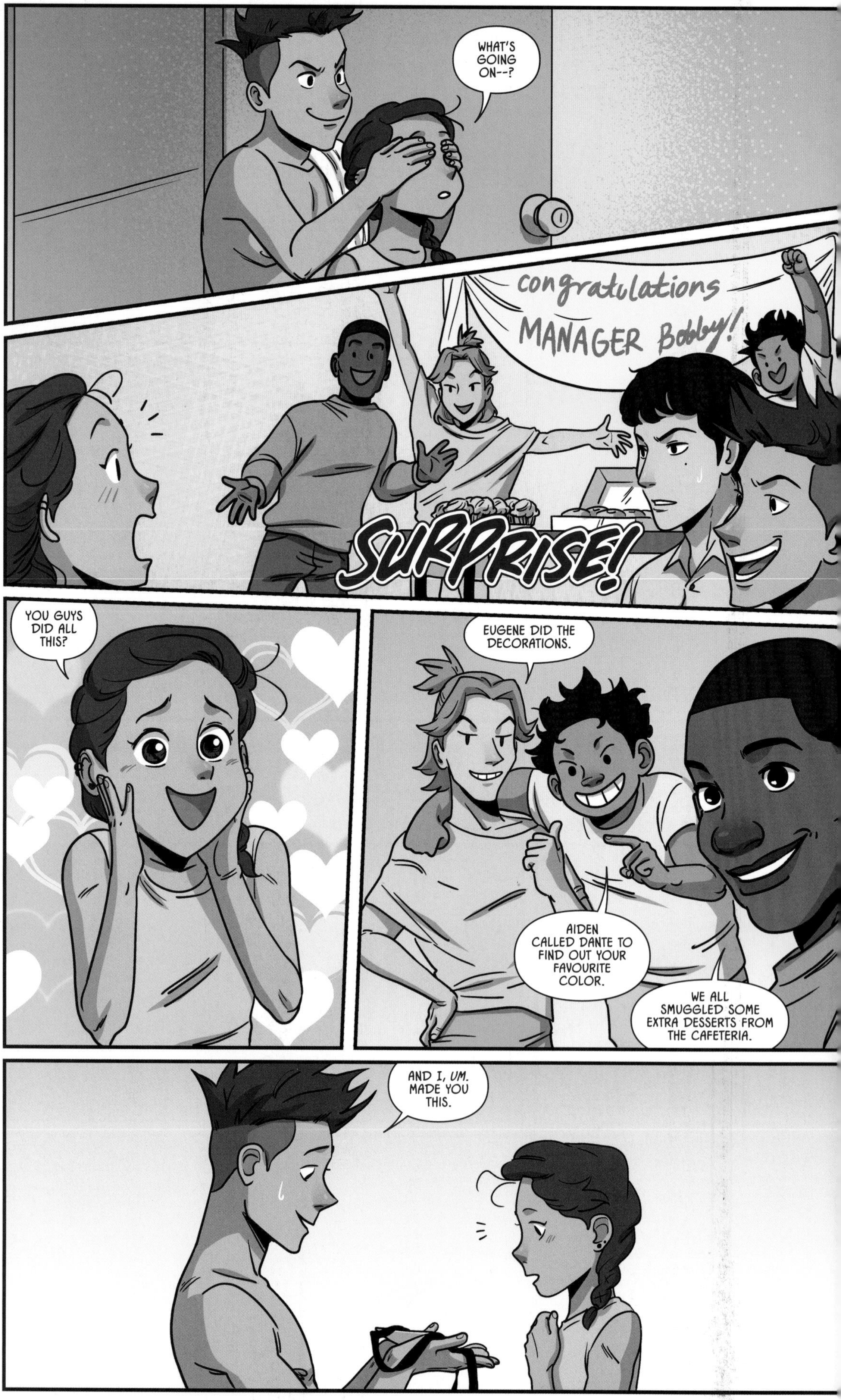
WHAT'S GOING ON--?
congratulations MANAGER Bobby!
SURPRISE!
YOU GUYS DID ALL THIS?
EUGENE DID THE DECORATIONS.
AIDEN CALLED DANTE TO FIND OUT YOUR FAVOURITE COLOR.
WE ALL SMUGGLED SOME EXTRA DESSERTS FROM THE CAFETERIA.
AND I, *UM.* MADE YOU THIS.

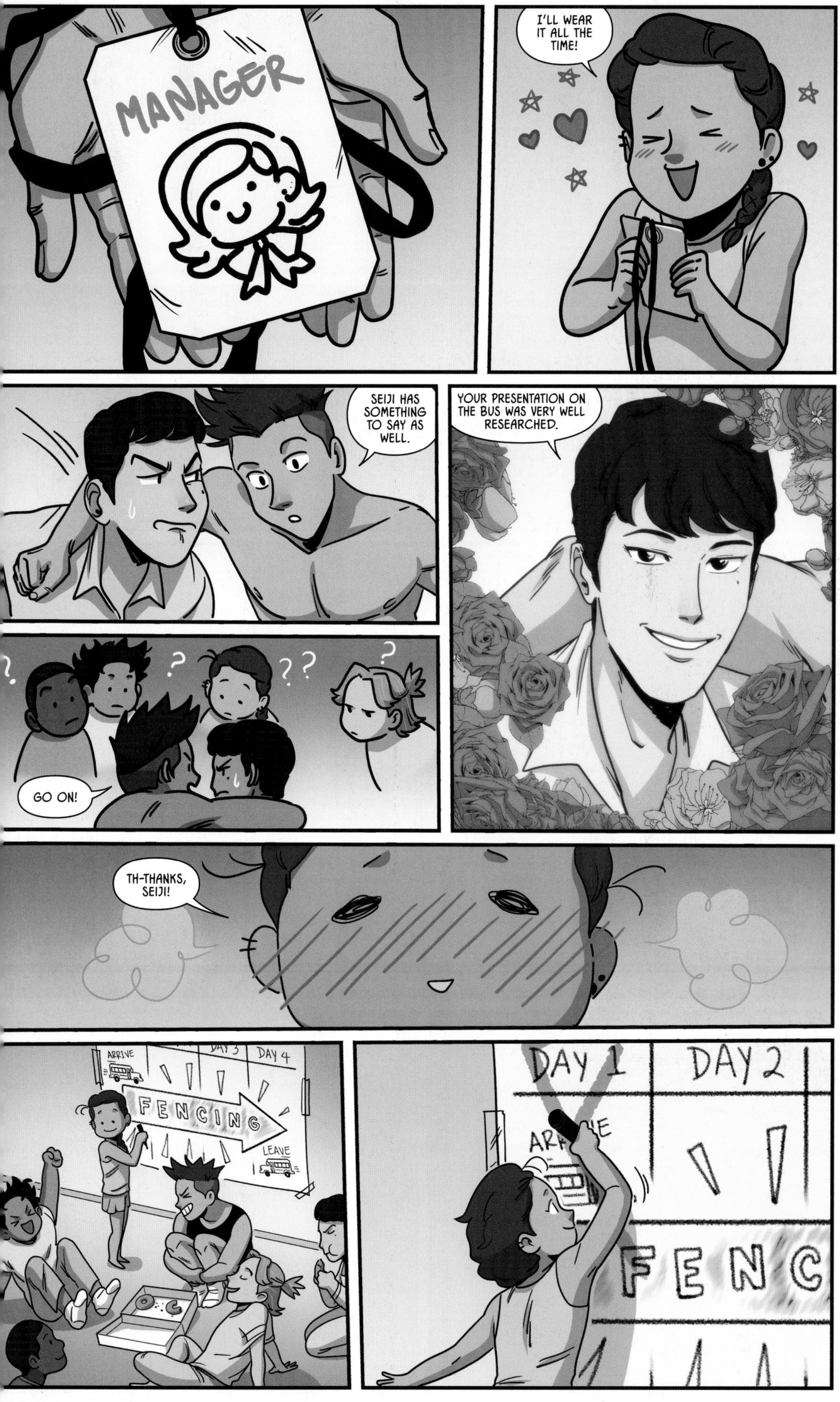
MANAGER
I'LL WEAR IT ALL THE TIME!
SEIJI HAS SOMETHING TO SAY AS WELL.
GO ON!
YOUR PRESENTATION ON THE BUS WAS VERY WELL RESEARCHED.
TH-THANKS, SEIJI!
ARRIVE
DAY 3
DAY 4
FENCING
LEAVE
DAY 1
DAY 2
FENC

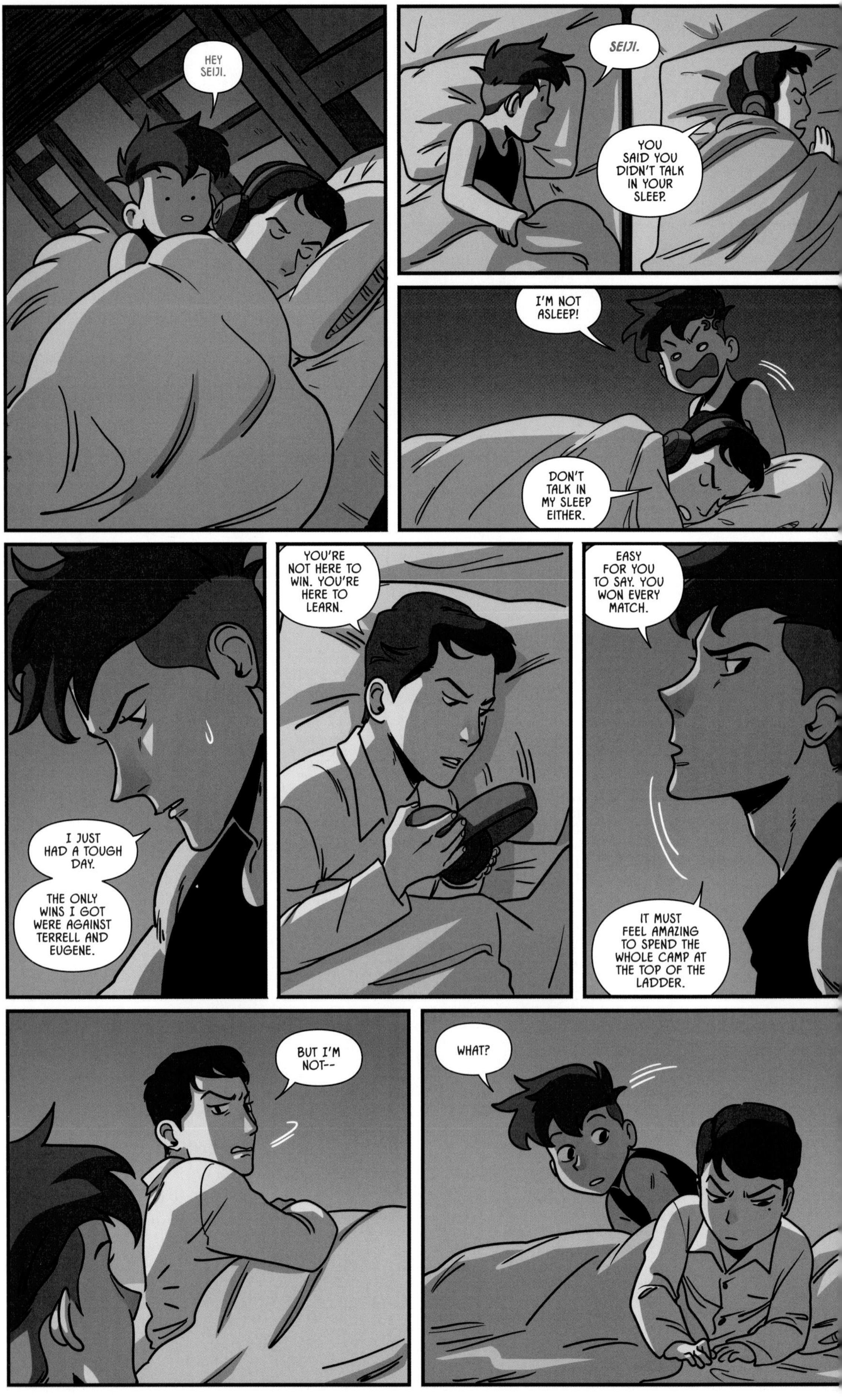
HEY SEIJI.
SEIJI.
YOU SAID YOU DIDN'T TALK IN YOUR SLEEP.
I'M NOT ASLEEP!
DON'T TALK IN MY SLEEP EITHER.
I JUST HAD A TOUGH DAY.
THE ONLY WINS I GOT WERE AGAINST TERRELL AND EUGENE.
YOU'RE NOT HERE TO WIN. YOU'RE HERE TO LEARN.
EASY FOR YOU TO SAY. YOU WON EVERY MATCH.
IT MUST FEEL AMAZING TO SPEND THE WHOLE CAMP AT THE TOP OF THE LADDER.
BUT I'M NOT--
WHAT?

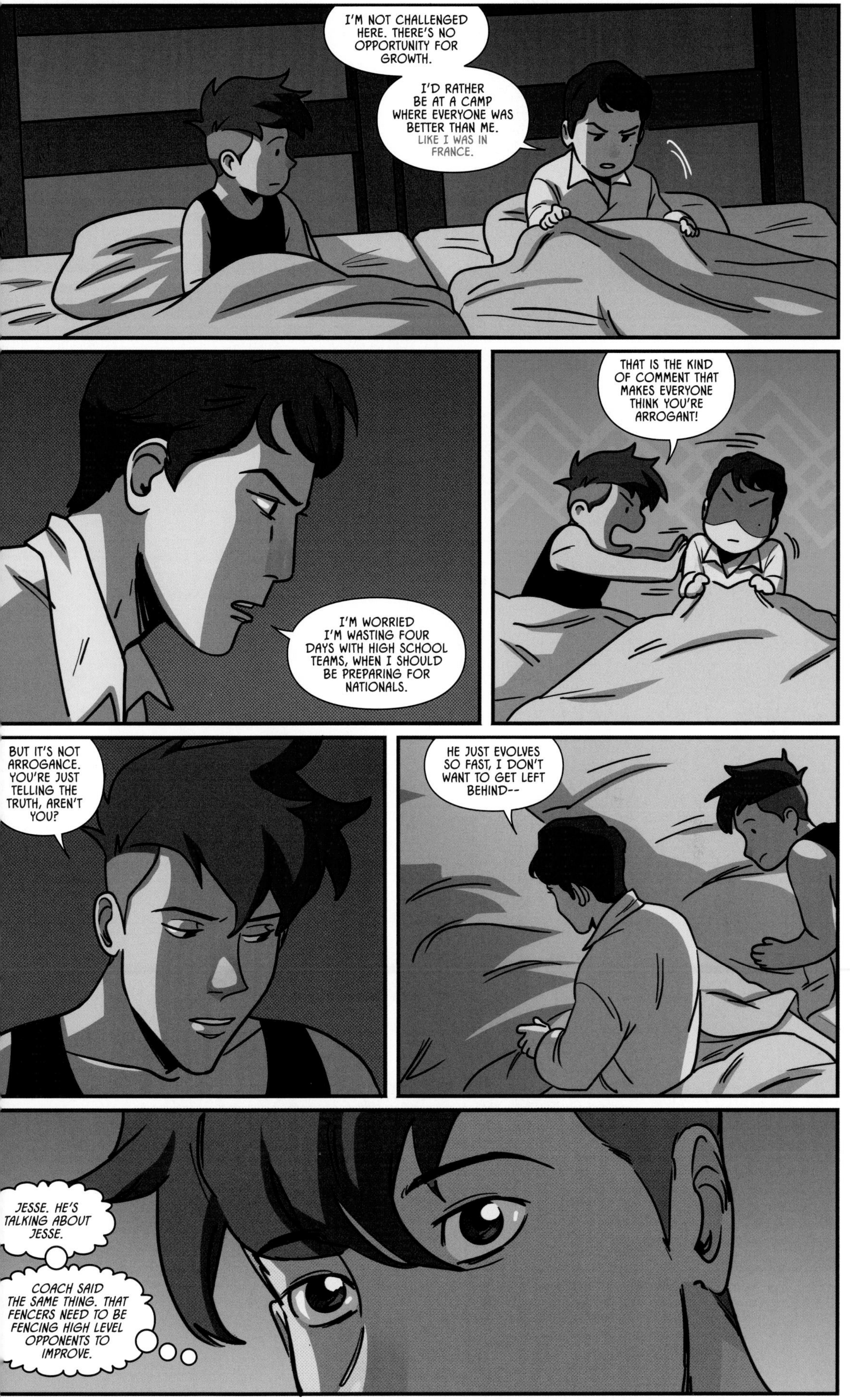
I'M NOT CHALLENGED HERE. THERE'S NO OPPORTUNITY FOR GROWTH.
I'D RATHER BE AT A CAMP WHERE EVERYONE WAS BETTER THAN ME. LIKE I WAS IN FRANCE.
I'M WORRIED I'M WASTING FOUR DAYS WITH HIGH SCHOOL TEAMS, WHEN I SHOULD BE PREPARING FOR NATIONALS.
THAT IS THE KIND OF COMMENT THAT MAKES EVERYONE THINK YOU'RE ARROGANT!
BUT IT'S NOT ARROGANCE. YOU'RE JUST TELLING THE TRUTH, AREN'T YOU?
HE JUST EVOLVES SO FAST, I DON'T WANT TO GET LEFT BEHIND--
JESSE. HE'S TALKING ABOUT JESSE.
COACH SAID THE SAME THING. THAT FENCERS NEED TO BE FENCING HIGH LEVEL OPPONENTS TO IMPROVE.

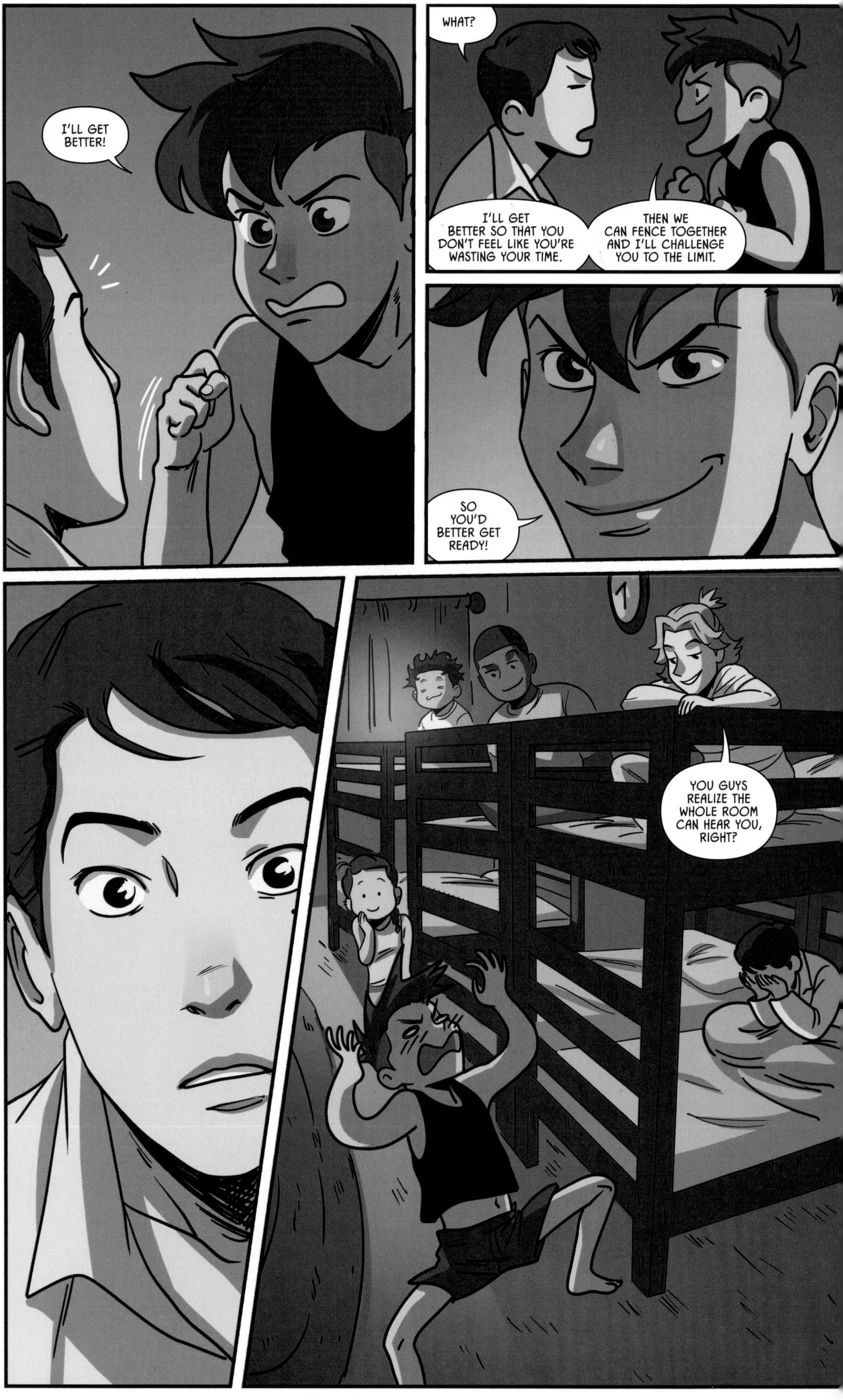
I'LL GET BETTER!
WHAT?
I'LL GET BETTER SO THAT YOU DON'T FEEL LIKE YOU'RE WASTING YOUR TIME.
THEN WE CAN FENCE TOGETHER AND I'LL CHALLENGE YOU TO THE LIMIT.
SO YOU'D BETTER GET READY!
YOU GUYS REALIZE THE WHOLE ROOM CAN HEAR YOU, RIGHT?

CHAPTER
TWENTY

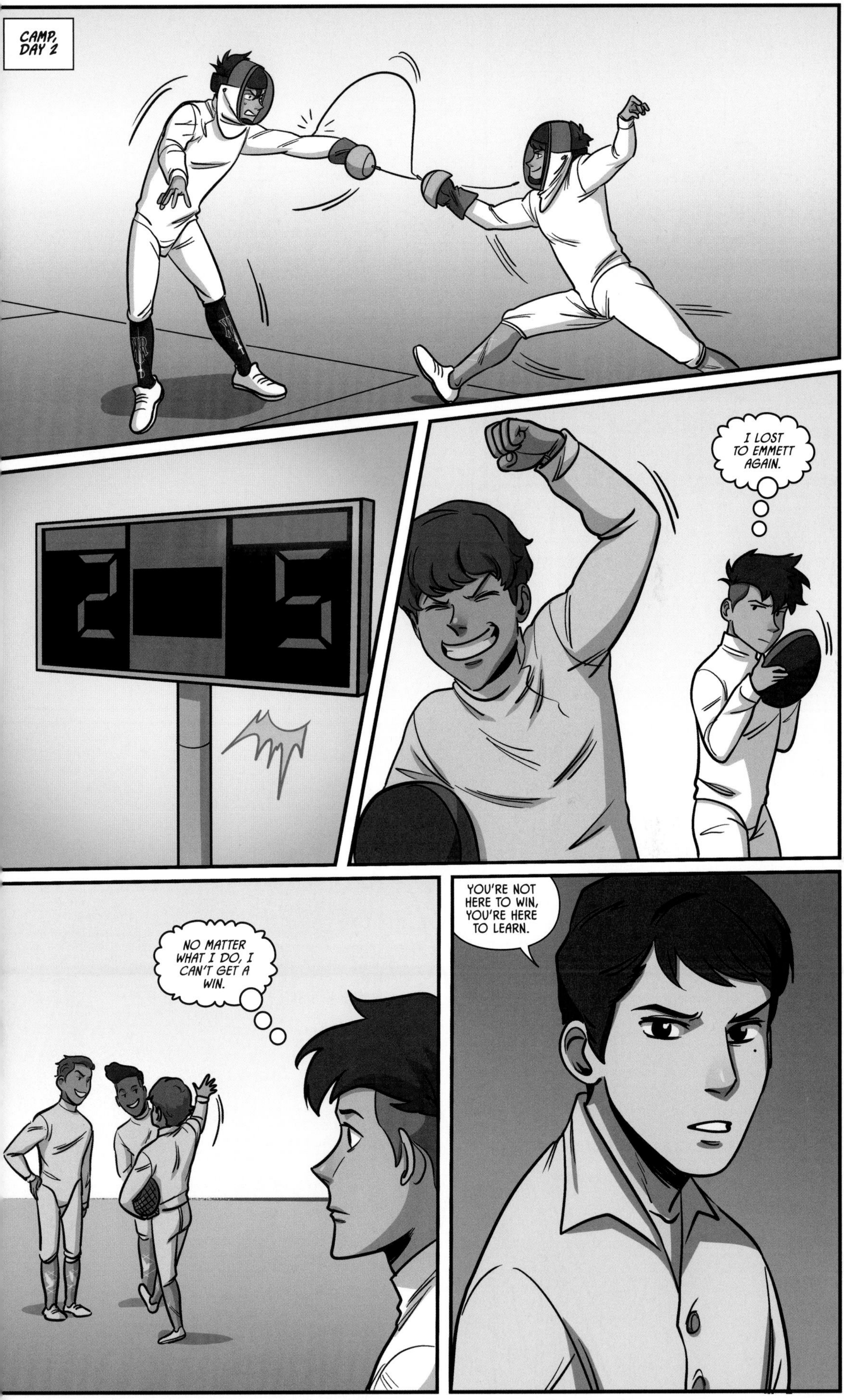
CAMP, DAY 2
I LOST TO EMMETT AGAIN.
NO MATTER WHAT I DO, I CAN'T GET A WIN.
YOU'RE NOT HERE TO WIN, YOU'RE HERE TO LEARN.

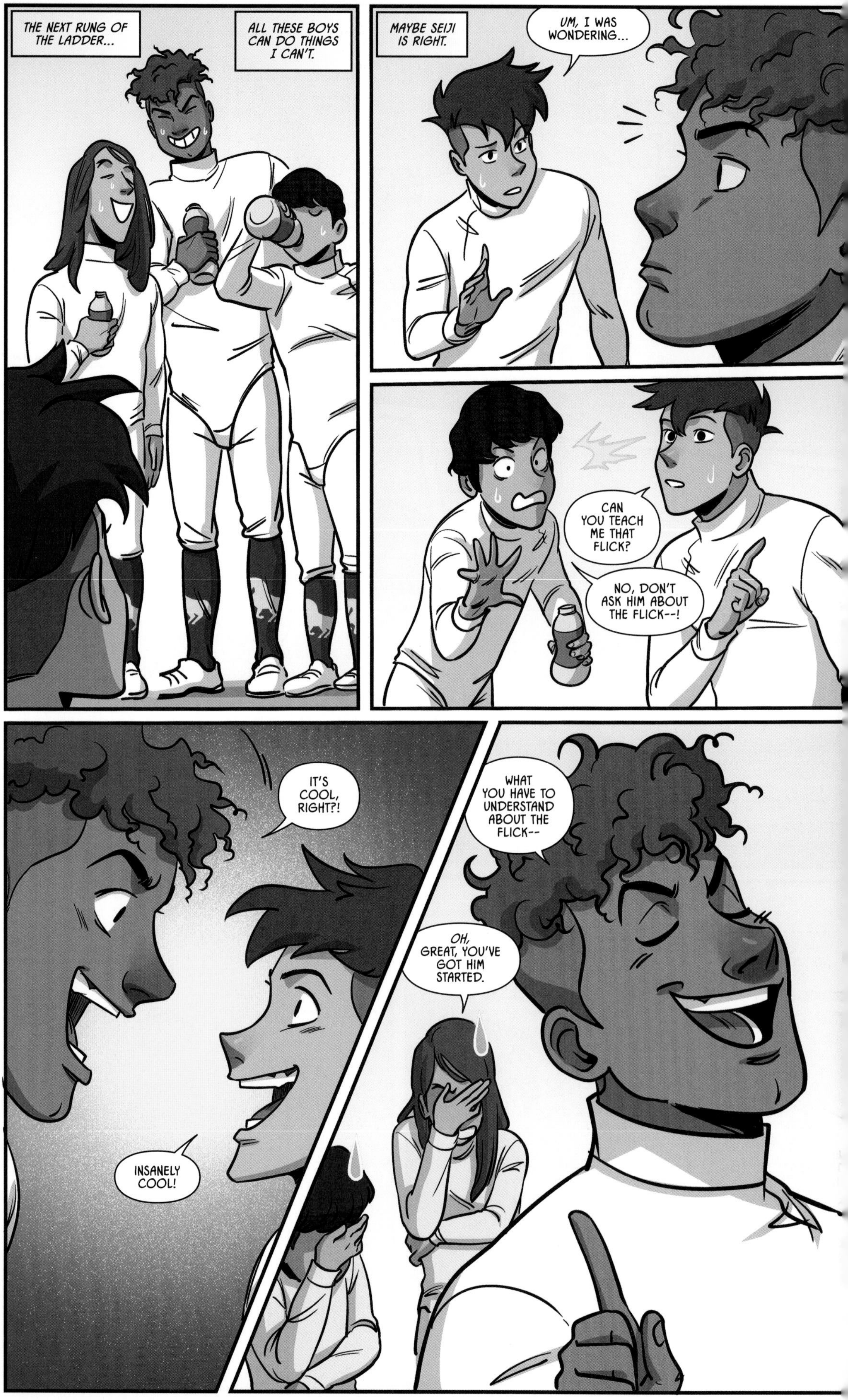
THE NEXT RUNG OF THE LADDER...
ALL THESE BOYS CAN DO THINGS I CAN'T.
MAYBE SEIJI IS RIGHT.
UM, I WAS WONDERING...
CAN YOU TEACH ME THAT FLICK?
NO, DON'T ASK HIM ABOUT THE FLICK--!
IT'S COOL, RIGHT?!
INSANELY COOL!
WHAT YOU HAVE TO UNDERSTAND ABOUT THE FLICK--
OH, GREAT, YOU'VE GOT HIM STARTED.

THE FLICK IS A FAST HIT THAT YOU MAKE WHEN YOU FLICK YOUR BLADE LIKE A WHIP.

"THE WHIPPING MOTION BENDS THE BLADE AROUND PARRIES, MAKING IT POSSIBLE TO HIT PLACES YOU COULDN'T OTHERWISE.

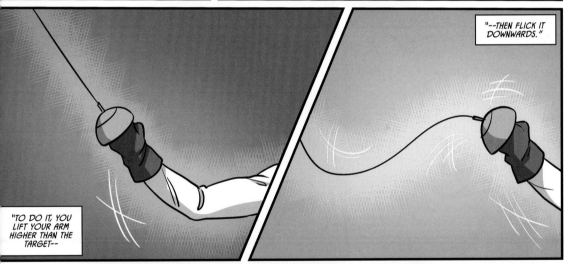

"TO DO IT, YOU LIFT YOUR ARM HIGHER THAN THE TARGET--

"--THEN FLICK IT DOWNWARDS."

NOW, WHEN YOU START OUT IN ÉPÉE IT'S BEST TO FLICK TO THE HAND, WRIST OR ARM--

AREN'T FLICKS QUITE RARE IN ÉPÉE?

YES, THEY ARE DIFFICULT TO DO. IT TAKES INCREDIBLE ACCURACY AND PRECISION.

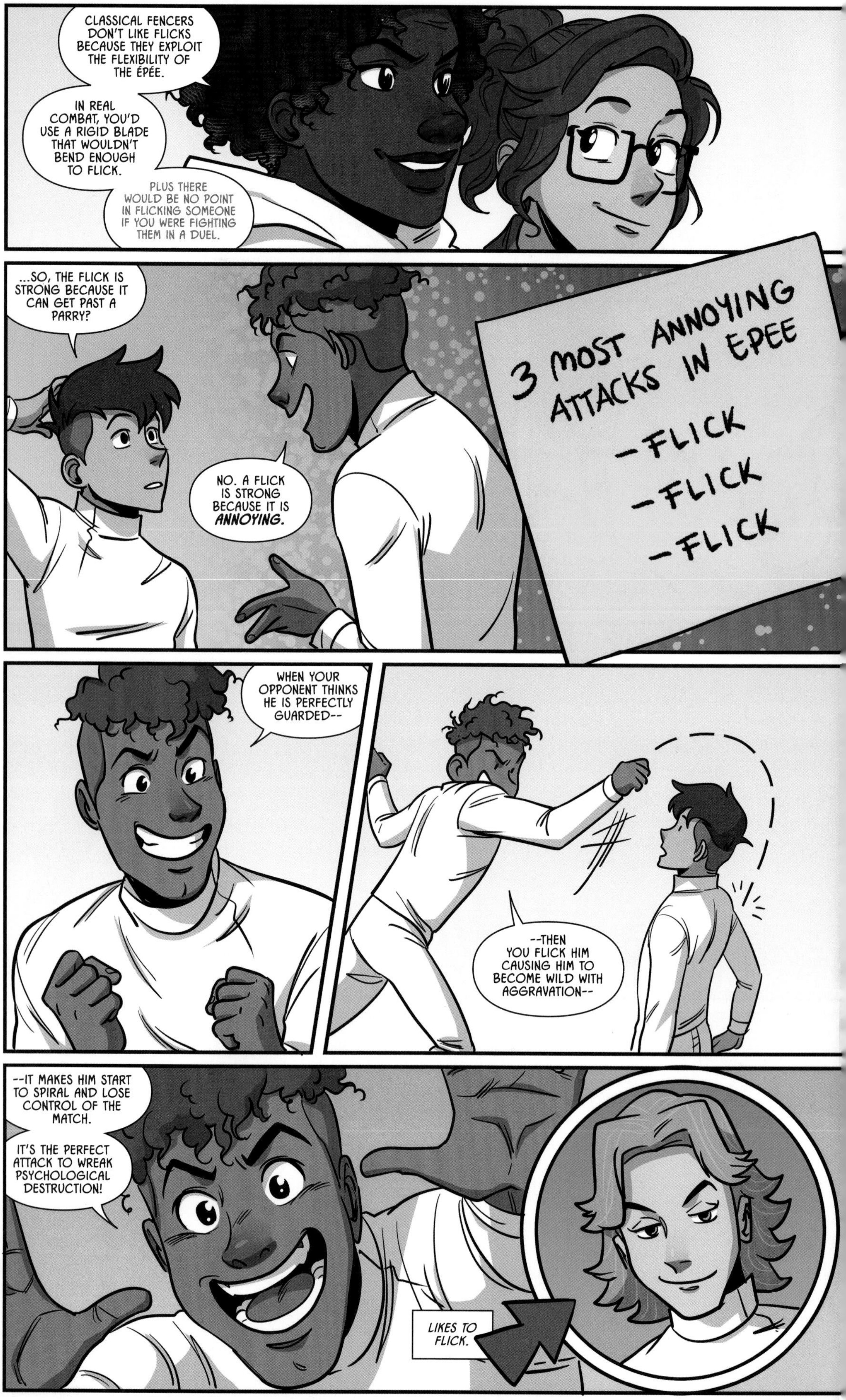
CLASSICAL FENCERS DON'T LIKE FLICKS BECAUSE THEY EXPLOIT THE FLEXIBILITY OF THE ÉPÉE.
IN REAL COMBAT, YOU'D USE A RIGID BLADE THAT WOULDN'T BEND ENOUGH TO FLICK.
PLUS THERE WOULD BE NO POINT IN FLICKING SOMEONE IF YOU WERE FIGHTING THEM IN A DUEL.
...SO, THE FLICK IS STRONG BECAUSE IT CAN GET PAST A PARRY?
NO. A FLICK IS STRONG BECAUSE IT IS ***ANNOYING.***
3 MOST ANNOYING ATTACKS IN EPEE
-FLICK
-FLICK
-FLICK
WHEN YOUR OPPONENT THINKS HE IS PERFECTLY GUARDED--
--THEN YOU FLICK HIM CAUSING HIM TO BECOME WILD WITH AGGRAVATION--
--IT MAKES HIM START TO SPIRAL AND LOSE CONTROL OF THE MATCH.
IT'S THE PERFECT ATTACK TO WREAK PSYCHOLOGICAL DESTRUCTION!
LIKES TO FLICK.

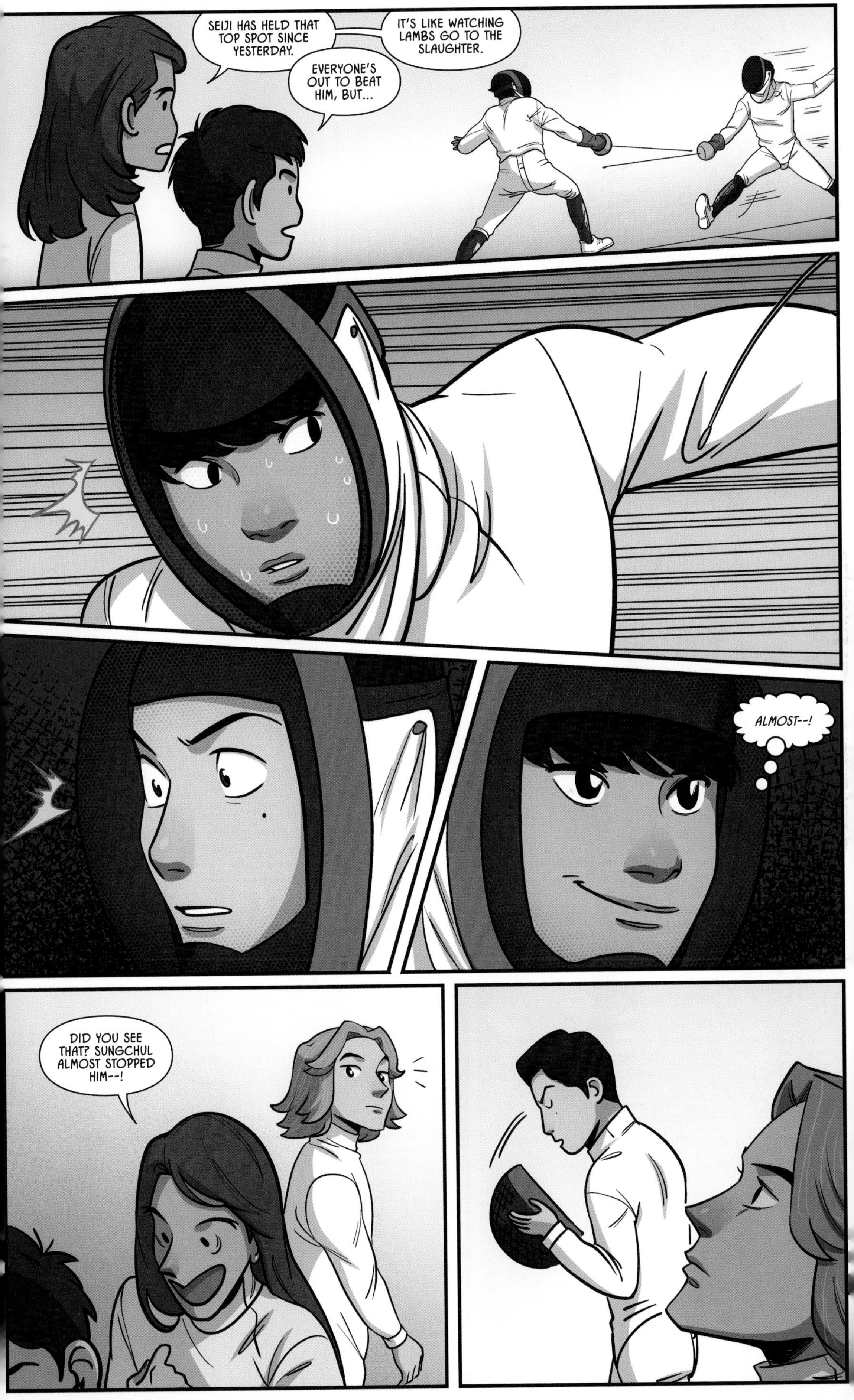

SEIJI HAS HELD THAT TOP SPOT SINCE YESTERDAY.
EVERYONE'S OUT TO BEAT HIM, BUT...
IT'S LIKE WATCHING LAMBS GO TO THE SLAUGHTER.
ALMOST--!
DID YOU SEE THAT? SUNGCHUL ALMOST STOPPED HIM--!

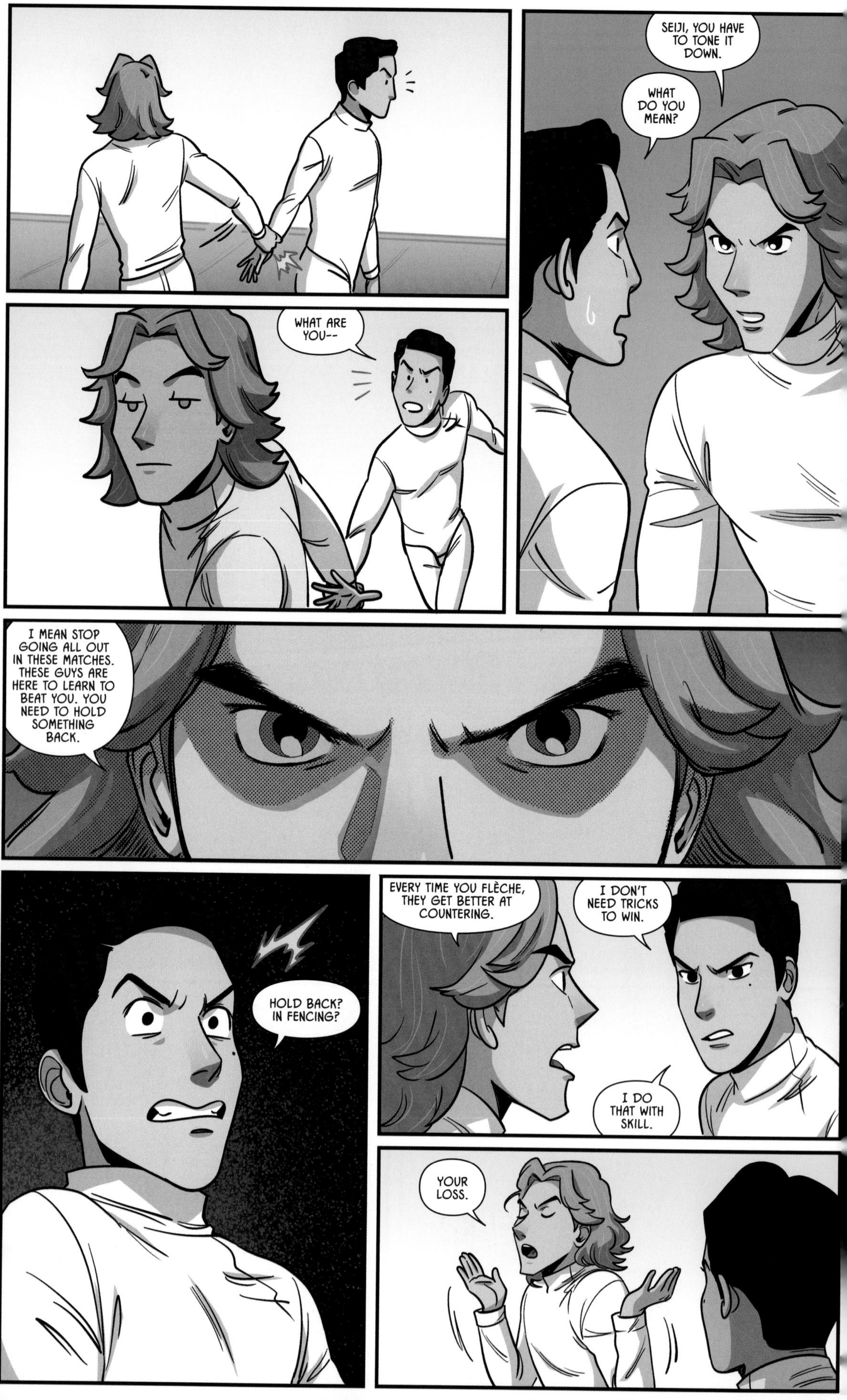
SEIJI, YOU HAVE TO TONE IT DOWN.
WHAT DO YOU MEAN?
WHAT ARE YOU--
I MEAN STOP GOING ALL OUT IN THESE MATCHES. THESE GUYS ARE HERE TO LEARN TO BEAT YOU. YOU NEED TO HOLD SOMETHING BACK.
HOLD BACK? IN FENCING?
EVERY TIME YOU FLÈCHE, THEY GET BETTER AT COUNTERING.
I DON'T NEED TRICKS TO WIN.
I DO THAT WITH SKILL.
YOUR LOSS.

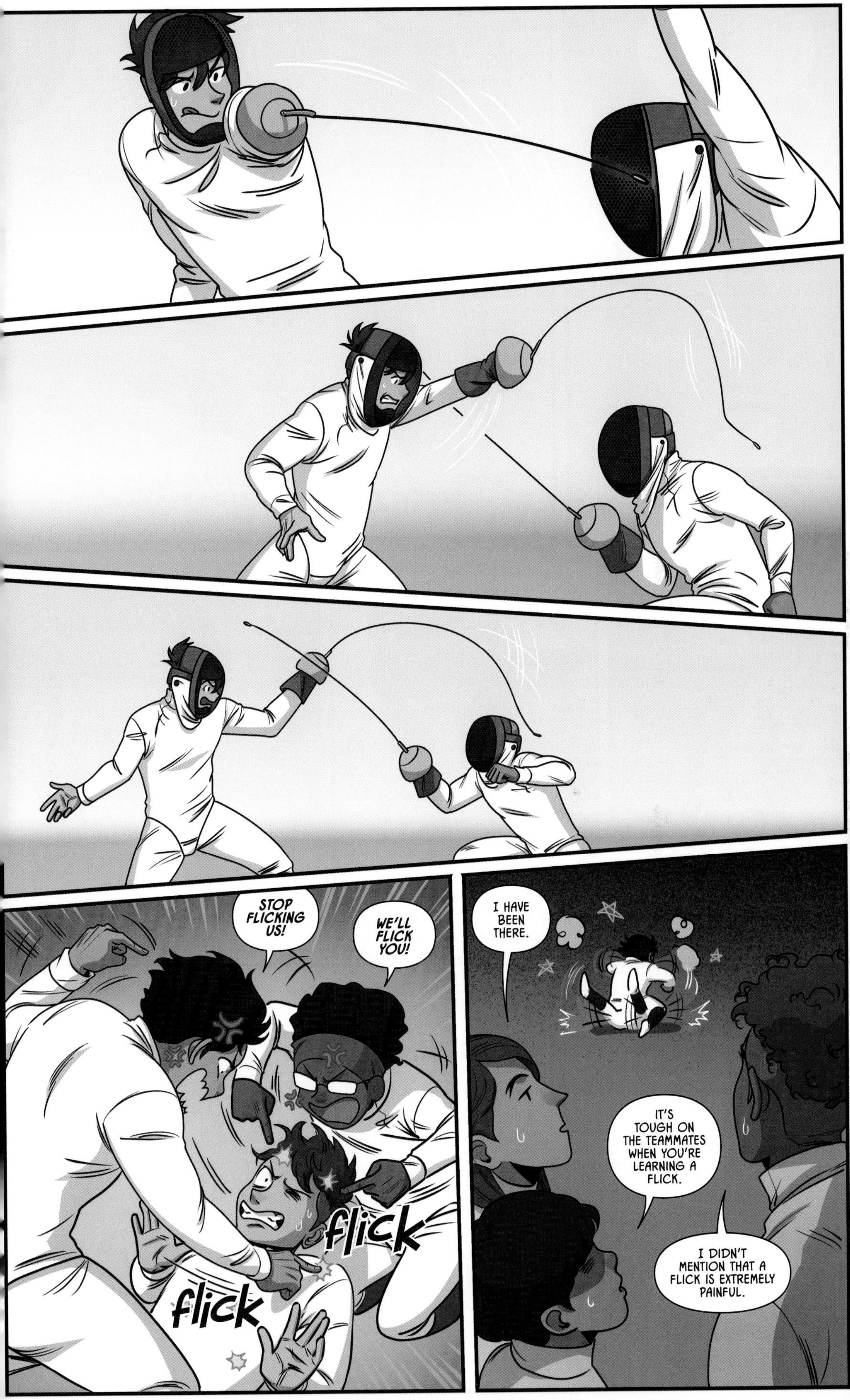
STOP FLICKING US!
WE'LL FLICK YOU!
flick
flick
I HAVE BEEN THERE.
IT'S TOUGH ON THE TEAMMATES WHEN YOU'RE LEARNING A FLICK.
I DIDN'T MENTION THAT A FLICK IS EXTREMELY PAINFUL.

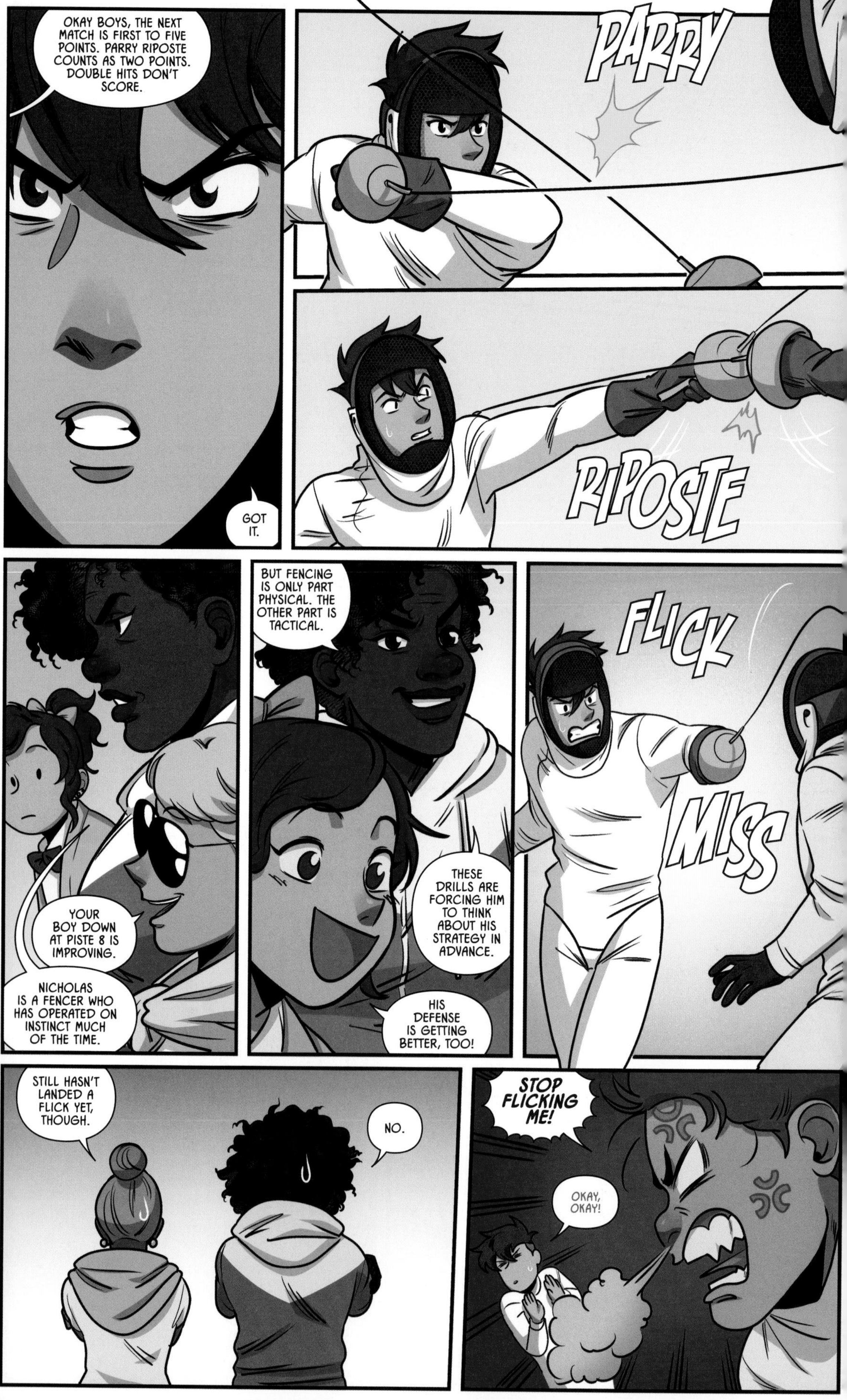
OKAY BOYS, THE NEXT MATCH IS FIRST TO FIVE POINTS. PARRY RIPOSTE COUNTS AS TWO POINTS. DOUBLE HITS DON'T SCORE.
GOT IT.
PARRY
RIPOSTE
YOUR BOY DOWN AT PISTE 8 IS IMPROVING.
NICHOLAS IS A FENCER WHO HAS OPERATED ON INSTINCT MUCH OF THE TIME.
BUT FENCING IS ONLY PART PHYSICAL. THE OTHER PART IS TACTICAL.
THESE DRILLS ARE FORCING HIM TO THINK ABOUT HIS STRATEGY IN ADVANCE.
HIS DEFENSE IS GETTING BETTER, TOO!
FLICK
MISS
STILL HASN'T LANDED A FLICK YET, THOUGH.
NO.
STOP FLICKING ME!
OKAY, OKAY!

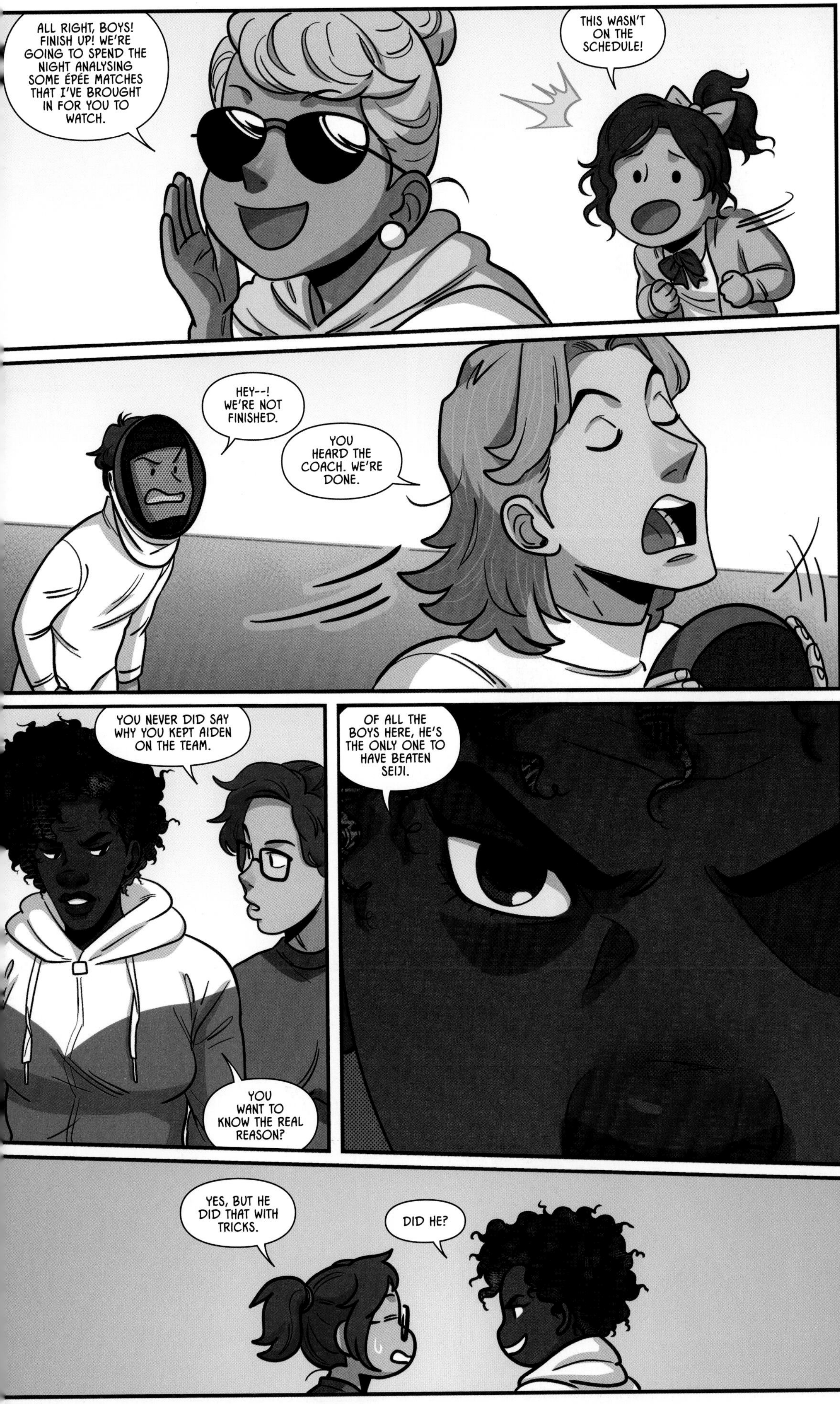
ALL RIGHT, BOYS! FINISH UP! WE'RE GOING TO SPEND THE NIGHT ANALYSING SOME ÉPÉE MATCHES THAT I'VE BROUGHT IN FOR YOU TO WATCH.
THIS WASN'T ON THE SCHEDULE!
HEY--! WE'RE NOT FINISHED.
YOU HEARD THE COACH. WE'RE DONE.
YOU NEVER DID SAY WHY YOU KEPT AIDEN ON THE TEAM.
YOU WANT TO KNOW THE REAL REASON?
OF ALL THE BOYS HERE, HE'S THE ONLY ONE TO HAVE BEATEN SEIJI.
YES, BUT HE DID THAT WITH TRICKS.
DID HE?

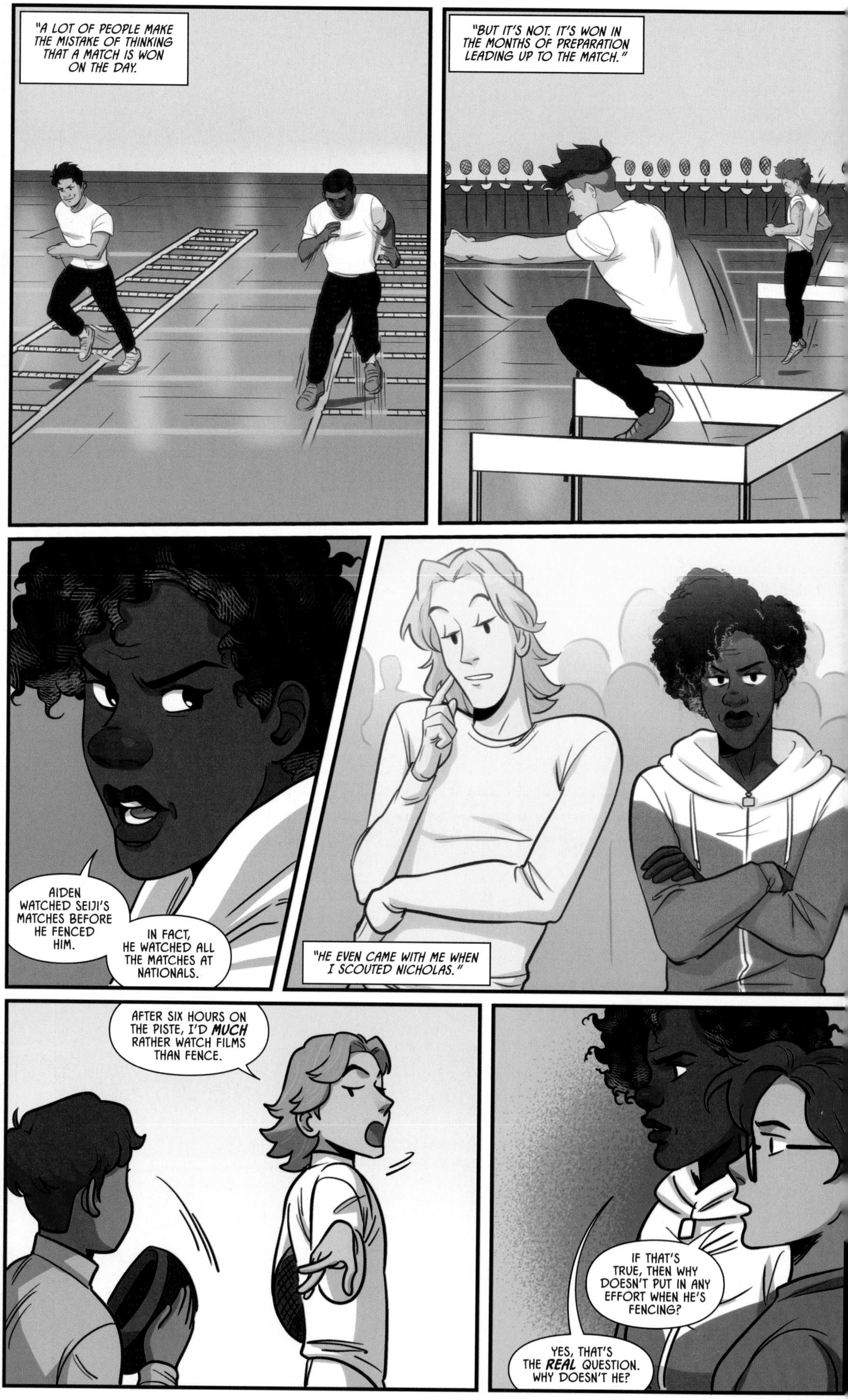
"A LOT OF PEOPLE MAKE THE MISTAKE OF THINKING THAT A MATCH IS WON ON THE DAY.
"BUT IT'S NOT. IT'S WON IN THE MONTHS OF PREPARATION LEADING UP TO THE MATCH."
AIDEN WATCHED SEIJI'S MATCHES BEFORE HE FENCED HIM.
IN FACT, HE WATCHED ALL THE MATCHES AT NATIONALS.
"HE EVEN CAME WITH ME WHEN I SCOUTED NICHOLAS."
AFTER SIX HOURS ON THE PISTE, I'D MUCH RATHER WATCH FILMS THAN FENCE.
IF THAT'S TRUE, THEN WHY DOESN'T PUT IN ANY EFFORT WHEN HE'S FENCING?
YES, THAT'S THE REAL QUESTION. WHY DOESN'T HE?

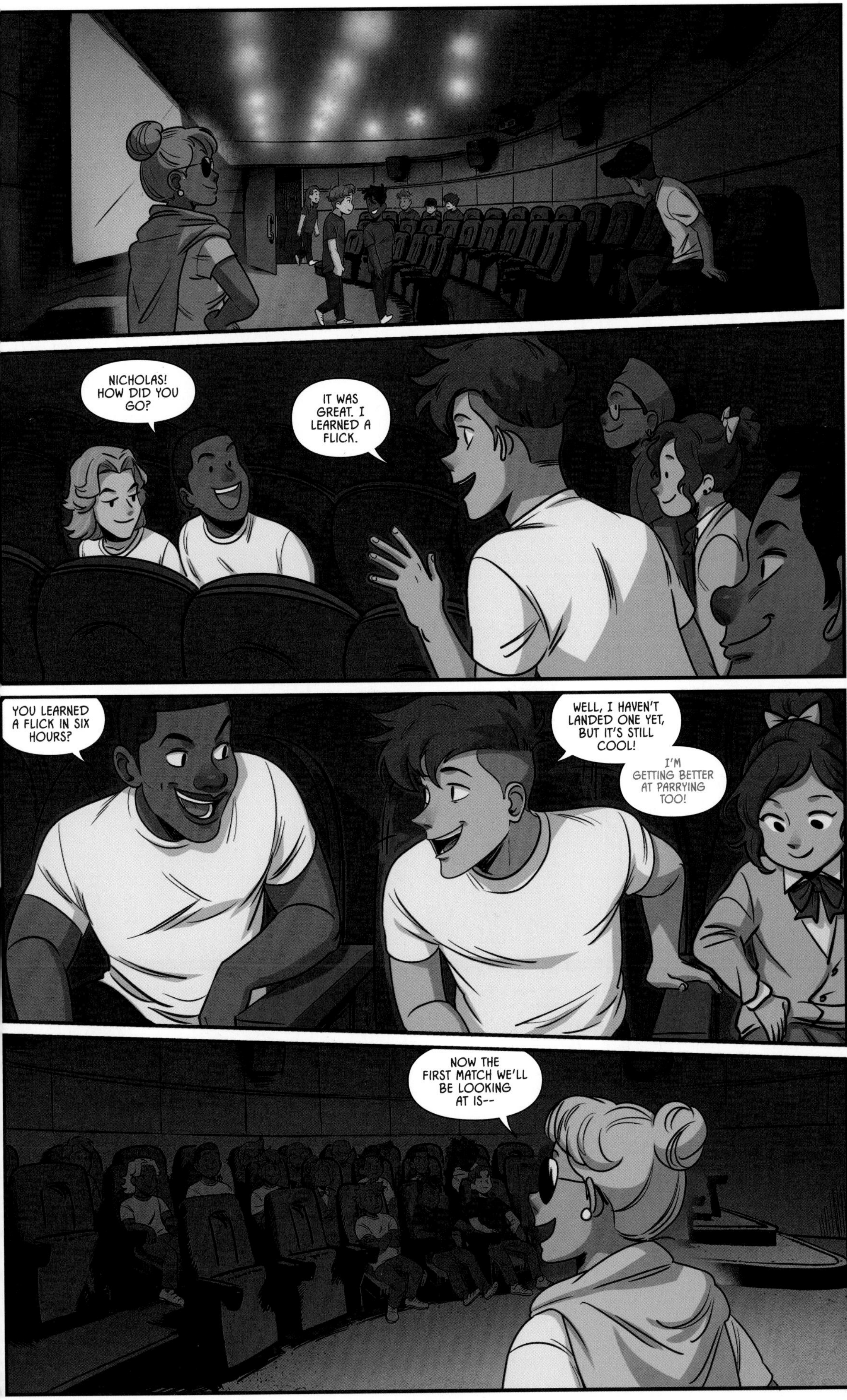
NICHOLAS! HOW DID YOU GO?
IT WAS GREAT. I LEARNED A FLICK.
YOU LEARNED A FLICK IN SIX HOURS?
WELL, I HAVEN'T LANDED ONE YET, BUT IT'S STILL COOL!
I'M GETTING BETTER AT PARRYING TOO!
NOW THE FIRST MATCH WE'LL BE LOOKING AT IS--

"LAST YEAR'S UNDER-16 FINALS AT NATIONALS."

KATAYAMA!

COSTE!

THE MATCH WHERE SEIJI LOST TO JESSE--!

EVERYONE TALKS ABOUT IT, BUT I'VE NEVER SEEN IT.

OH, THIS MATCH IS INCREDIBLE. I'VE WATCHED IT ON YOUTUBE A HUNDRED TIMES.

NOW AS THE MATCH STARTS, YOU WILL SEE IMMEDIATELY THAT BOTH BOYS--

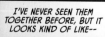

THAT'S SEIJI, AND DMITRI, HIS COACH.

AND THAT'S JESSE, AND--

--ROBERT COSTE.

I'VE NEVER SEEN THEM TOGETHER BEFORE, BUT IT LOOKS KIND OF LIKE--

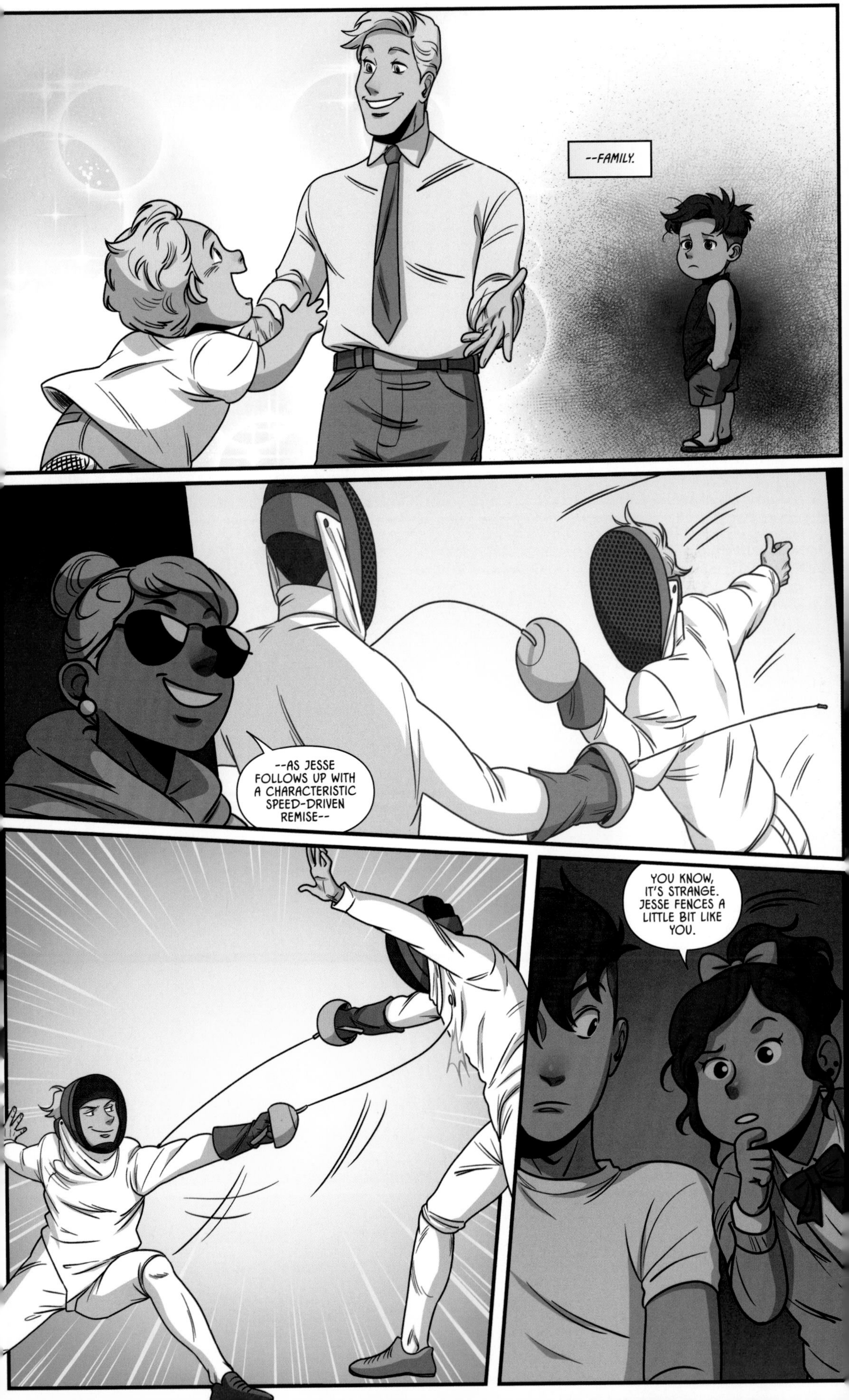
--FAMILY.
--AS JESSE FOLLOWS UP WITH A CHARACTERISTIC SPEED-DRIVEN REMISE--
YOU KNOW, IT'S STRANGE. JESSE FENCES A LITTLE BIT LIKE YOU.

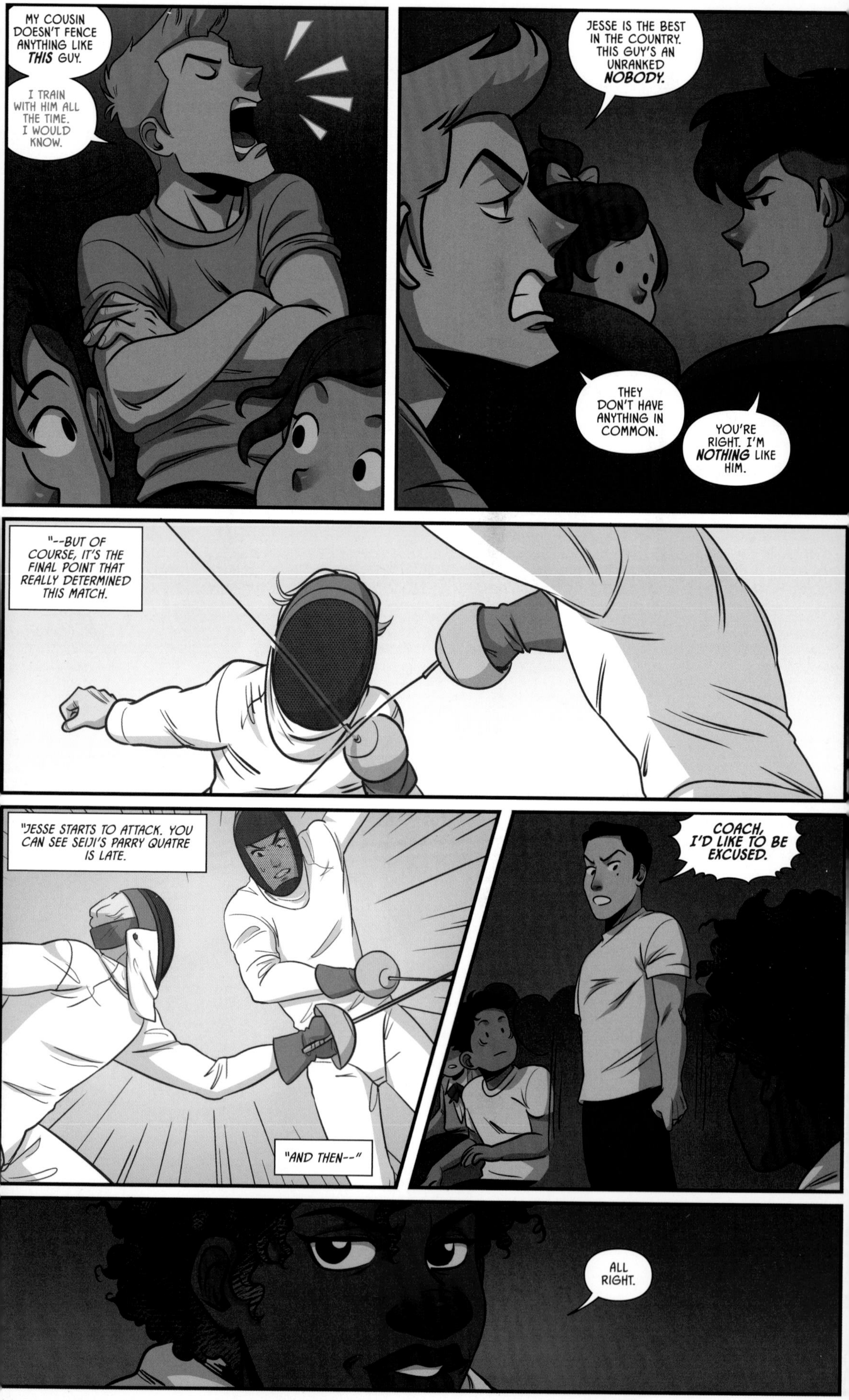

MY COUSIN DOESN'T FENCE ANYTHING LIKE ***THIS*** GUY.
I TRAIN WITH HIM ALL THE TIME. I WOULD KNOW.
JESSE IS THE BEST IN THE COUNTRY. THIS GUY'S AN UNRANKED ***NOBODY.***
THEY DON'T HAVE ANYTHING IN COMMON.
YOU'RE RIGHT. I'M ***NOTHING*** LIKE HIM.
"--BUT OF COURSE, IT'S THE FINAL POINT THAT REALLY DETERMINED THIS MATCH.
"JESSE STARTS TO ATTACK. YOU CAN SEE SEIJI'S PARRY QUATRE IS LATE.
"AND THEN--"
COACH, I'D LIKE TO BE EXCUSED.
ALL RIGHT.

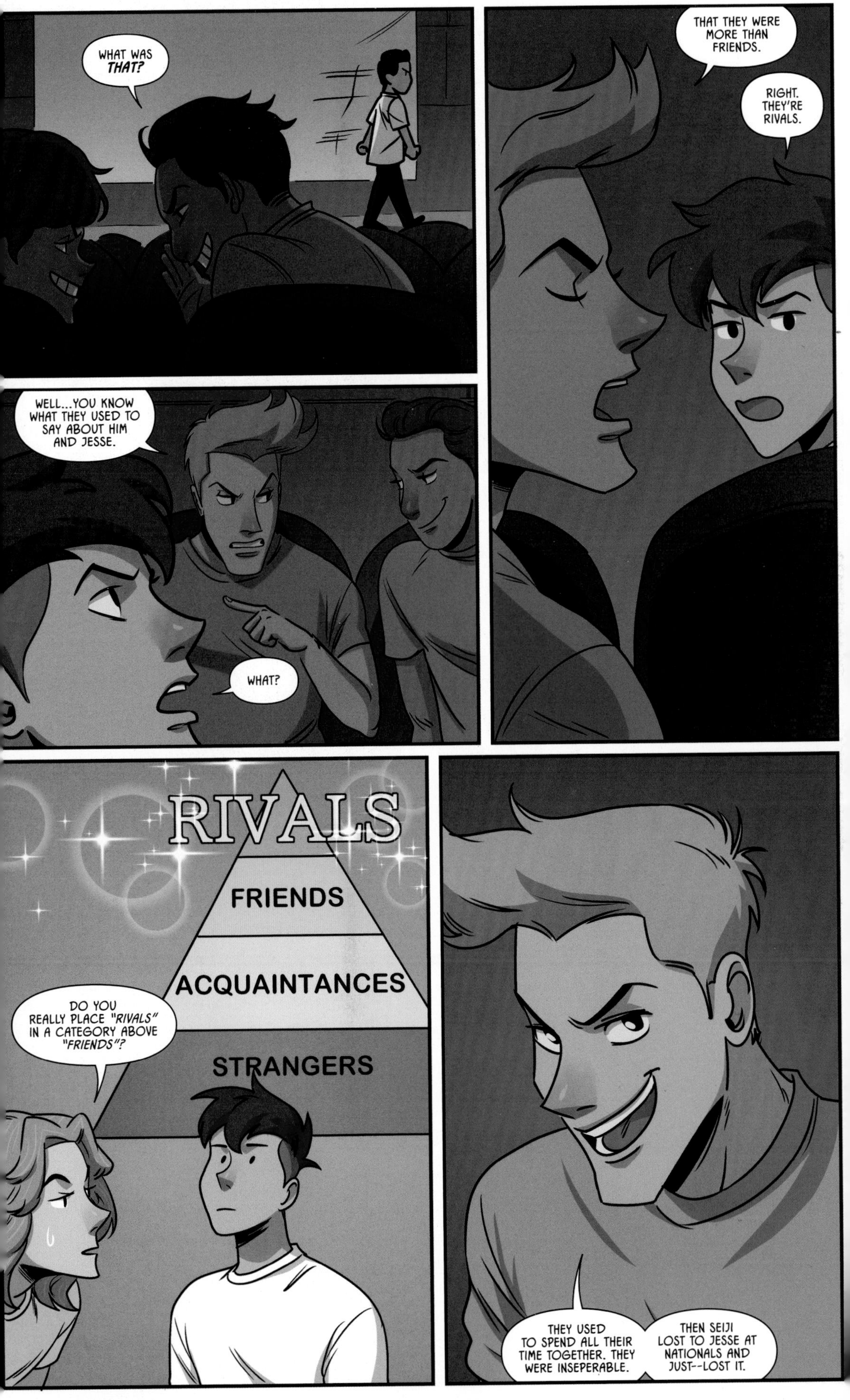
WHAT WAS *THAT?*
THAT THEY WERE MORE THAN FRIENDS.
RIGHT. THEY'RE RIVALS.
WELL...YOU KNOW WHAT THEY USED TO SAY ABOUT HIM AND JESSE.
WHAT?
RIVALS
FRIENDS
ACQUAINTANCES
STRANGERS
DO YOU REALLY PLACE *"RIVALS"* IN A CATEGORY ABOVE *"FRIENDS"*?
THEY USED TO SPEND ALL THEIR TIME TOGETHER. THEY WERE INSEPERABLE.
THEN SEIJI LOST TO JESSE AT NATIONALS AND JUST--LOST IT.

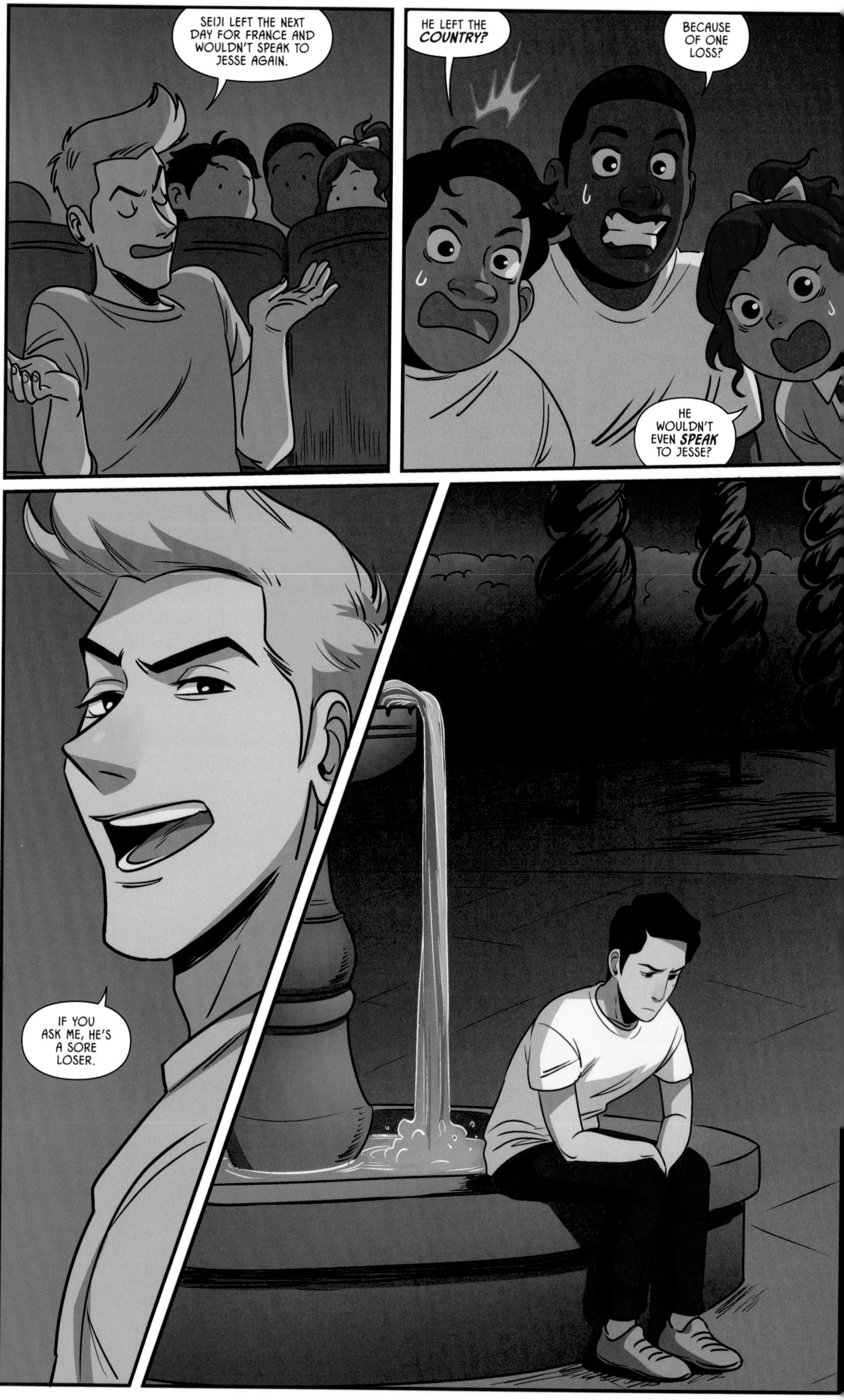
SEIJI LEFT THE NEXT DAY FOR FRANCE AND WOULDN'T SPEAK TO JESSE AGAIN.
HE LEFT THE ***COUNTRY?***
BECAUSE OF ONE LOSS?
HE WOULDN'T EVEN ***SPEAK*** TO JESSE?
IF YOU ASK ME, HE'S A SORE LOSER.

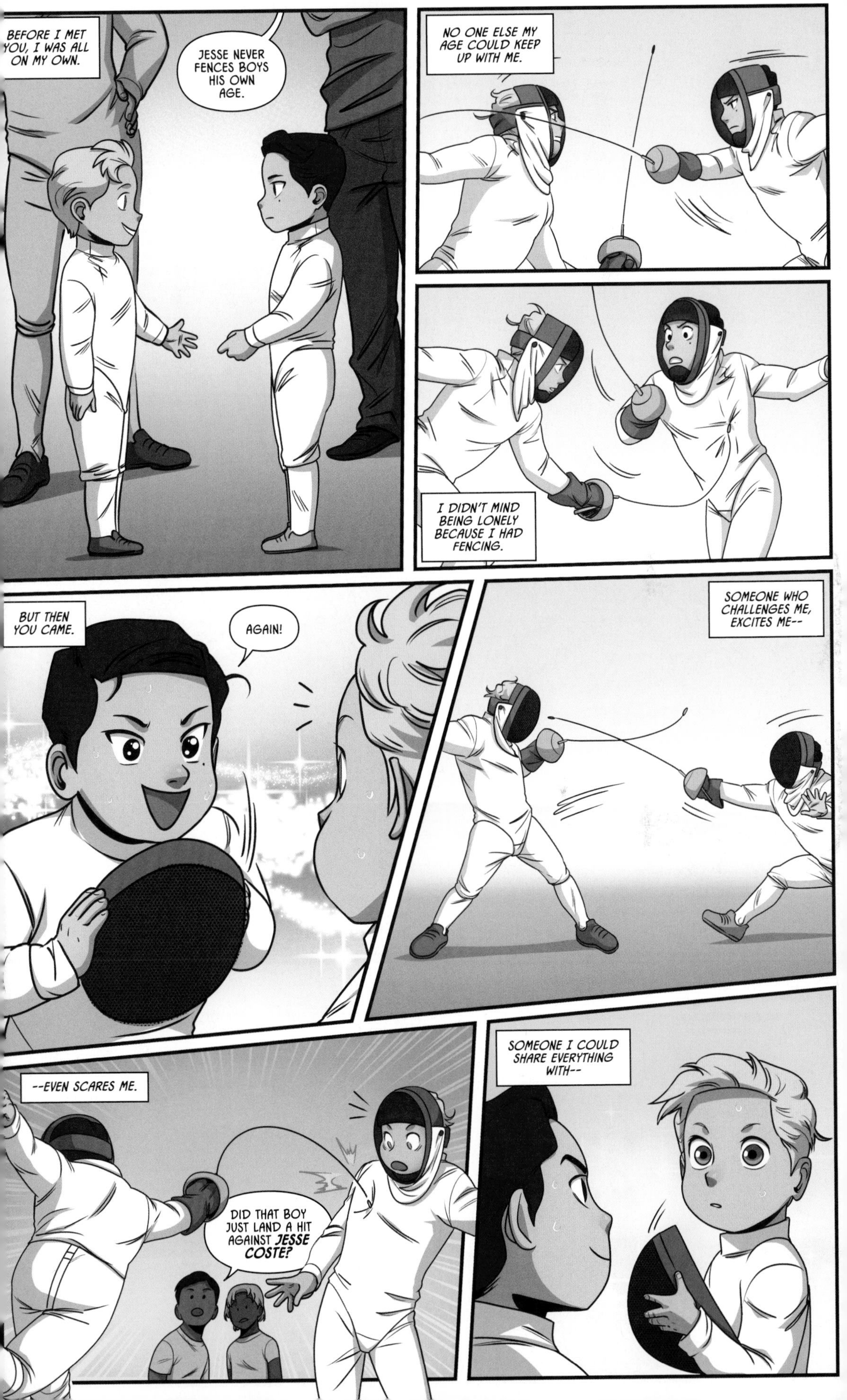
BEFORE I MET YOU, I WAS ALL ON MY OWN.
JESSE NEVER FENCES BOYS HIS OWN AGE.
NO ONE ELSE MY AGE COULD KEEP UP WITH ME.
I DIDN'T MIND BEING LONELY BECAUSE I HAD FENCING.
BUT THEN YOU CAME.
AGAIN!
SOMEONE WHO CHALLENGES ME, EXCITES ME--
--EVEN SCARES ME.
DID THAT BOY JUST LAND A HIT AGAINST JESSE COSTE?
SOMEONE I COULD SHARE EVERYTHING WITH--

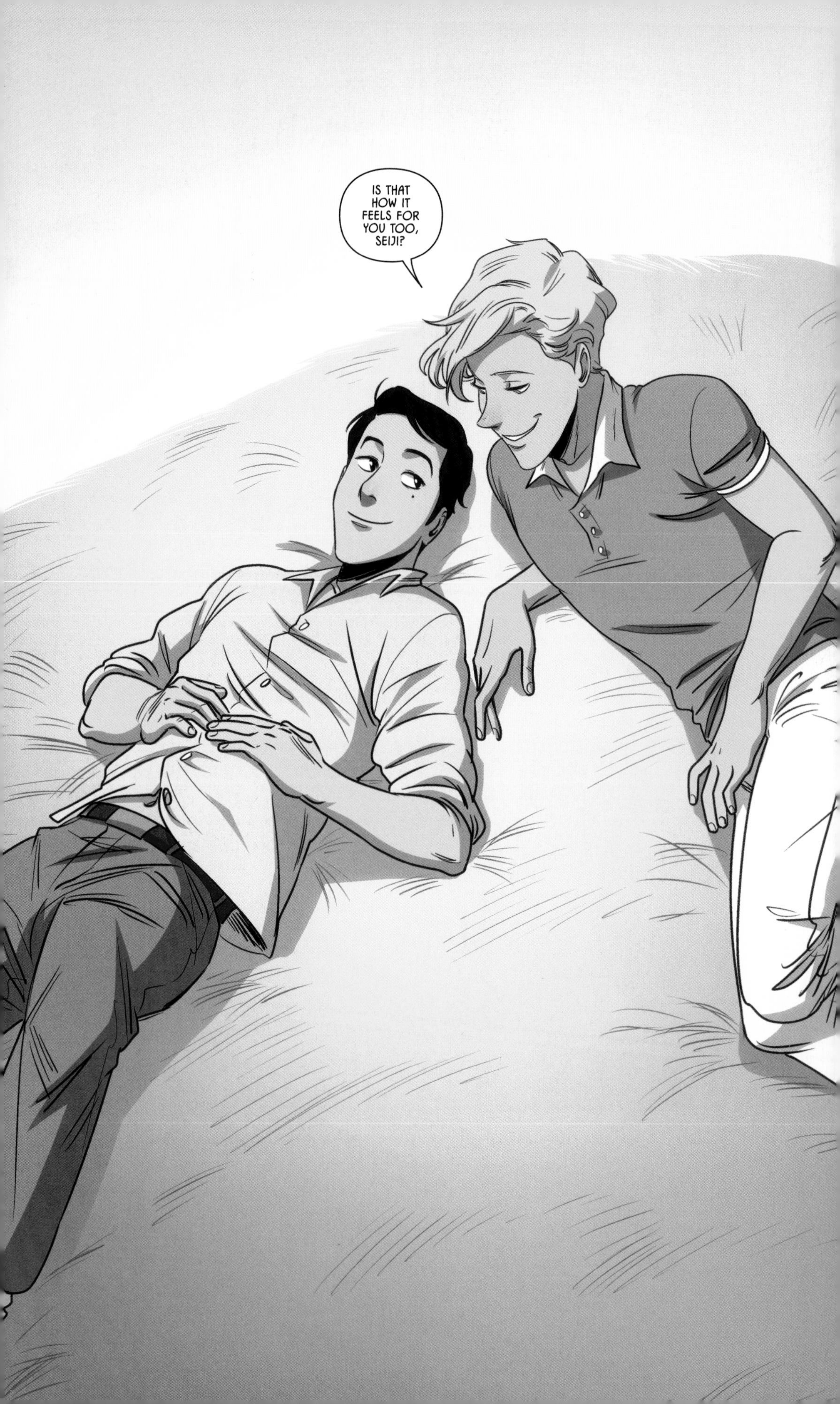
IS THAT HOW IT FEELS FOR YOU TOO, SEIJI?

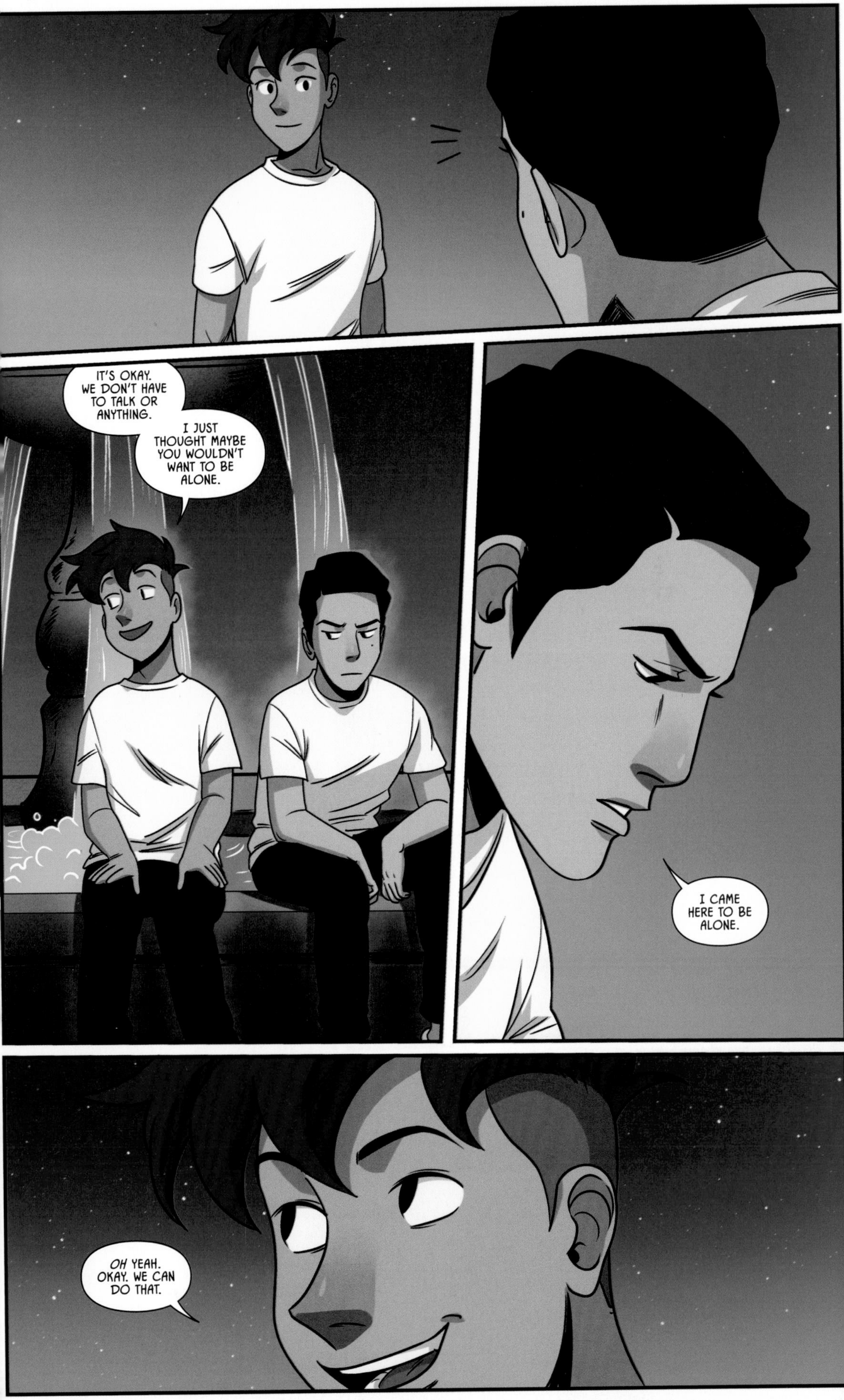
IT'S OKAY. WE DON'T HAVE TO TALK OR ANYTHING.
I JUST THOUGHT MAYBE YOU WOULDN'T WANT TO BE ALONE.
I CAME HERE TO BE ALONE.
OH YEAH. OKAY. WE CAN DO THAT.

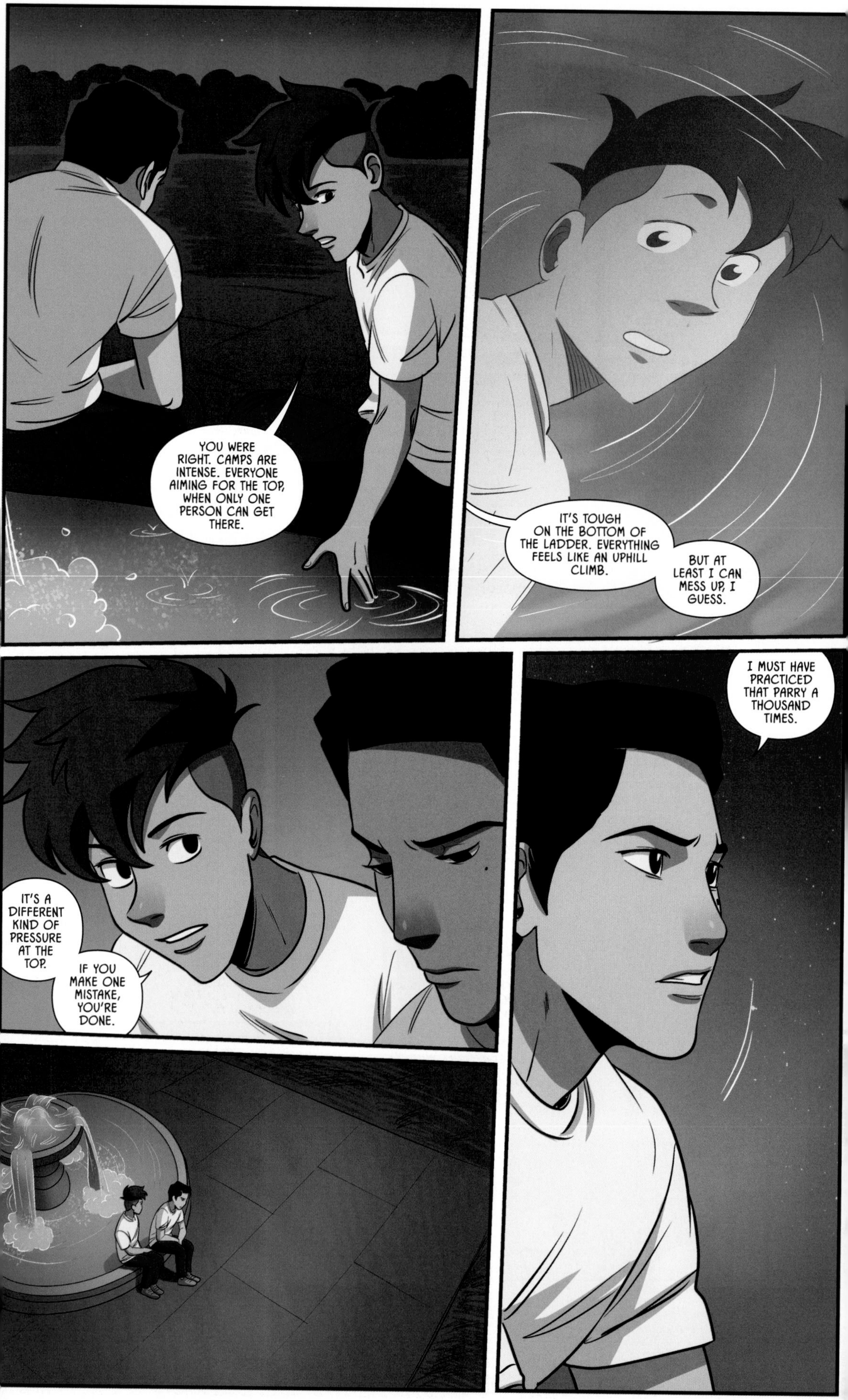
YOU WERE RIGHT. CAMPS ARE INTENSE. EVERYONE AIMING FOR THE TOP, WHEN ONLY ONE PERSON CAN GET THERE.
IT'S TOUGH ON THE BOTTOM OF THE LADDER. EVERYTHING FEELS LIKE AN UPHILL CLIMB.
BUT AT LEAST I CAN MESS UP, I GUESS.
IT'S A DIFFERENT KIND OF PRESSURE AT THE TOP.
IF YOU MAKE ONE MISTAKE, YOU'RE DONE.
I MUST HAVE PRACTICED THAT PARRY A THOUSAND TIMES.

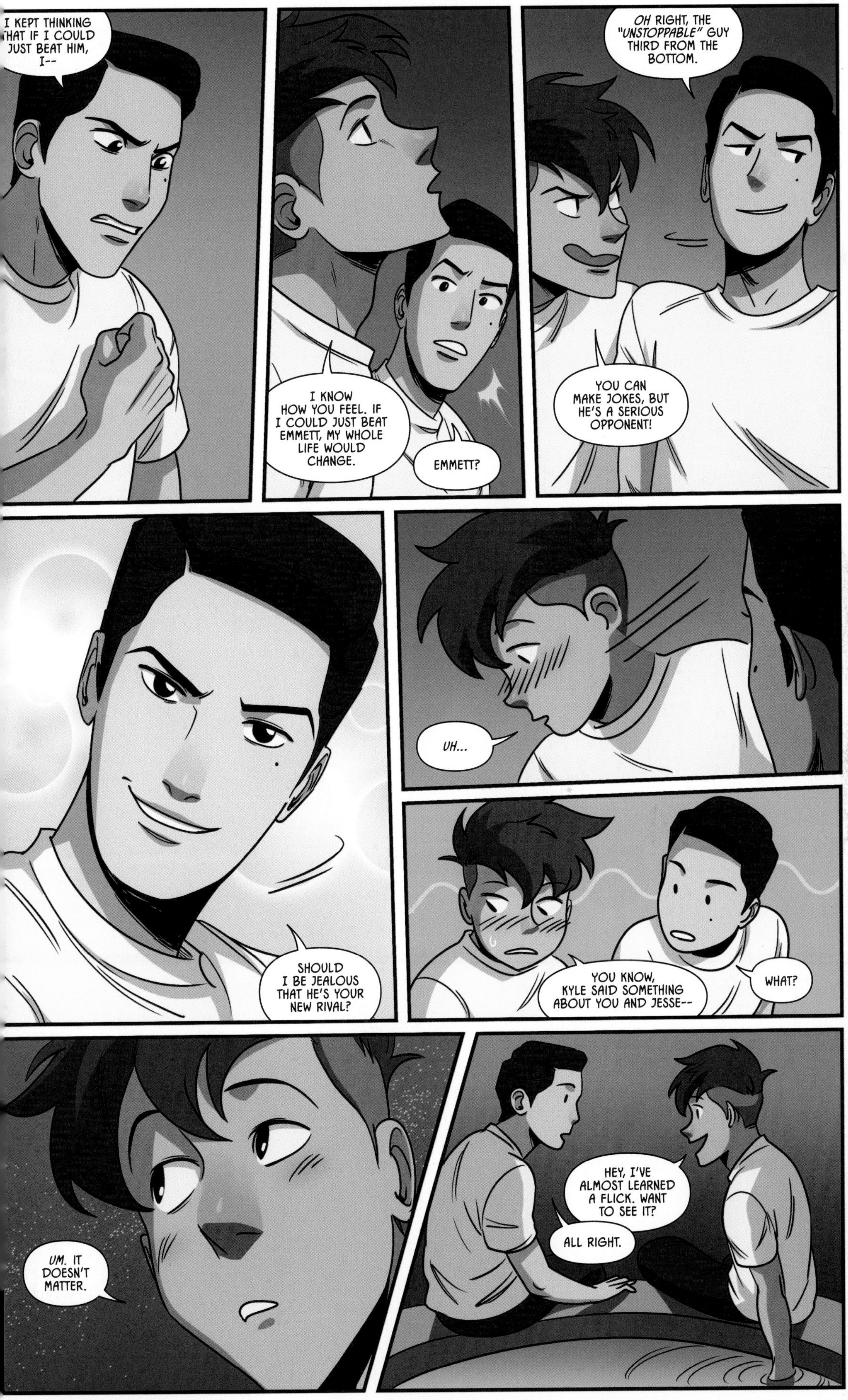
I KEPT THINKING THAT IF I COULD JUST BEAT HIM, I--
I KNOW HOW YOU FEEL. IF I COULD JUST BEAT EMMETT, MY WHOLE LIFE WOULD CHANGE.
EMMETT?
OH RIGHT, THE *"UNSTOPPABLE"* GUY THIRD FROM THE BOTTOM.
YOU CAN MAKE JOKES, BUT HE'S A SERIOUS OPPONENT!
SHOULD I BE JEALOUS THAT HE'S YOUR NEW RIVAL?
UH...
YOU KNOW, KYLE SAID SOMETHING ABOUT YOU AND JESSE--
WHAT?
UM. IT DOESN'T MATTER.
HEY, I'VE ALMOST LEARNED A FLICK. WANT TO SEE IT?
ALL RIGHT.

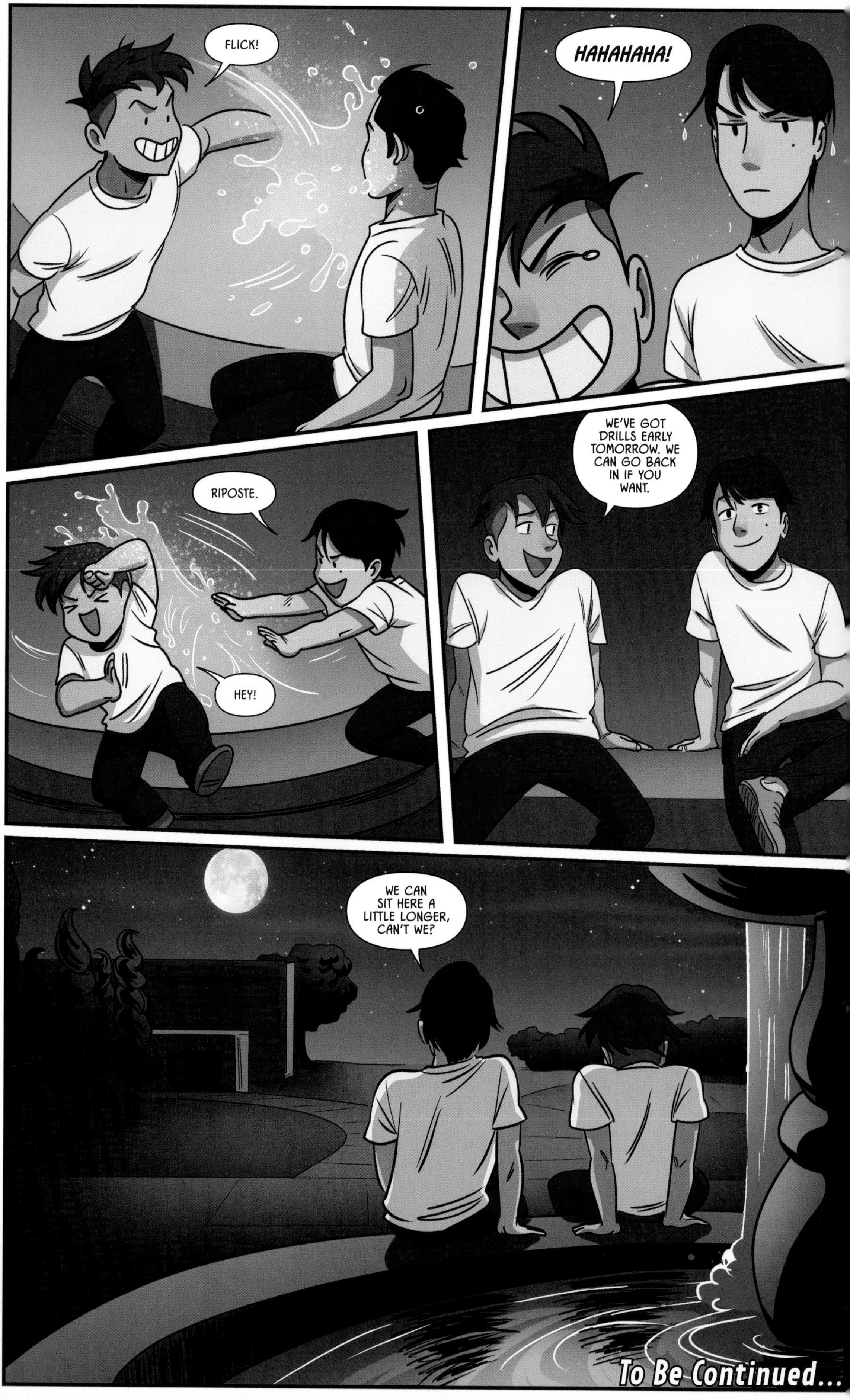
FLICK!
HAHAHAHA!
RIPOSTE.
HEY!
WE'VE GOT DRILLS EARLY TOMORROW. WE CAN GO BACK IN IF YOU WANT.
WE CAN SIT HERE A LITTLE LONGER, CAN'T WE?
To Be Continued...

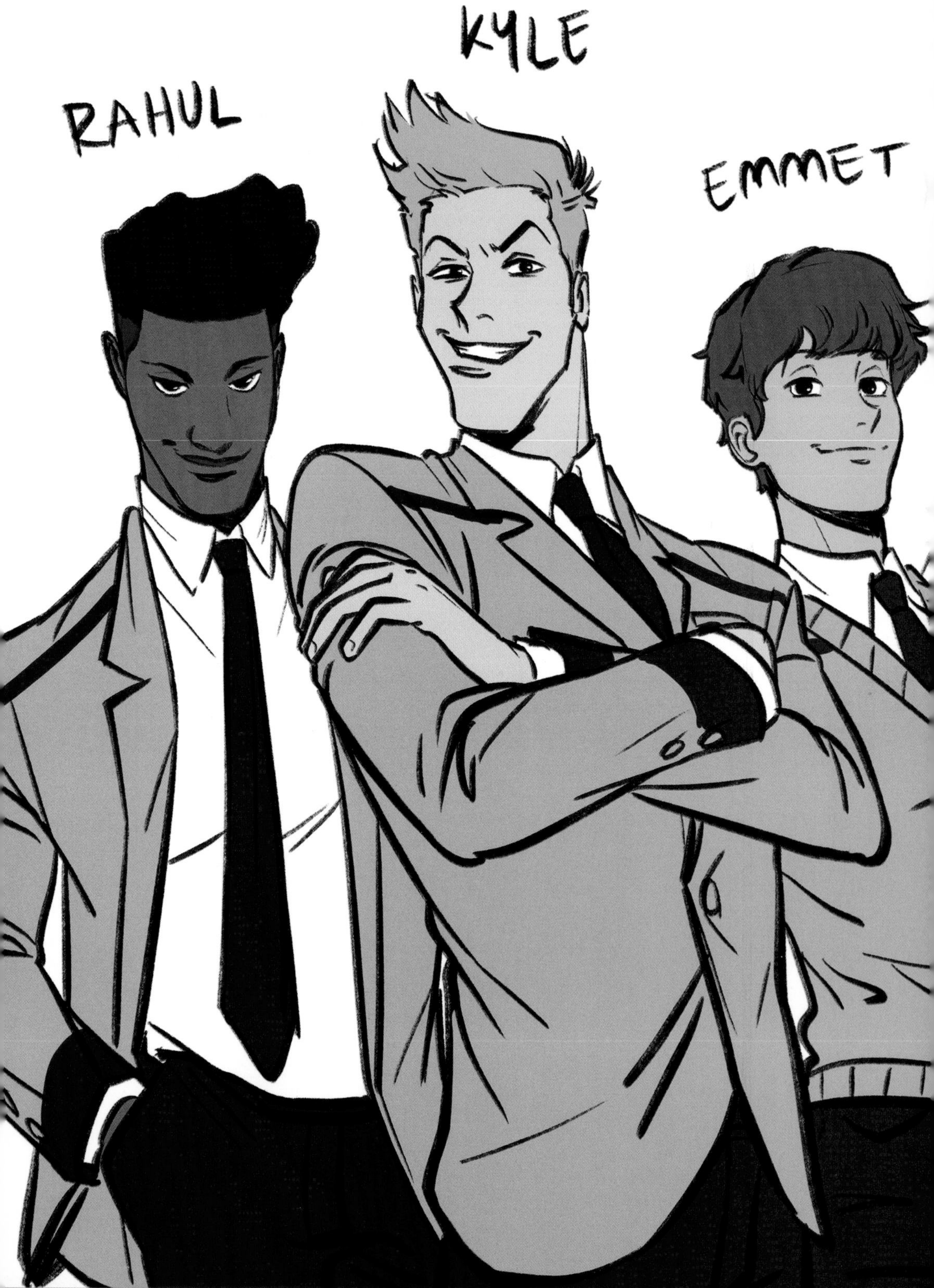
RAHUL
KYLE
EMMET

LOWTHER HALL

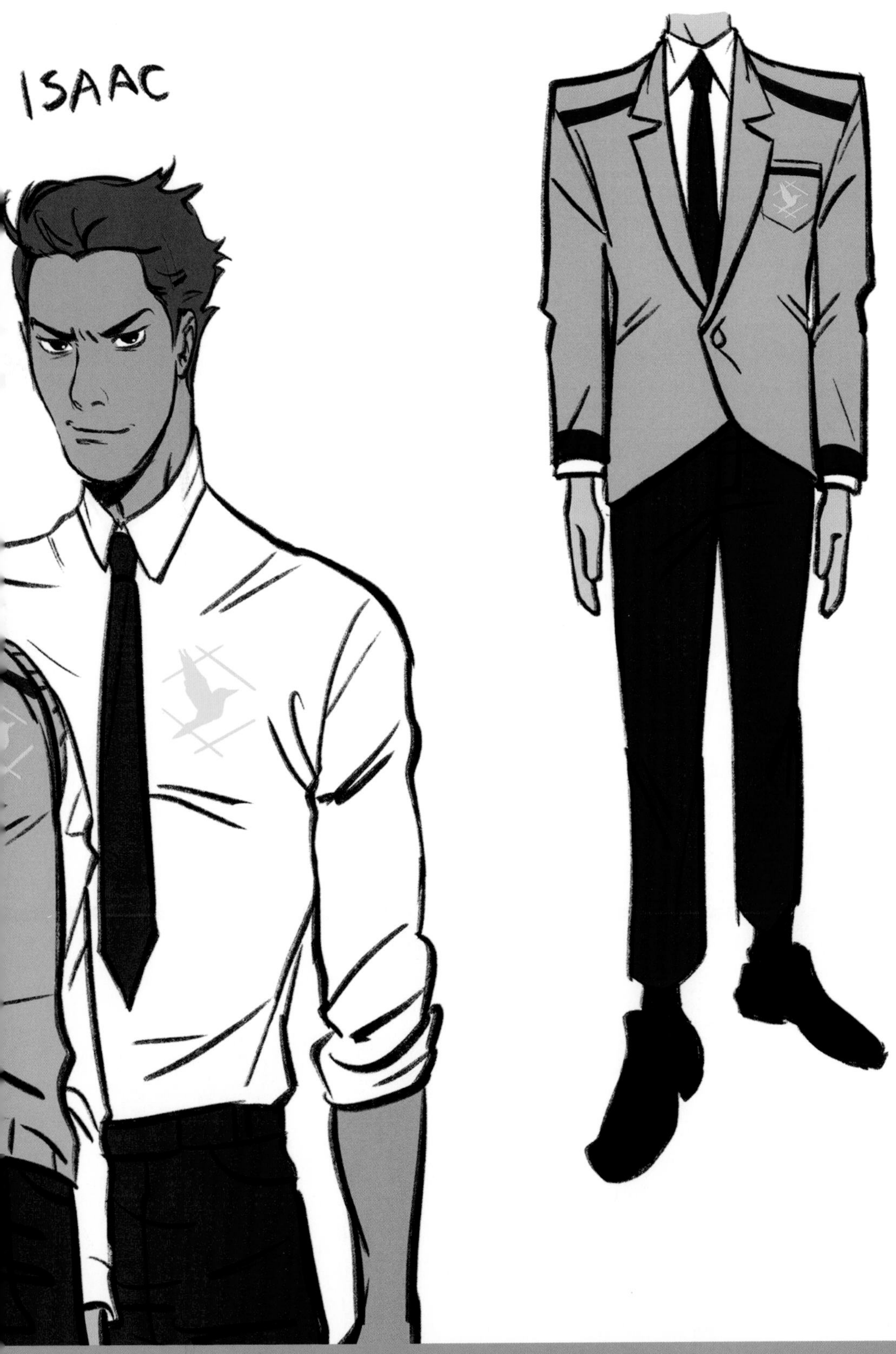
ISAAC

CHARACTER DESIGNS BY **JOHANNA THE MAD**

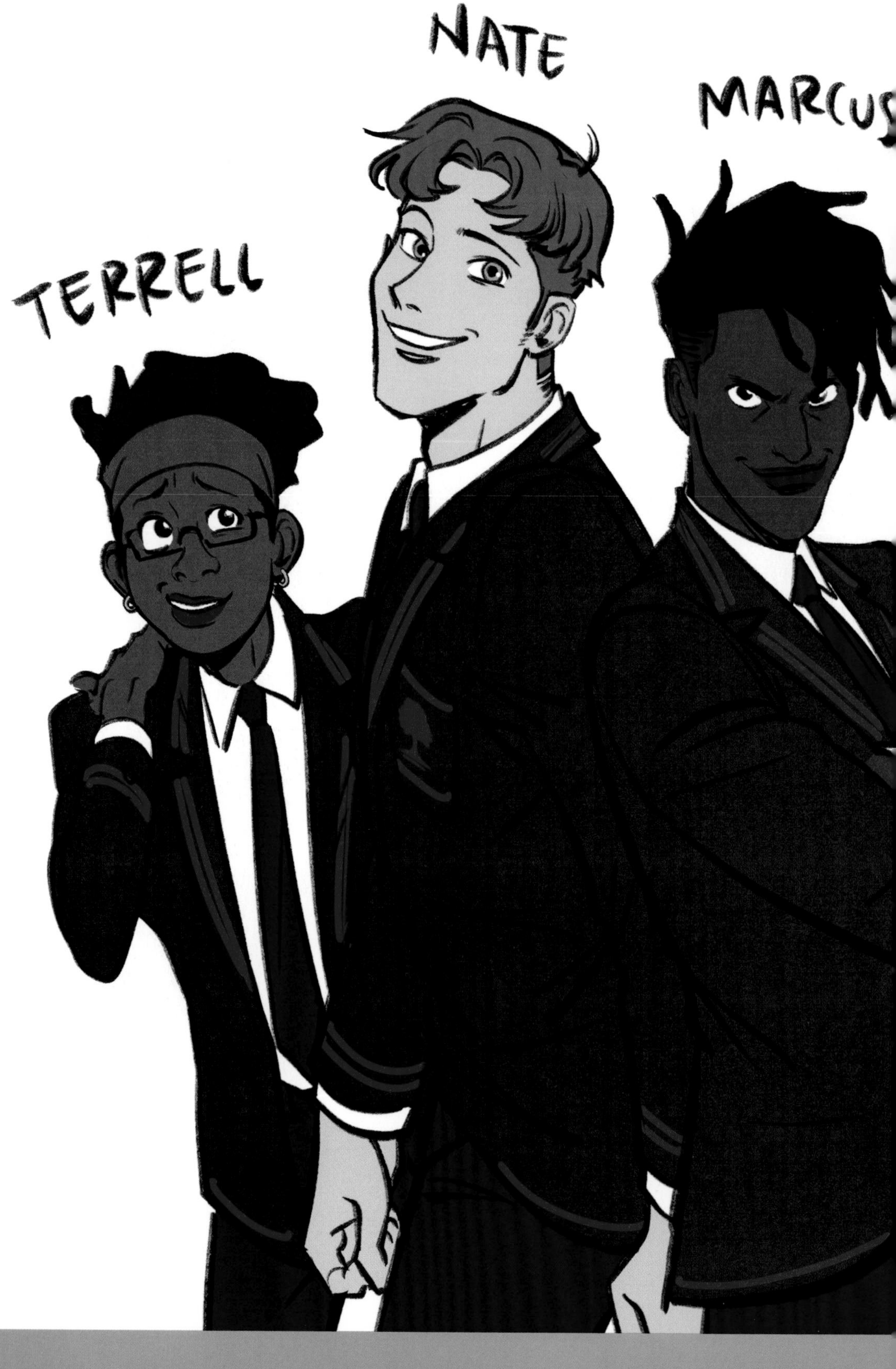
NATE
MARCUS
TERRELL

MACROBERTSON

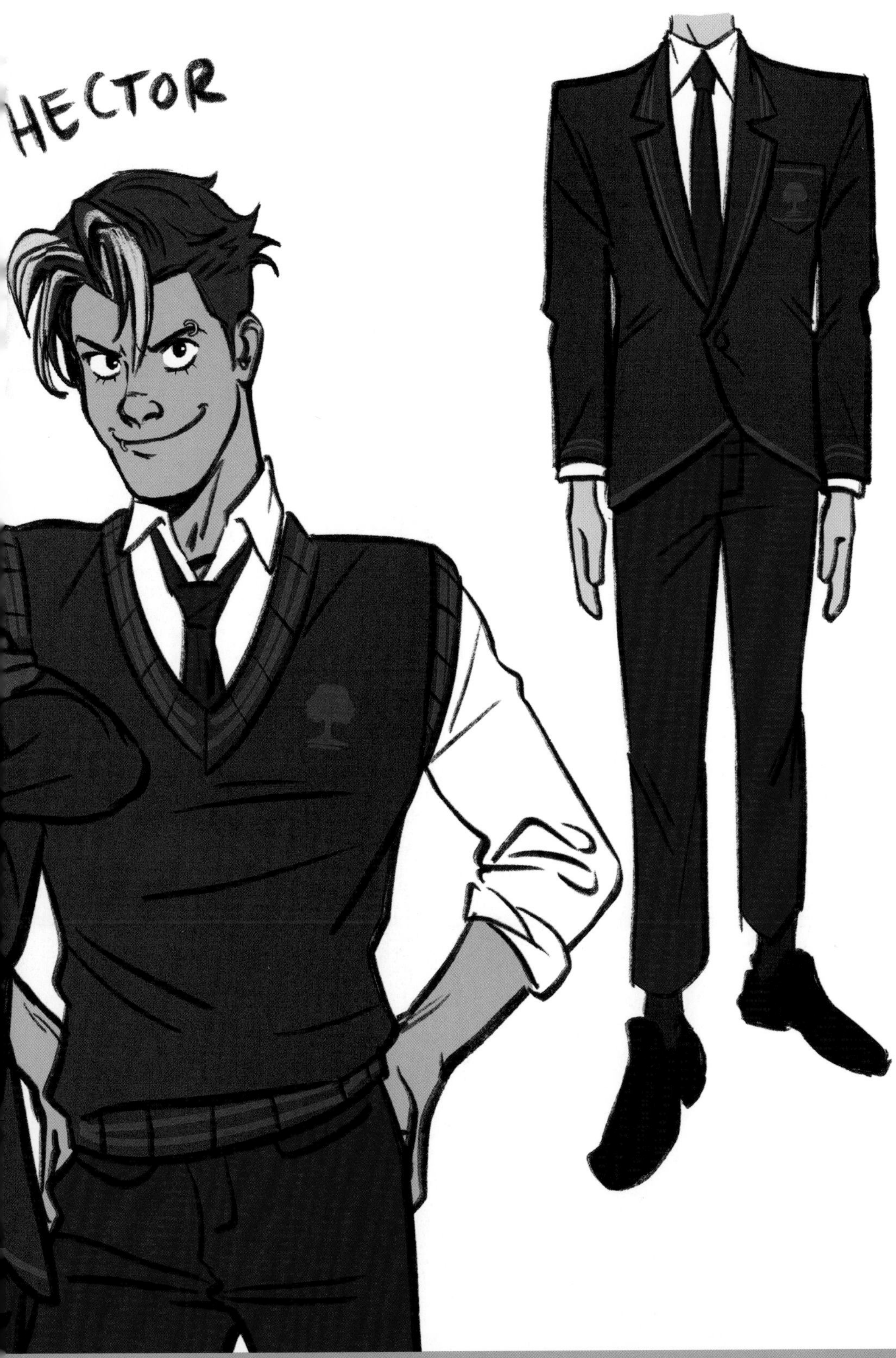
HECTOR

CHARACTER DESIGNS BY **JOHANNA THE MAD**

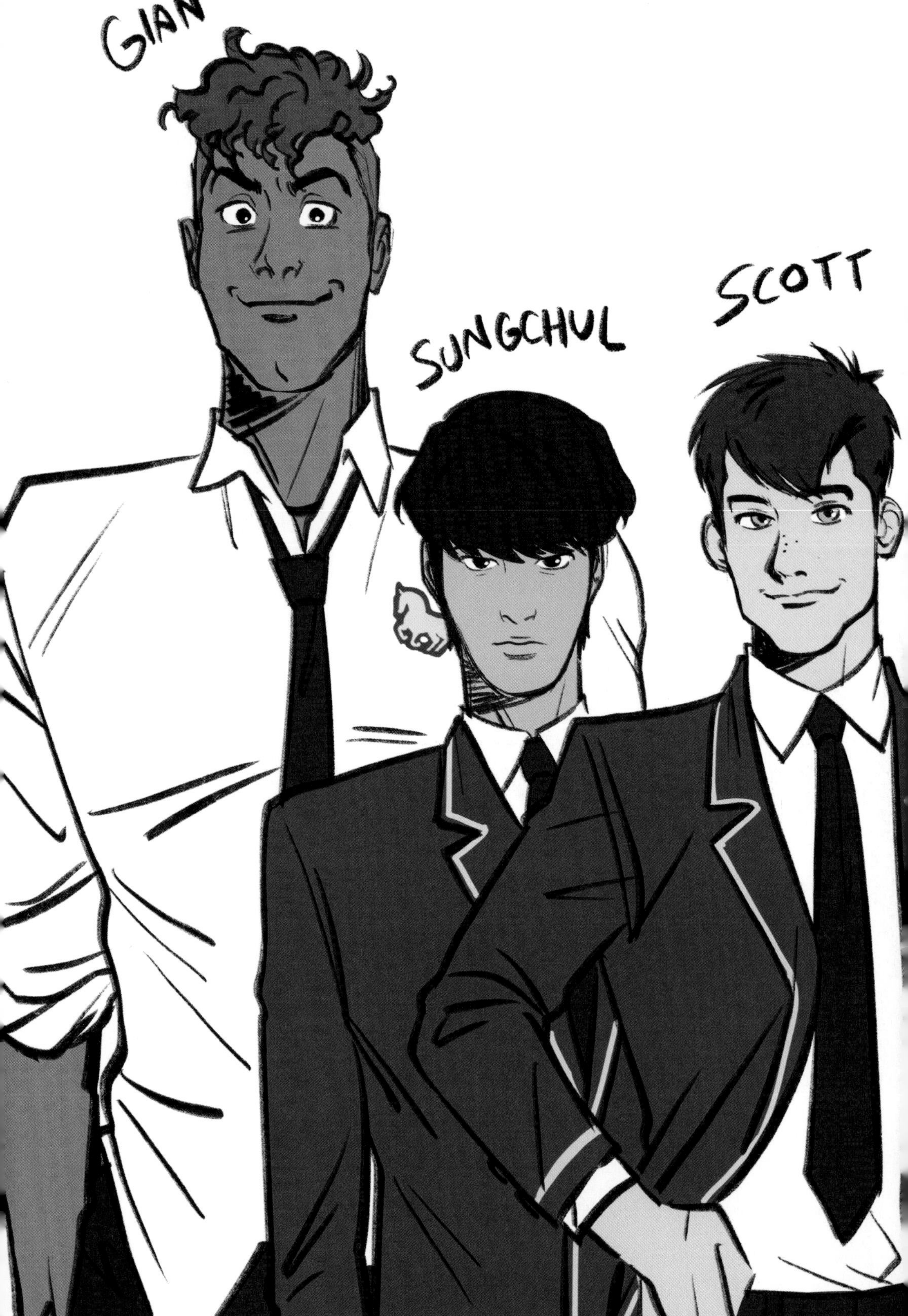
GIAN
SUNGCHUL
SCOTT

HALVERTON

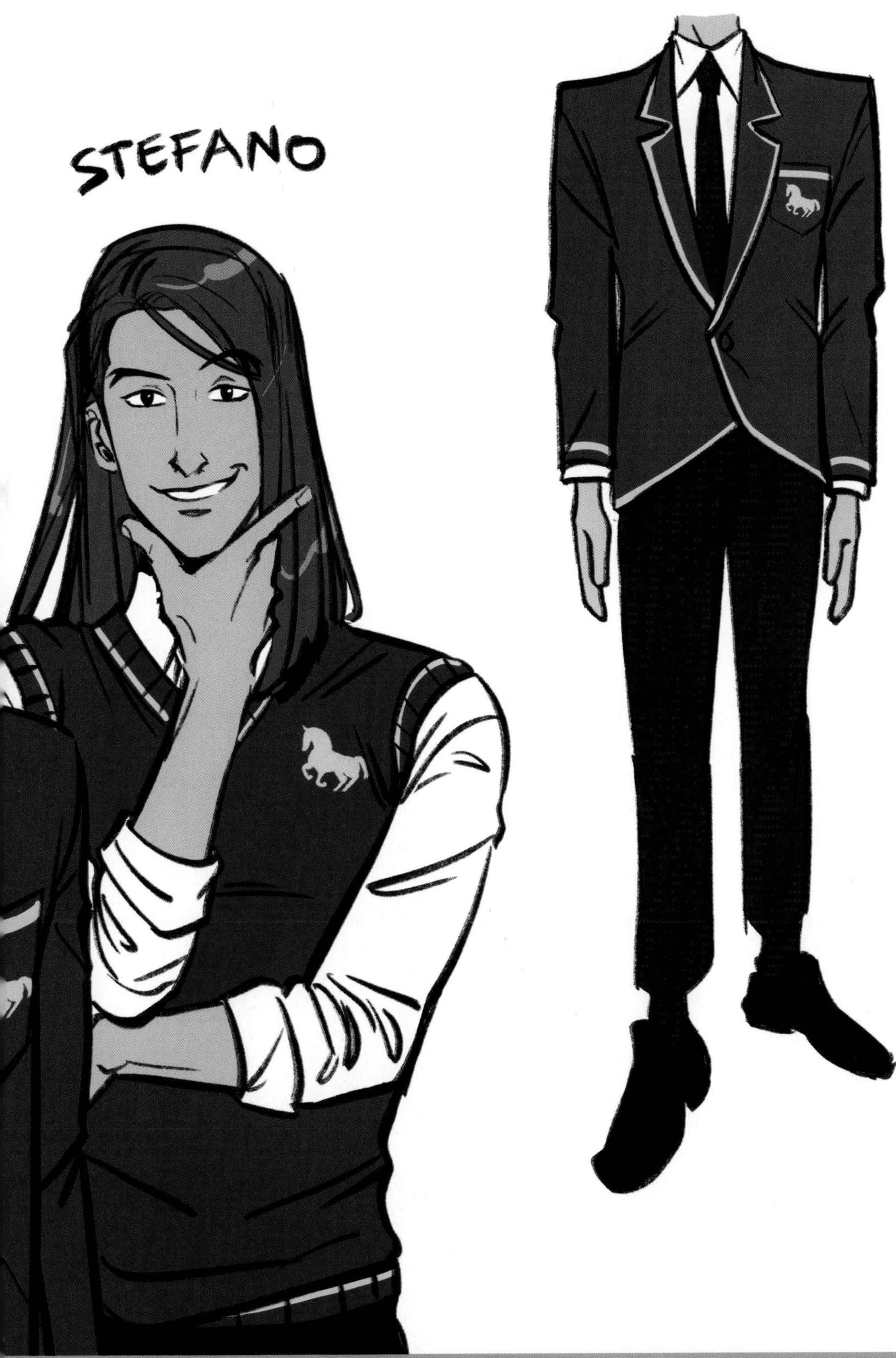
STEFANO

CHARACTER DESIGNS BY **JOHANNA THE MAD**

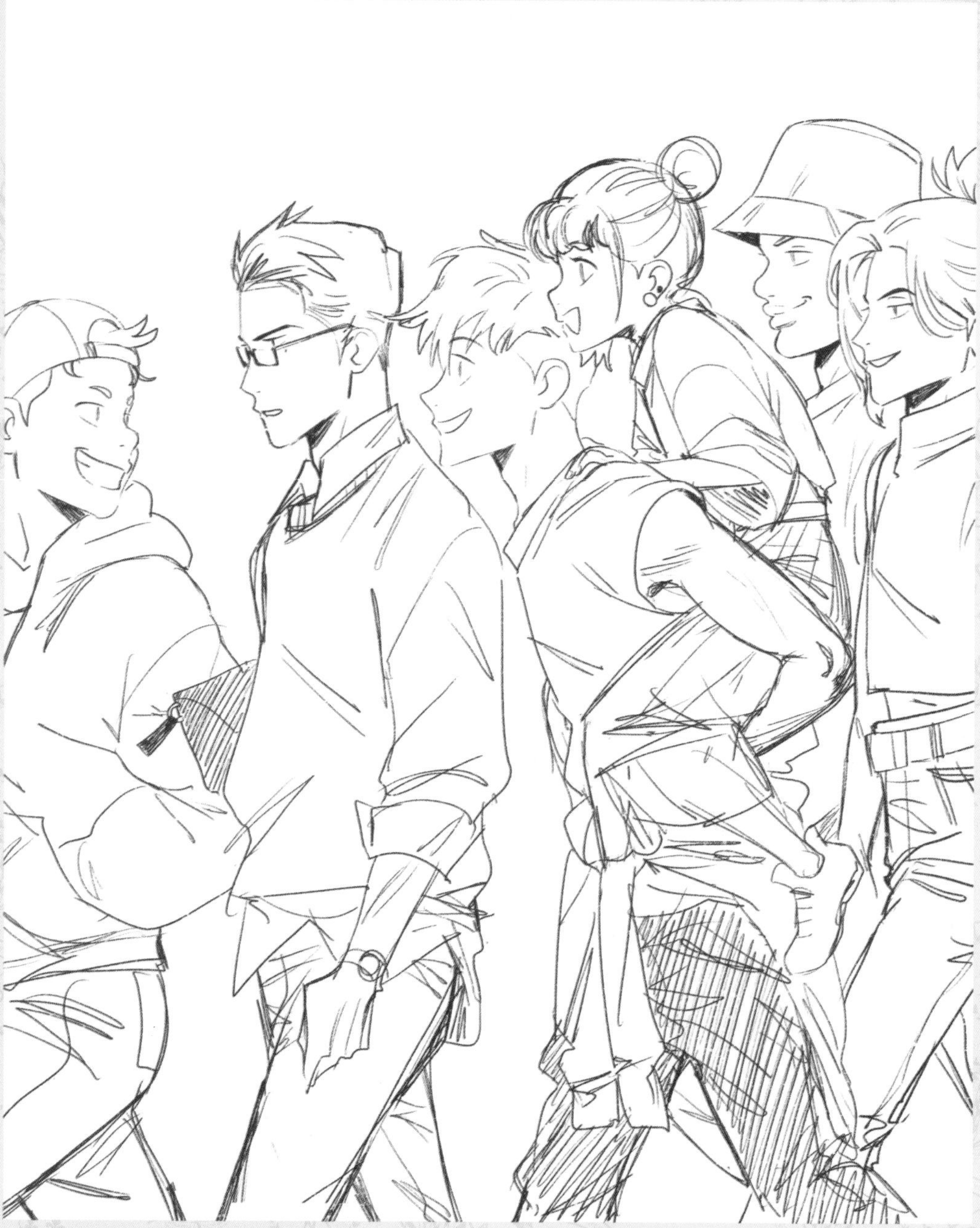

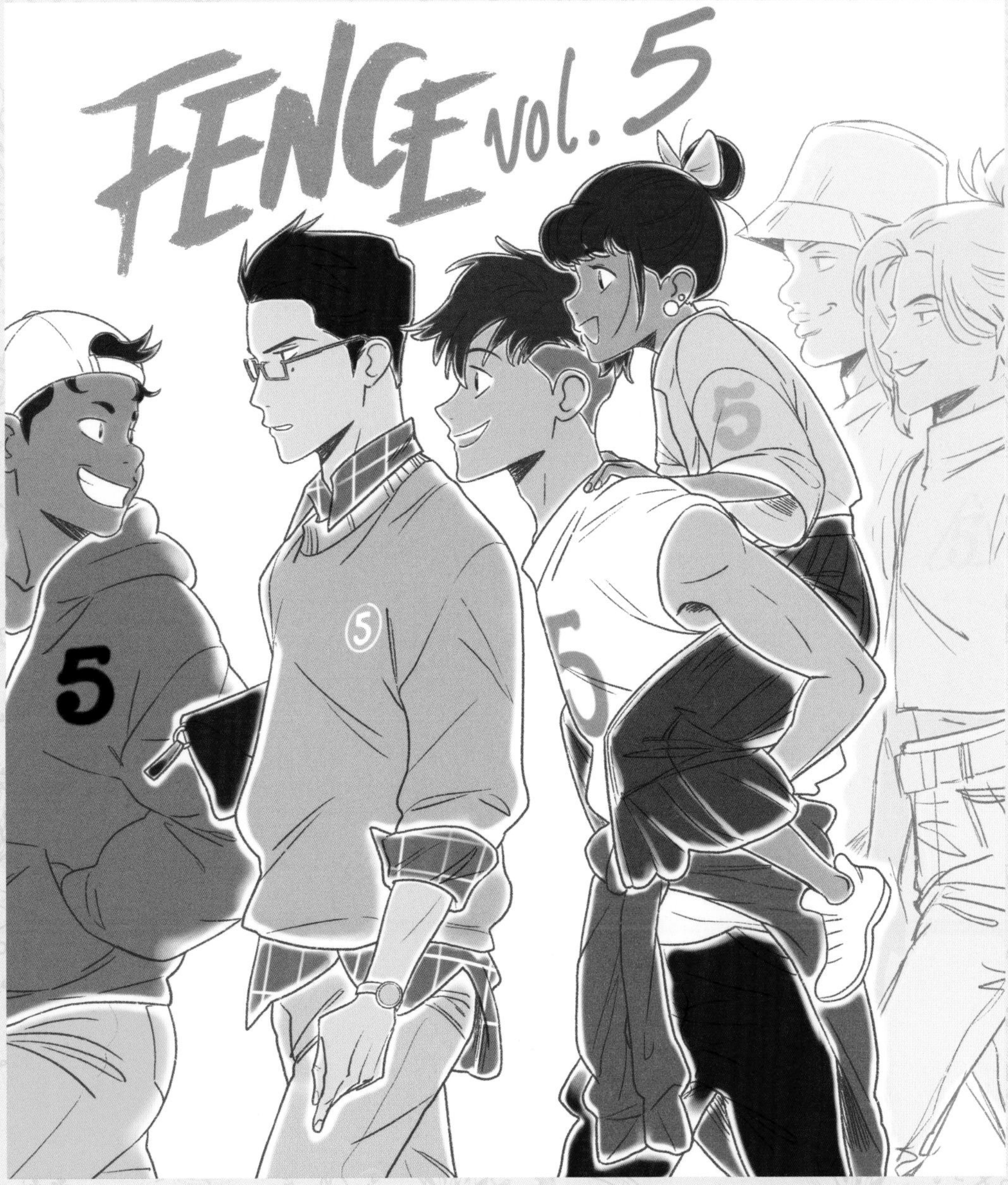
FENCE vol. 5

PENCILS BY **JOHANNA THE MAD**

FAKE DATING.
REAL SWORDS.

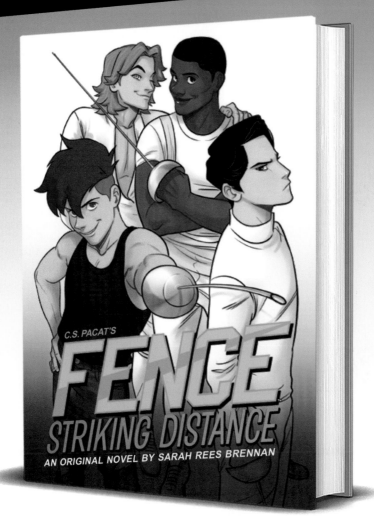

An original novel based on the C.S. Pacat series

Bestselling author Sarah Rees Brennan
brings the boys of Kings Row to life
in the first-ever Fence novel,
featuring art by Johanna The Mad

 thenovl.com/fence

DISCOVER
ALL THE HITS

STEVENSON • ELLIS • WATTERS • ALLEN
LUMBERJANES
BEWARE THE KITTEN HOLY
NEW YORK TIMES BESTSELLING SERIES

Allison + Treiman + Cogar
GIANT DAYS
VOLUME ONE

From a writer of Disney's Moana
RIBON • FISH • PEER
SLAM!
VOLUME ONE

Hope Larson • Brittney Williams • Sarah Stern
GOLDIE VANCE
"Scoot over Nancy Drew..." —Los Angeles Times
Volume One

JAMES TYNION IV • RIAN SYGH • WALTER BAIAMONTE
THE BACKSTAGERS

TYSON HESSE'S
DIESEL
IGNITION

BOOM! BOX

AVAILABLE AT YOUR LOCAL COMICS SHOP AND BOOKSTORE

To find a comics shop in your area, visit www.comicshoplocator.com

WWW.**BOOM-STUDIOS**.COM

Lumberjanes
ND Stevenson, Shannon Watters, Grace Ellis, Gus Allen, and Others
Volume 1: Beware the Kitten Holy
ISBN: 978-1-60886-687-8 | $14.99 US
Volume 2: Friendship to the Max
ISBN: 978-1-60886-737-0 | $14.99 US
Volume 3: A Terrible Plan
ISBN: 978-1-60886-803-2 | $14.99 US
Volume 4: Out of Time
ISBN: 978-1-60886-860-5 | $14.99 US
Volume 5: Band Together
ISBN: 978-1-60886-919-0 | $14.99 US

Giant Days
John Allison, Lissa Treiman, Max Sarin
Volume 1
ISBN: 978-1-60886-789-9 | $9.99 US
Volume 2
ISBN: 978-1-60886-804-9 | $14.99 US
Volume 3
ISBN: 978-1-60886-851-3 | $14.99 US

Jonesy
Sam Humphries, Caitlin Rose Boyle
Volume 1
ISBN: 978-1-60886-883-4 | $9.99 US
Volume 2
ISBN: 978-1-60886-999-2 | $14.99 US

Slam!
Pamela Ribon, Veronica Fish, Brittany Peer
Volume 1
ISBN: 978-1-68415-004-5 | $14.99 US

Goldie Vance
Hope Larson, Brittney Williams
Volume 1
ISBN: 978-1-60886-898-8 | $9.99 US
Volume 2
ISBN: 978-1-60886-974-9 | $14.99 US

The Backstagers
James Tynion IV, Rian Sygh
Volume 1
ISBN: 978-1-60886-993-0 | $14.99 US

Tyson Hesse's Diesel: Ignition
Tyson Hesse
ISBN: 978-1-60886-907-7 | $14.99 US

Coady & The Creepies
Liz Prince, Amanda Kirk, Hannah Fisher
ISBN: 978-1-68415-029-8 | $14.99 US

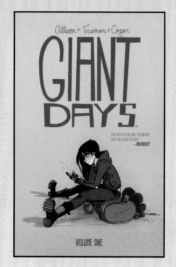